FAMILIES OUTSIDE MARRIAGE

Second edition

Jacqueline Priest LLB

Lecturer in Law,
University of Durham

FAMILY LAW
1993

Published by Family Law
an imprint of Jordan Publishing Limited
21 St Thomas Street
Bristol BS1 6JS

British Library Cataloguing-in-Publication Data

A catalogue record for this book is available from the British Library.

ISBN 0 85308 186 7

Typeset by Rowland Phototypesetting Limited, Bury St Edmunds, Suffolk
Printed in Great Britain at Henry Ling Limited, The Dorset Press, Dorchester.

FOREWORD

The marriage rate declines, and all the evidence – not only the statistics, but reported cases and experience of everyday legal practice – points to a great increase in the number of people who are living together outside marriage. No longer do couples marry as soon as children come along: the number of births outside marriage has almost trebled in a decade, and in many cases the parents are living together on a permanent basis and register the birth jointly. It seems clear that many unmarried couples have no intention of marrying. How dated the phrase 'stable illicit union' seems today – twenty-five years after it was given prominence in the campaign to liberalise the divorce laws.

The first edition of Jacqueline Priest's book soon established itself as a secure guide through the jungle of case-law and legislation, and the second edition comes at a particularly opportune time. The Family Law Reform Act 1987 has been overtaken by the massive reforming codification of child law embodied in the Children Act 1989, while the Child Support Act 1991 is about to come into force – and it will certainly have a dramatic effect. With the aid of this book, the busy practitioner will be able to give clients the advice they need; students will be able to unravel the complexities of the law, and all who value legal scholarship will admire the author's achievement.

STEPHEN CRETNEY
February 1993

v

PREFACE

The aim of this book is to offer a guide to the legal position of those whose relationship subsists outside the bonds of matrimony. It includes treatment of substantive and procedural rules generally regarded as belonging to 'family law' and 'property law', but it also deals with a range of other provisions which have an impact on the position of unmarried couples and any children of their relationship.

In April 1989, when the first edition of this book was in preparation, the implementation of several major provisions of the Family Law Reform Act 1987 appeared to have inaugurated a new era with respect to the legal consequences of parenthood of a child of unmarried parents. In the event, completion of the first edition was postponed in order to accommodate (as an Appendix) the far more sweeping changes to be effected by the Children Act 1989, albeit that no rules of court had then been published and no confirmation given as to the date of implementation. Since then, the Children Act 1989 has come into force, sweeping away much of the law relating to children described in Part III of the first edition. Moreover, the Child Support Act 1991, which comes into force on 5 April 1993, has created a wholly new extra-judicial machinery for the assessment of child maintenance. This substantially supplants the powers of the court described in Part II of the first edition, with significant repercussions for those aspects of financial provision in respect of which the court's powers remain, at least ostensibly, unscathed.

The period of preparation of this second edition saw the publication of the most important sets of Regulations made under the Child Support Act 1991. It also coincided with the appearance of the first reported decisions under the Children Act 1989. The typescript of this edition was delivered to the publishers at the end of October 1992, but it has been possible to incorporate references to reported decisions as at the end of January 1993.

The purpose of this edition, as of the first edition, is to offer a guide to the law as it now stands. It is beyond the scope of such an undertaking to consider changes which *may* come about in the future. There is, however, little indication that the pace of change in family law will abate: The Law Commission has put forward proposals for reform of the law relating to remedies for domestic violence which, if implemented, would have a profound effect on the availability and practical value of the remedies at the court's disposal. Incidental to its proposals for reform of the law relating to intestacy, the Law Commission has also recommended special treatment for surviving cohabitants under the Inheritance Act 1975 by means of an amendment which could have a significant impact on the court's treatment of 'widowed' cohabitants, albeit that only a relatively small number of applicants might need to rely upon it. Finally, the Government's Adoption Law Review proposes modifications to the law relating to the acquisition of parental responsibility by step-fathers, and the use of *inter vivos* guardianship as an adjunct to residence orders, with the intention of reducing the number of step-parent and intra-family adoption applications. As these examples demonstrate, while much has been achieved since the process of gradual direct or indirect recognition of the special position of unmarried couples first started to gather momentum in the mid-1970s, a great deal remains on the agenda.

JACQUELINE PRIEST
February 1993

CONTENTS

PART I: THE HOME

PART II: MONEY

TABLE OF CASES

TABLE OF STATUTES

TABLE OF STATUTORY INSTRUMENTS

Part I
THE HOME

1 OWNERSHIP

1.1 General principles

'There is not one law of property applicable where a dispute as to property is between spouses . . . and another law of property where the dispute is between others' (*Gissing v Gissing* [1971] AC 886, per Lord Dilhorne at 899). If a dispute arises between husband and wife as to title to property, that question of title 'must be decided by the principles of law applicable to the settlement of claims between those not so related, while making full allowances in view of that relationship' (*Pettitt v Pettitt* [1970] AC 777, per Lord Upjohn at 813). Thus, if any distinction is to be drawn between cases involving spouses and cases not involving spouses, that distinction must lie not in the substantive rules to be applied (but see further §1.2 below), but in the *allowances* that the court will be prepared to make in view of the spousal relationship such as, for instance, a greater readiness to draw the inference of an intention by the parties to confer proprietorial benefits upon each other.

It is now clear that, in cases involving cohabitants, the court will be prepared to make full allowances equivalent to those made for married couples, but that this will be permissible only if, apart from the absence of a marriage certificate, the relationship bears all the hallmarks of a marital relationship, and in *Bernard v Josephs* (1983) FLR 178 at 186–7, Griffiths LJ warned against the 'blithe assumption' that all couples living together are to be regarded as no different from a married couple: 'The judge must look carefully at the nature of the relationship, and only if satisfied that it was intended to involve the same degree of commitment as marriage will it be legitimate to regard them as no different from a married couple'. Thus, for example, the decision of the parties to live together without marrying may be reached because each of them values his independence and does not wish to make the commitment of marriage. In such a case it would be misleading to make the same assumptions and draw the same inferences as in the case of a married couple. On the other hand, the underlying basis of a relationship can change with the passage of time, and the attitudes and expectations present at the commencement of cohabitation may give way to an unspoken commitment to each other so that a relationship supervenes which is sufficiently marriage-like to affect subsequent transactions.

1.2   Special rules

Notwithstanding the general approach outlined above, certain rules are exclusively applicable to married couples and their property. The following, in particular, are inapplicable to cohabitants, save where extended to formerly engaged couples by the Law Reform (Miscellaneous Provisions) Act (LR(MP)A) 1970.

1.2.1   The Married Women's Property Act 1964

The Married Women's Property Act 1964 imposes the rule that, in the absence of an agreement to the contrary, money or property derived from a housekeeping allowance paid by a husband to a wife shall be treated as belonging to them both in equal shares. It reverses the common-law rule that any surplus fund or property bought therewith belonged to the husband (see *Hoddinott v Hoddinott* [1949] 2 KB 406, where reference was made to the potential for injustice resulting from the common law's failure to grant recognition to skill and economy in household management). It may be assumed that the common-law rule remains applicable to housekeeping allowances paid as between cohabitants. Nevertheless, its operation may be displaced by evidence of a contrary intention and, even in the absence of an express agreement, the facts in any given case may support the inference of an intention that the recipient of the housekeeping allowance be allowed to reap the benefit of domestic economies and retain any surplus as her own (for a passing reference to this possibility, see *Windeler v Whitehall* [1990] 2 FLR 505 at 516–517).

Dealings with a housekeeping allowance could be a relevant consideration in determining interests in the home if, for example, a cohabitant's cash contribution to the purchase of a new home were derived from savings previously accumulated from a housekeeping allowance.

1.2.2 The Matrimonial Proceedings and Property Act 1970, s 37

Section 37 of the Matrimonial Proceedings and Property Act 1970, expressed as a declaratory provision, places beyond doubt the rule that, in the absence of any express or implied agreement to the contrary, a husband or wife who makes a substantial contribution in money or money's worth to the improvement of property belonging to the other spouse, or to them both, thereby acquires a share (or an enlarged share) in the property. The size of the share acquired or enlarged will be determined by any agreement made by the parties at the time of the improvement or, in default of agreement, by a decision of the court as to what share would be just in all the circumstances. The limited case-law indicates that a just assessment will be one which takes into account the extent to which the value of the property was enhanced by the improvement, and which attributes to the improving spouse a corresponding proportionate share (see *Re Nicholson* [1974] 2 All ER 386).

Section 37 is limited by its terms to improvements effected by spouses. It is also applicable to engaged couples whose agreement to marry is terminated (LR(MP)A 1970, s 2(1); see §1.2.5 below), but it is not directly applicable to other cohabitants. However, a similar claim may lie where a cohabitant has carried out improvements to property, based on the general principles relating to constructive trusts (see §1.3.4 below).

1.2.3 The presumption of advancement

The presumption of advancement; that is, the presumption of an intention to make a gift, can be invoked where a wife claims to be entitled to property purchased or funds provided by her husband, but put into her name. The presumption of advancement may also be invoked where a man has property conveyed into his fiancée's name (*Moate v Moate* [1948] 2 All ER 486, and see now LR(MP)A 1970, s 2(1), and *Mossop v Mossop* [1988] 2 FLR 173), but this will not be possible where there is no question of any agreement to marry.

A presumption of fact is merely an assumption without evidence, and is therefore rebuttable by evidence as to the actual state of affairs. In practice, the presumption of advancement has little significance today. In *Pettitt v Pettitt* [1970] AC 777, the warning was given that such presumptions, evolved by judges dealing with the disputes of the propertied classes of the last century, are of little weight in modern conditions: some explanation of the parties' conduct will usually be available to eliminate the need to rely on *presumed* intent (per Lord Diplock at 824, and see per Lord Reid at 793).

1.2.4   Matrimonial proceedings

It has been stressed that property disputes between cohabitants are so similar to disputes between husbands and wives that they should be taken to the Family Division rather than the Chancery Division to enable the case to be heard by a court accustomed to the 'family law' approach to such matters (see *Bernard v Josephs*, above, per Lord Denning at 185). Nevertheless, with one exception (see below), the only procedures and powers available are essentially those applicable to disputes between legal strangers. This is particularly significant in two respects.

(i) A married couple who are in dispute over the ownership of property may have the dispute resolved in proceedings brought by either spouse under the Married Women's Property Act 1882, s 17. Although the court in s 17 proceedings has extensive powers to regulate the use and enjoyment of property (see Matrimonial Causes (Property and Maintenance) Act 1958, s 7), its powers do not include any power to *redistribute* matrimonial property. It may only declare what ownership interests exist, on an application of the principles described in this chapter (*Pettitt v Pettitt*, above; *Burns v Burns* [1984] FLR 216). In procedural terms, however, a cohabitant is at a disadvantage compared to a spouse insofar as, except in circumstances noted below, a cohabitant will be unable to make use of the summary procedure provided by s 17. This may be particularly disadvantageous where there is substantial property involved since the county court has jurisdiction to hear an application under s 17 whatever the value of the property in dispute. The county court also has jurisdiction unlimited by value over applications under the Law of Property Act 1925, s 30 for an order for sale in respect of real property held on a trust for sale, but it seems that this jurisdiction without limit may be confined to cases where there is no dispute as to beneficial entitlements since, where the relief sought is a declaration of trust (as where a constructive trust is alleged against a sole legal owner), the jurisdictional limitation by reference to the value of the property remains applicable. In such cases, the consent of both parties will be required in order to confer jurisdiction on the county court where the value of a property is in excess of the current county court jurisdictional limit.

The s 17 summary procedure is available to cohabitants who fulfil the requirements of the LR(MP)A 1970, that is to say, persons between whom there has been an agreement to marry which has been terminated (see, eg *Marsh v von Sternberg* [1986] 1 FLR 526). In such cases, the application under s 17 must be made within three years of the termination of the agreement (LR(MP)A 1970, s 2(2)). Some caution is required in this respect if there is likely to be dispute as to whether the parties ever entered into an agreement to marry: failure to prove such an agreement will mean that the proceedings have been incorrectly initiated under s 17 and additional costs will be incurred in correcting the procedural defect.

(ii) When a marriage is ended by divorce, property matters can be dealt with by the divorce court under the Matrimonial Causes Act 1973, which gives the court very extensive powers to redistribute both capital assets and income, and any settlement between the parties can be negotiated against the background of those extensive powers. A cohabitant obviously has no right of recourse to divorce proceedings and, whether formerly engaged or not, is unable to invoke the divorce court's redistributive powers (see *Mossop v Mossop*, above).

1.2.5 Parties between whom there has been an agreement to marry

Reference has been made in preceding paragraphs to the Law Reform (Miscellaneous Provisions) Act 1970 which extends to formerly engaged couples certain rules of law and one procedural provision applicable to property disputes between spouses. It may be noted that the Act gives no guidance as to what constitutes an 'agreement to marry'. Certainly, it does not expressly require there to have been a formal, publicly announced 'engagement'. In practice, an assertion that the parties had agreed to marry may well be disputed (as in *Mossop v Mossop*, above; alleged agreement to marry followed by cohabitation for four years) and, as was noted by Lord Denning in *Bernard v Josephs* (above) at 184, the relationship of 'engaged' or 'not engaged' to be married is often undetermined and indeterminable: a consideration which he used in further justification of the court's preparedness to take a broad view of cases involving cohabitants.

The provisions of the LR(MP)A 1970 apply to *all* agreements to marry, notwithstanding that a particular agreement might have been unenforceable at common law (eg because it was entered into at a time when one of the parties was already married) (*Shaw v Fitzgerald* [1992] 1 FLR 357, but query whether this judgment confuses enforceability with *validity*; see further *Fender v St John Mildmay* [1938] AC 1).

1.3   Legal and equitable interests

Legal ownership of property will be disclosed by the conveyance. Beneficial ownership of property depends, in the first instance, upon the agreement of the parties with respect thereto at the time of acquisition. Where there is a conveyance to joint legal owners the document may also declare in whom the beneficial interests are to vest. The Court of Appeal has many times stressed that, when the legal estate in a house is acquired by two persons in their joint names, it is very much to be deplored if their solicitors fail to take steps to ascertain and declare their intentions with respect to the beneficial interests (see *Springette v Defoe* [1992] 2 FLR 388, per Dillon LJ at 390; see also *Cowcher v Cowcher* [1972] 1 All ER 943 at 959; *Bernard v Josephs* (1983) FLR 178 at 187; *Marsh v von Sternberg* [1986] 1 FLR 526 at 528). In *Walker v Hall* [1984] FLR 126 at 129, Dillon J raised the possibility that a solicitor who fails to do so may be liable in negligence. An express declaration of trust will be especially desirable where the parties are contributing unequally to the purchase price of the property but where it is their intention to create a trust in equal shares, and in any other case where the intention is to share in proportions other than those in which the purchase price is provided.

1.3.1   Joint legal ownership with express declaration

If the conveyance or form of transfer (or lease) not only declares in whom the legal title is to vest, but also declares in whom the beneficial title is to vest, that necessarily concludes the question of title for all time unless the document can be set aside as the result of fraud or mistake (see *Pettitt v Pettitt* [1970] AC 777, per Lord

Upjohn at 813; see also *Goodman v Gallant* [1986] 1 FLR 513).

Any such declaration will usually appear in the conveyance itself, but may be found elsewhere, as in *Leake v Bruzzi* [1974] 1 WLR 1528 where, the wife being a minor, the property was conveyed into the husband's sole name but where the parties executed a deed of trust on the same day as the transfer declaring that the husband held the property on trust for both parties as beneficial joint tenants. Any such declaration of trust must satisfy the formal requirements of the Law of Property Act 1925, which provides that a declaration of trust in respect of land is unenforceable unless it is evidenced in writing and signed by the party declaring the trust (s 53(1)(b); see also s 53(1)(c); disposition of an *existing* equitable interest must be in writing and signed by the person making the disposition).

There is no reason why a contemporaneous declaration of trust should not be embodied in an agreement which also deals, for instance, with the liability of the parties *inter se* with respect to mortgage instalments if one party leaves the home, or with the right of the party remaining in occupation to buy out the other party's interest, perhaps specifying the period he is to be allowed to attempt to make arrangements to do so before the property is placed on the open market for sale.

Joint tenants

The express declaration may describe the parties as beneficial joint tenants, the effect of which is that, until severance of the joint tenancy, each joint tenant has an identical interest in the whole land and every part of it and, if sold, in the proceeds of sale. The interest of each tenant is identical in size, nature and duration. On the death of a joint tenant, his interest in the property passes to the remaining tenant(s) by virtue of the right of survivorship and does not form part of the deceased tenant's estate. On severance of a joint tenancy (see below), the parties become tenants in common, each entitled to an equal divided share and, on death after severance, that interest will not pass by the rule of survivorship but will form part of the deceased tenant's estate for distribution according to the terms of that tenant's will or the rules governing intestate succession.

Where title to the property is registered, any transfer to joint owners will be notified to the Land Registry and recorded using Form 19(JP). That form sets out the names of the legal owners of the property and provides sufficient space for a declaration of the

beneficial interests. There follows a declaration that 'the survivor
of them can/cannot give a valid receipt for capital money arising on
a disposition of the land', with a marginal note requesting deletion
of 'can' or 'cannot' as appropriate. In *Re Gorman* [1990] 1 WLR
616, the Divisional Court considered the effect of words entitling
the survivor to give a valid receipt for capital monies and held that
such a declaration 'clearly and unequivocally' pointed to a joint
beneficial tenancy but, in *Huntingford v Hobbs* [1992] Fam Law
437, the Court of Appeal held (applying *Harwood v Harwood* [1991]
2 FLR 274) that such a declaration is not to be treated as an implied
declaration of trust.

Tenants in Common

Where the declaration is of a tenancy in common, each tenant in
common enjoys a right to a specific divided share. On the death of
a tenant in common that tenant's share does not pass automatically
to the remaining tenant(s) but forms part of the deceased tenant's
estate.

Other possibilities

In *Goodman v Gallant*, above, the court expressly noted the possibility of a hybrid declaration; that is to say, one which provides for
beneficial interests to be equivalent to those of joint tenants unless
and until severance occurs, but with interests in *unequal* shares if
severance takes place. Such a declaration could fulfil a useful role
where an unmarried couple wish to make provision for the survivor
should either party die while the relationship is still subsisting but
also wish to deal with the possibility of relationship breakdown
during their joint lives in a manner which recognises inequality of
contributions to the purchase.

Fraud and mistake

Where the form of a conveyance has been procured by fraud, the
conveyance may be set aside. Where the form of the conveyance is
the result of a mistake as to the common intention of the parties
and thus fails accurately to give effect to that intention, rectification
may be sought, as in *Thames Guaranty Ltd v Campbell* [1985]
QB 210, where the entire purchase price was provided by the wife

but where it was agreed that, as a matter of courtesy, the property would be conveyed to the spouses as joint legal owners. It was further agreed between the spouses that, in equity, the property should belong entirely to the wife. The wife succeeded in an application for rectification of the conveyance, which had described the spouses as holding the property as joint tenants in law *and in equity* as a result of their solicitors' mistaken assumption that this was their intention.

Rectification will not be granted to the prejudice of a bona fide purchaser for value without notice who has taken an interest under the instrument in its unrectified form (eg, a mortgage lender).

The situation where the conveyance fails to embody the parties' common intention may be distinguished from cases where the parties are simply at cross-purposes with each other, as in *Burgess v Rawnsley* [1975] Ch 429, where both parties had contributed equally to the purchase of a house conveyed into their joint names with an express declaration that the beneficial interests were also jointly held. The man intended that the house would become the parties' matrimonial home but the woman's evidence was that at the time of the purchase he had never mentioned marriage to her and that she never contemplated marriage. She had agreed to the purchase in order to have a place of her own on division of the property into two flats. On the man's death, his administratrix claimed a half-share in the house. The Court of Appeal held that the absence of a common purpose was not sufficient to defeat the express declaration and raise a resulting trust. (On the facts of *Burgess v Rawnsley*, however, the administratrix succeeded on the basis of behaviour subsequent to the conveyance which had the effect of severing the beneficial joint tenancy.)

Severance

There are various methods by which a beneficial joint tenancy may be severed so as to create a tenancy in common. The simplest and most certain is by giving notice in writing in accordance with the Law of Property Act 1925, s 36(2). Other methods were considered in *Burgess v Rawnsley*, above, where it was made clear that an agreement between joint tenants to sever the tenancy will be effective whether the agreement is oral or in writing, and that negotiations between joint tenants which do not result in any agreement but which indicate a common intention that the joint tenancy be regarded as severed will also effect a severance (*Burgess v Rawnsley*, above). Neither an uncommunicated declaration of severance nor, it seems, a mere verbal notice will suffice. However, there may be unilateral *actions* by one tenant which will effect a severance, such as a sale or mortgage to a third party (see eg, *Ahmed v Kendrick* [1988] 2 FLR 22; *First National Securities Ltd v Hegerty* [1985] FLR 80), or the issuing of proceedings for an order for sale under the Law of Property Act 1925, s 30 (see *Re Draper* [1969] Ch 486) or the bankruptcy of one tenant (see *Re Gorman* [1990] 1 WLR 616; and see *Re Dennis* [1992] 3 All ER 436).

1.3.2   Joint legal ownership with no express declaration

Where property is conveyed into the names of joint legal owners with no express declaration of trust, this raises a presumption of an intention to share the beneficial interest so that, unless the facts are very unusual, the parties will each be entitled to a share in the beneficial interest (*Burns v Burns* [1984] FLR 216 per May LJ at 241).

There is, however, no presumption that the parties are entitled to equal shares in the property (see *Bernard v Josephs* (1983) FLR 178; and see *B v B (Real Property: Assessment of Interests)* [1988] 2 FLR 490). It will be necessary to ascertain the intentions of the parties at the time of the purchase (considered further at 1.4 below).

Moreover, the presumption of shared beneficial interests will yield to evidence of an alternative explanation for the form of the conveyance. For instance, the form of the conveyance may have been dictated by the requirements of the building society which granted a mortgage for the purchase of the property, although the joint legal owners themselves had no intention that the beneficial interest be shared.

Such circumstances arose in *Grzeczkowski v Jedynska* (1971) 115 SJ 126, and it was held that the husband and wife, as joint legal owners, held the property on trust for the wife's sole benefit. In that case, in accordance with the parties' original intention, the mortgage repayments had been entirely met by rents paid by lodgers. However, it has been said that the fact that a house could not be bought as a family home unless both parties assumed liability under a mortgage is some ground for inferring that each person so liable is to acquire a beneficial interest (*Young v Young* [1984] FLR 375).

1.3.3 Sole legal ownership

Where property is conveyed into the name of one person as sole legal owner then *prima facie* the sole legal ownership will carry with it the whole of the beneficial interest (*Burns v Burns* [1984] FLR 216). However, it may be possible to establish that the beneficial interest is not vested exclusively in that person, but rather is held on trust for some other person who is entitled to a beneficial interest, either solely or in common with the sole legal owner, on the basis of an implied, resulting or constructive trust.

1.3.4 Resulting, implied and constructive trusts

The Law of Property Act 1925, s 53(2), expressly excludes the creation and operation of resulting, implied and constructive trusts from the formal requirements of the Act.

The failure of the judges to adopt a consistent terminology and discriminate clearly between those species of trust creates considerable difficulties of exposition (for example, see *Burns v Burns* above, per Fox LJ at 224; see also *Grant v Edwards* [1987] 1 FLR 87, per Mustill LJ at 101).

Resulting trusts

A presumed resulting trust arises where property is purchased in the name of a person who has contributed none, or not all, of the purchase price. Equity presumes an intention at the time of acquisition that the non-owning contributor shall take a share in the beneficial interest proportionate to his contribution to the purchase price, and the resulting trust arises to give effect to that presumed intention. The presumption may be rebutted by evidence of an alternative intention, such as an intention that the money be provided by way of gift, loan or rent. In *Richards v Dove* [1974] 1 All ER 888, the woman cohabitant had contributed to the deposit insofar as it was paid with funds from the parties' joint bank account, but the man's evidence was that the contribution was accepted as a loan which he had promised to repay, and that he had made clear his intention to purchase the property in his sole name. After the purchase, the parties' financial arrangements continued as during their previous occupation of rented accommodation: the woman paying for food and gas, the man for electricity, rates and other outgoings, including the mortgage. It was held that the presumption of a resulting trust was rebutted (but see also *Sekhon v Alissa* [1989] 2 FLR 94; unsuccessful attempt to establish that mother's 60 per cent contribution to purchase price was intended as a gift; and see further *Passee v Passee* [1988] 1 FLR 263).

Constructive trusts

The constructive trust is based essentially on the actual common intention of the parties and arises where the non-owning party has acted to his or her detriment in reliance on a common intention that the beneficial interests be shared. In *Lloyds Bank v Rosset* [1990] 2 FLR 155 at 163, Lord Bridge stressed the critical distinction to be drawn between two categories of case. First, there are cases where there is evidence of express discussions between the parties which resulted in an agreement, arrangement or understanding between them as to the sharing of the beneficial interests (and neither a common intention by the parties that a house is to be renovated as a 'joint venture' nor a common intention that the house is to be shared by parents and children as the family home throws any light on their intentions with respect to the beneficial ownership; *ibid* at 161). Once the arrangement to share is established, it remains only to be shown that the non-owning party has acted to his or her detriment, or has significantly altered his or her position in reliance on the agreement. The second category of case arises where there is no evidence to support a finding of an express agreement or express representation that the non-owning party is to have a share (however reasonable it might have been for the parties to have reached such an agreement if they had applied their minds to the question). In these cases, the court must rely on the conduct of the parties both as the basis from which to infer a common intention to share the beneficial interests, and as constituting the detrimental acts in reliance on the common intention.

(a) *Expressed intention*

The reference to 'an express agreement *or express representation*' requires further comment. In *Grant v Edwards* [1987] 1 FLR 87, the defendant told the plaintiff, his cohabitant, that her name was not going onto the title because this might prejudice her position in her divorce proceedings. The trial judge found that the defendant never actually intended the plaintiff to have a share in the property and had simply given an untruthful excuse for not doing something which he never intended to do. However, this absence of any actual common intention was not fatal to the plaintiff's claim since the nature of the excuse which the defendant gave must have led the plaintiff to believe that she had some interest in the house, and his conduct precluded him from denying that the case was analogous to those in which a genuine common intention existed (see also *Eves v Eves* [1975] 1 WLR 1338; man's conduct in giving excuse for not putting property into joint names raised the inference of an understanding between them that the woman was to have a share, otherwise no excuse would have been needed).

Once a common intention is established, the plaintiff must have significantly altered her position *in reliance upon it* and, in *Grant v Edwards*, above, at 95, Nourse J commented that 'the law is not so cynical as to infer that a woman will only go to live with a man to whom she is not married if she understands that she is to have an interest in their home . . . [there] must be conduct on which the woman could not reasonably have been expected to embark unless she was to have an interest in the house'.

In that case, the woman had made substantial contributions to the household finances without which the man could not have kept up the mortgage payments, and the court was able to infer that she had been acting in reliance on the common intention (and see *Stokes v Anderson* [1991] 1 FLR 391 where the claimant made payments to enable her cohabitant to acquire his ex-wife's share in the property and to reduce the mortgage debt on the ex-wife's new home; a debt for which he had undertaken liability. See also *Risch v McFee* [1991] 1 FLR 105 where, once the common intention had crystallised, the woman acted upon it by providing money to reduce the mortgage debt, and by not seeking repayment of a sum previously advanced as a loan to enable her cohabitant to buy out his ex-wife's share in the property).

The necessary link between the claimant's actions and the common intention can also be inferred in the absence of financial contributions. For example, in *Eves v Eves*, above, the woman cohabitant had undertaken extensive work on the property including considerable heavy manual labour, and the court readily drew the inference of a link between her labours and the established common intention (see also *Cooke v Head* [1972] 1 WLR 518).

(b) *Inferred intention*

The cases considered above may be contrasted with cases in which attempts have been made to persuade the court to infer from the parties' conduct an intention to share the beneficial interest in the absence of any express understanding to that effect. In *Thomas v Fuller-Brown* [1988] 1 FLR 237, an unemployed man was kept by the woman in whose house they lived. When she obtained an improvement grant, the parties agreed that he would carry out the work, which was very substantial. After that agreement the parties' domestic arrangements continued on the same basis as before save that the man received some money additional to his keep by way of 'pocket-money'. There was no express discussion between them with respect to the beneficial interests in the property. The court felt unable to infer a common intention as to the sharing of the beneficial interests since, on the facts, the parties' conduct was capable of a perfectly rational alternative explanation. Slade LJ observed (at 247) that 'a man who does work by way of improvement to his cohabitee's property without a clear understanding as to the financial basis on which the work is to be done does so at his own risk'.

In *Lloyd's Bank v Rosset*, above, the husband acquired a semi-derelict property which the wife prepared for occupation by, amongst other things, supervising and coordinating the work of builders, ordering and collecting building materials, and carrying out some decorating work herself. In Lord Bridge's opinion, this activity could not possibly justify the inference of a common intention that the beneficial interest be shared. He observed: 'it would be the most natural thing in the world for any wife, in the absence of her husband abroad, to spend all the time she could spare and to employ any skills she might have . . . in doing all she could do to accelerate progress of the work quite irrespective of any expectation she might have of enjoying a beneficial interest in the property'. Furthermore, the monetary value of her work in relation to the total cost of the property was trifling, so that, even if there had been independent evidence of a common intention that she should share in the property, Lord Bridge doubted whether her contribution would have sufficed to support a claim to a constructive trust. (Compare *H v M (Property: Beneficial Interest)* [1992] 1 FLR 229, which concerned homes in England and Spain, both in the man's sole name. In relation to the English home, Waite J found that there had been express discussions sufficient to amount to an understanding that the home was to be shared beneficially. The woman's actions in giving full support to speculative commercial ventures which put the home at hazard were found to constitute the required detrimental reliance. In relation to the house in Spain, there having been no express discussions as to ownership, the woman's claim to an interest failed: her commercial activities in Spain were inadequate to justify the inference of intended proprietary interest.)

It may be noted that (at 164) Lord Bridge referred to both *Eves v Eves*, above, and *Grant v Edwards*, above, and commented that the conduct of the woman in each of these cases fell far short of such conduct as would by itself have supported the claim in the absence of an express representation by the male partner that she was to have such an interest – an observation which underlines the difficulties likely to be encountered by those seeking to establish a constructive trust, bearing in mind that the claimant in *Grant v Edwards* had in fact made substantial contributions to the household budget without which the mortgage instalments could not have been maintained by her partner.

The position is likely to present less difficulty where there is a financial contribution directly linked to the mortgage. In *Lloyds Bank v Rosset*, above, Lord Bridge acknowledged (at 164), that direct contributions to the purchase price, whether initially or by payment of mortgage instalments, will readily justify the drawing of the necessary inference but continued: 'as I read the authorities, it is at least extremely doubtful whether anything less will do'.

Mortgages

A cohabitant's claim to an interest in the parties' home will often rest on an assertion that she has contributed, directly or indirectly, to the discharge of the mortgage commitment. It may be helpful therefore to reproduce here the propositions advanced by May LJ in *Burns v Burns* [1984] FLR 216 at 242:

'Where a matrimonial or family home is bought in the man's name alone on mortgage by the mechanism of deposit and instalments, then if the woman pays or contributes to the initial deposit this points to a common intention that she should have *some* beneficial interest in the house. If thereafter she makes direct contributions to the instalments, then the case is *a fortiori* and her rightful share is likely to be greater. If the woman, having contributed to the deposit, but although not making direct contributions to the instalments, nevertheless uses her own money for other joint household expenses so as to enable the man the more easily to pay the mortgage instalments out of his money, then her position is the same.'

In *Gissing v Gissing* [1971] AC 886, Lord Diplock observed (at 907–8) that in the circumstances described above the payment of general household expenses may be regarded as corroborative of an intention at the time of acquisition to share the beneficial interest, it being recognised that it may be no more than a mere matter of convenience which partner meets particular household outgoings, and that the payment of household expenses may be intended by both parties to be treated as including a contribution to the purchase price of the home.

May LJ continued:

'Where a woman has made no contribution to the original deposit, but makes regular and substantial contributions to the mortgage instalments, it may still be reasonable to infer a common intention that she should share the beneficial interest from the outset or infer a fresh agreement after the original conveyance that she should acquire a share.'

An intention to share can thus be found even where the contributions do not commence until some time after the original transaction, provided either that the court can infer such an intention at the outset on the basis of an expectation that the party not then contributing (eg a woman not then gainfully employed because of the need to care for children) would contribute as and when she could, or that there is evidence to justify a finding of changed intention (see also *Gissing v Gissing*, above, per Lord Diplock at 908).

It may be added that, just as anticipated participation in the payment of mortgage instalments can point to a common intention to share, so too can an expectation that one party will make a single capital payment in the future, as in *Re Nicholson* [1974] 2 All ER 386, where at the time of the purchase of the home in the husband's sole name, the wife contributed to the deposit and gave an (unenforceable) undertaking to use an expected legacy to pay off the capital sum outstanding on the mortgage, the husband paying the instalments in the meantime. The legacy was in fact applied as anticipated. The court drew the inference of an intention at the outset that the property should belong to them in equal shares.

With respect to changed or supervening intention, in *Grant v Edwards*, above, Mustill LJ specifically observed (at 101) that 'the event happening between the parties which, if followed by the relevant type of conduct on the part of the claimant, can lead to the creation of an interest in the claimant, may itself occur after acquisition. The beneficial interests may change in the course of the relationship'.

The question of changed or supervening intention commonly arises where cohabitation commences after the sole legal owner has already embarked on the purchase of the property with the aid of a mortgage. In *Gissing v Gissing*, above, Viscount Dilhorne observed (at 901) that it might well be difficult to establish a change of common intention but specifically noted that such an assertion could be supported, for instance, by proof that up to the time when the change of intention is said to have occurred, the mortgage repayments were made by one party, but were made thereafter by the other. In the light of Lord Bridge's remarks in *Lloyds Bank v Rosset* (quoted above) it is difficult to envisage any other circumstances which would justify the drawing of an inference of a changed intention.

According to May LJ's final proposition in *Burns v Burns*:

'when the house is taken in the man's name alone, if the woman makes no "real" or "substantial" financial contribution towards either the purchase price, deposit or mortgage instalments by means of which the family home was acquired, then she is not entitled to any share in the beneficial interest in that home even though over a very substantial number of years she may have worked just as hard as the man in maintaining the family, in the sense of keeping house, giving birth to and looking after and helping to bring up the children of the union.'

This proposition flows inevitably from what has gone before, and is well-illustrated by the facts of *Burns v Burns* itself, where the parties had lived together for 19 years, 17 of which had been spent in the property in question, a house bought in the man's sole name by way of mortgage. The woman was without paid employment for 12 years after the purchase and had made no direct cash contribution to the purchase price. The court held that it could not infer a common intention that the woman was to have a beneficial interest merely from the fact that she had lived with the man for 19 years, had performed domestic duties and had looked after the couple's two children, or from the fact that she had bought chattels for the household from her earnings and had redecorated the house (see also *Gissing v Gissing*, above).

Resulting and constructive trusts contrasted

(i) The constructive trust is potentially more flexible than the resulting trust. The resulting trust arises from a contribution to the costs of acquisition of the property whereas if a common intention is established by evidence of express discussions, the acts invoked as establishing the detrimental reliance may take forms which would not qualify as contributions to the purchase within the resulting trust framework.

(ii) The resulting trust arises from an intention presumed to have been present at the time of acquisition of the legal estate. A constructive trust arises from a common intention which may have existed at the time of the original acquisition, but which may equally come into existence after the legal estate is acquired.

(iii) In resulting trust cases, the parties' interests are quantified by reference to their respective contributions to the purchase. By contrast, in constructive trust cases the court need not limit itself to the value of the detrimental acts in assessing the size of the claimant's share. Indeed, the common intention in respect of which the detrimental acts are pleaded may involve a wholly different basis for ascertaining the parties' shares, as where there is an intention to share the beneficial interest equally notwithstanding inequality of contributions.

(iv) A resulting trust may be 'waiting in the wings' in cases where it is not possible to establish or give effect to a constructive trust. For example, in *Re Densham* [1975] 1 WLR 1519, the husband had become a constructive trustee in consequence of an express agreement between the parties that they were to be jointly entitled to the property. That agreement fell foul of statutory provisions which rendered certain transactions void as against a trustee in bankruptcy. However, the wife having contributed indirectly (through joint savings) to the deposit on the property, she was entitled to a one-ninth share in the property under a resulting trust.

1.3.5 Bankruptcy

As *Re Densham*, above, illustrates, an agreement whereby one partner becomes a constructive trustee is, in essence, a disposition by
that party. The beneficiary's interest may therefore be vulnerable
to an application to have the transaction set aside. The same would
apply to cases where the conveyance itself declares the parties to
be trustees for themselves in proportions which do not reflect their
actual contributions to the costs of acquisition.

The Insolvency Act 1986, s 423 provides for the setting aside of
transactions entered into at an undervalue with the intention of
defeating the claims of creditors. By s 339, the court may also
intervene where there has been a transaction at an undervalue in
the five years preceding the presentation of the petition for bankruptcy. If the transaction occurred more than two years prior to
that date the court may intervene only if the bankrupt was insolvent
at the time of the transaction or became insolvent as a result of it,
but there is a rebuttable presumption that this condition is satisfied
if the transaction was entered into with 'an associate', which
includes a spouse and a 'reputed spouse'.

1.4 Quantification of shares

1.4.1 Determining the size of shares

Where it has been established that the parties share the beneficial
interest in the home, the size of each party's share is dependent
upon the parties' common intention. Where the parties have made
their intention clear by means of an enforceable declaration of trust,
it remains only to carry out whatever equitable accounting is appropriate in the particular circumstances of the case (see §1.4.3 below).
In the absence of a formal record of the parties' intention, the court
will look for other external signs of common intention. As Dillon
LJ emphasised in *Springette v Defoe* [1992] 2 FLR 388 at 393: 'the
common intention of the parties must, in my judgment, mean a
shared intention communicated between them. It cannot mean an
intention which each happened to have in his or her mind but had
never communicated to the other'. Steyn LJ made the same point
more succinctly (at 394): 'Our trust law does not allow property
rights to be affected by telepathy'.

Generally, the external signs of common intention will be found, if at all, in discussions between the parties, but the court may also derive assistance from the parties' *actions*, as in *Grant v Edwards* [1987] 1 FLR 87 where, following a fire at the home, the sum remaining from insurance moneys after completion of the repairs was paid by the man into the parties' joint bank account. Viewed against the background of the woman's substantial indirect contributions to mortgage repayments in reliance on the common intention that she was to have a share, that act was regarded as evidence of an intention to share the beneficial interest equally.

Where there is no evidence as to the parties' intention with respect to the size of their respective shares, the court is driven back to the equitable principle that the shares are presumed to be in proportion to the contributions. Where the property is purchased outright for cash, the extent of the respective contributions to the purchase price will generally be readily ascertainable. It is now clear that the legal expenses of the purchase are to be regarded as an integral part of the acquisition costs, so that contributions to the incidental expenses of the purchase are to be brought into the account (see eg *Walker v Hall* [1984] FLR 126; *Grant v Edwards* above, *Huntingford v Hobbs* [1992] Fam Law 437).

Cash may be contributed indirectly, as in *Walker v Hall*, above, where the parties had pooled their earnings to meet their household expenses and the mortgage repayments on their home – a property already acquired by the man before the commencement of their relationship. The proceeds of sale of that home were applied to the purchase of a new home and it was held that the woman's contributions (via the common pool) to the mortgage payments in respect of the previous home constituted an indirect contribution to the purchase price of the new home, since they had resulted in more 'free' money being available to meet the cost of the new house (and see *Nixon v Nixon* [1969] 1 WLR 1676).

A contribution to the acquisition need not be in the form of cash, but may be the equivalent of cash, as where a sitting tenant is able to buy the freehold at a discounted price (see *Marsh v von Sternberg* [1986] 1 FLR 526; relied upon in *Springette v Defoe*, above: council tenant exercising 'right to buy' at a discount of 41 per cent from market value treated as having made a direct cash contribution of that sum).

The exercise becomes more difficult where the purchase involves commitment to a mortgage stretching many years into the future.

In such cases, the tendency of the court is to treat the person(s) liable under the mortgage as having contributed the capital sum thus raised. Thus, for example, parties who assumed joint liability in respect of a loan were held to have contributed the capital sum in equal shares in *Walker v Hall*, *Marsh v von Sternberg* and *Springette v Defoe*. However, this approach will yield to evidence of any agreement between the parties as to how their joint mortgage liability is to be discharged.

This result is well illustrated by *Huntingford v Hobbs*, above, where the purchase price, inclusive of expenses, was £63,860 of which the woman provided a cash contribution of £38,860. The balance was raised by way of an endowment mortgage taken in the parties' joint names but there was an express agreement between the parties that the man would make all payments of mortgage interest and premiums in respect of the associated insurance policy. It was held, therefore, that the man was to be treated as having contributed the entire sum raised by the mortgage. Thus, the parties were beneficially entitled as to 61 per cent to the woman and 39 per cent to the man. In that case, the man moved out of the home just over two years after the purchase and ceased to make any further payments; the mortgage interest being paid thereafter by the woman. This was held not to affect the size of his share in the property. However, in view of the agreement, the sum outstanding in respect of the mortgage was held to be a charge on the defendant's share alone in calculating the sum he should receive in respect of his interest (though an element of 'double compensation' appears to have been introduced by the manner in which the Court of Appeal carried out its calculations on this aspect of the case).

A possible alternative approach is to examine the whole period of repayment and to assess each party's share on the basis of the contributions actually made. According to Lord Diplock in *Gissing v Gissing* [1971] AC 886, at 908–9, there is nothing inherently improbable in spouses acting on the understanding that the wife should be entitled to a share which is not to be quantified immediately upon the acquisition of the home but is left to be determined when the mortgage is repaid or the property disposed of, on the basis of what is fair having regard to the total contributions, direct or indirect, which each spouse has made by that date. That approach was applied in *Young v Young* [1984] FLR 375 where the purchase price was partly provided by the woman and partly raised by a mortgage in respect of which the parties were joint mortgagors. The instalments were paid from a joint account in which their earnings were pooled. By the date of the separation some 16 months after the purchase, the capital sum owing (originally £11,750) had been reduced by only £200. Instalments thereafter were paid by the woman. The court granted a declaration that the woman was solely entitled to the entire beneficial interest. It was described as 'wholly unrealistic' to decide that even a very small proportion of the equity was held beneficially for the man. This approach was applied by the judge at first instance in *Huntingford v Hobbs*, above, but the Court of Appeal made clear that such a course will only be appropriate where the evidence discloses no clear arrangement between the parties at the time of the purchase as to the manner in which the mortgage payments are to be provided for (per Sir Christopher Slade at Fam Law 438; see also *Marsh v von Sternberg*, above).

When the court finds itself obliged to measure actual contributions to the purchase, a particular difficulty will often arise if the parties' respective incomes and the pattern of their household expenditure have varied over the years of the purchase. Such a difficulty does not justify swift resort to the maxim 'equality is equity' (*Gissing v Gissing*, above), though it may mean that the size of shares has to be decided using a fairly 'broad brush' approach. A broad approach will also be inevitable where contributions have taken a form which cannot be quantified in cash terms, such as the manual labour of the woman in *Eves v Eves*, above, or the stimulus and organisational efforts of the wife in *B v B (Real Property: Assessment of Interests)* [1988] 2 FLR 490: house in joint names; wife's interest assessed at 15 per cent; her financial contribution 'minimal', but she was the 'driving force' in organising and supervising design and construction work.

1.4.2   Date of valuation

It is now settled that the shares of persons beneficially entitled under a trust are to be valued at the date of realisation by sale or notional sale. Such interests are absolute and indefeasible (see *Brykiert v Jones* (1981) FLR 373) and cannot be defeated or diminished, either automatically or by the exercise of some discretion, on the happening of some other event, such as the cessation of cohabitation (*Turton v Turton* [1988] 1 FLR 23).

1.4.3   Equitable accounting

Although the cessation of cohabitation will not trigger the valuation of the parties' interests, it may nevertheless mean that adjustments are necessary to take account of the post-separation discharge of burdens with respect to the property: the absent party will retain his share in full during the period of separation and must therefore contribute fairly to expenditure which preserves or enhances that investment. Thus, for example, if a party has spent money on recent redecoration of the property which results in an improved value at sale he should have credit for that expenditure (*Bernard v Josephs* (1983) FLR 178).

Where the party in occupation pays the whole of mortgage instalments for which both parties had assumed liability, that party will be credited with one half of the sum by which the capital debt has been reduced, in addition to his own share in the net proceeds (*Suttill v Graham* [1977] 1 WLR 819; and see *Brykiert v Jones* (1981) FLR 373: beneficial joint tenants separated one year after purchase; application for sale 30 years later).

It seems now to be accepted that payments of interest due under the mortgage are also to be brought into account as payments which have protected and preserved the capital investment (see *Re Gorman* [1990] 2 FLR 284). However, since the party who remains in the property has the benefit of exclusive occupation, the matter of occupation rent arises. The traditional view was that, while an occupation rent was clearly payable where one party had forced the other to leave by violence or other expulsive conduct (*Dennis v McDonald* (1982) FLR 409) or where the party remaining in occupation had resisted a sale (*Suttill v Graham*, above), no occupation rent was payable if a co-owner left the property voluntarily (*Jones (AE) v Jones (FW)* [1977] 1 WLR 438). However, the present view seems to be that it is not necessary to distinguish cases of voluntary departure, and an occupation rent is payable whatever the circumstances of the separation (see eg *Bernard v Josephs*, above; *Huntingford v Hobbs*, above).

As between equal co-owners, the occupation rent payable is one-half of a 'fair rent' as assessed under the Rent Act 1977, disregarding any scarcity value (*Dennis v McDonald*, above) but, to avoid possibly expensive and protracted inquiries and accounts, a 'rule of convenience' has been adopted which, in effect, sets off the interest element of mortgage repayments against a notional occupation rent (see eg *Re Gorman*, above; *Huntingford v Hobbs*, above).

1.5 Protection of interests

1.5.1 Legal ownership

No effective dealing with the entire legal interest in property can occur without the concurrence of each and every legal owner. Thus, if one joint legal owner ('the forger') forges the other ('innocent') owner's signature on documents purporting to effect an outright sale of the property to a bona fide purchaser, this purported sale by the forger will not operate to pass legal title, and cannot be an effective transfer of the innocent owner's beneficial interest. Nevertheless, the purported sale will have the effect of severing the beneficial joint tenancy (if any) and, if the purchaser so elects, under the doctrine of partial performance the transaction will effect the transfer to the purchaser of such beneficial interest as the forger has. Thereafter, the forger and the innocent owner will hold the legal estate on trust for the innocent owner and the purchaser. However, if the innocent owner at no time agreed to a sale of the property at the price paid by the purchaser, any necessary quantification of the share of the innocent owner cannot be carried out by reference to that price (*Ahmed v Kendrick* [1988] 2 FLR 22).

If a joint legal owner ('owner A') purports to effect a mortgage of property by deposit of title deeds (or, in the case of registered land, by deposit of the land certificate) without the consent of the other legal owner ('owner B'), owner B will be entitled to demand the return of the documents so deposited. Again, however, the purported creation of the legal charge may serve to create an equitable charge over owner A's equitable interest. Nevertheless, the person claiming the benefit of the charge will not necessarily be granted an order for partial performance. The court will consider the potential hardship to owner B and, if an order would cause substantial prejudice to owner B, the order may be refused.

The mere fact that an order would give the chargee *locus standi* to apply under the Law of Property Act 1925, s 30 for an order for the sale of the property would not by itself necessarily justify refusal of the remedy of partial performance. Nevertheless, that consequence of an order may amount to substantial prejudice on the particular facts of a given case (see *Thomas Guaranty Ltd v Campbell* [1988] QB 210: where further prejudice would have arisen in respect of the wife's application for rectification of the conveyance, as to which see §1.3.1 above).

1.5.2   Beneficial ownership

Where there is only one legal owner but more than one beneficial owner, the legal owner holds the property under a trust for sale. In principle, a second trustee should be appointed before a sale takes place. The legal owner may appoint another trustee (who need not be the other beneficial owner), and the conveyance can be endorsed with the notice of appointment. Alternatively, if the legal owner refuses to make an appointment, an application may be made under the Trustee Act 1925, s 41 for the appointment of another trustee by the court. In an emergency, an injunction can be sought restraining dealings with the property pending the outcome of the s 41 application (see *Waller v Waller* [1967] 1 WLR 451). A beneficial owner is entitled to have her wishes considered by the trustees before a sale is effected (Law of Property Act 1925, s 26(3); and see *Waller v Waller*, above). However, conveyance of the legal estate or the creation of a legal interest does not require the signature of a beneficial owner. Moreover, a sale by a sole trustee will be effective to pass good title to the legal estate, and the purchaser may be unaware of the beneficial owner's existence. In considering the consequences of such a transaction it is necessary to examine separately cases involving unregistered title, and those involving registered land.

Unregistered land

The fundamental rule in relation to trusts for sale is that, on sale, the interests of persons beneficially entitled are overreached and attach to the proceeds of sale in the hands of the vendor, from whom they may be recovered by an action for money had and received. The purchaser thus takes the property free of any such interest, which is overreached. However, a beneficial owner's interest will not be overreached and a purchaser will take subject to it *as an interest in the property* if the purchaser has actual or constructive notice of the existence of that interest. Actual notice means, simply, actual knowledge on the part of the purchaser. Constructive notice means, essentially, knowledge that the purchaser is deemed to have had in circumstances where the facts would have been uncovered by the making of such enquiries and inspections as ought reasonably to have been made by the purchaser or by his solicitor or other agent (Law of Property Act 1925, s 199(1)(ii)(a) and (b)).

An equitable interest arising under a resulting or constructive trust is not registrable as a land charge under the Land Charges Act 1972. Thus, constructive notice cannot be established by reference to an entry in the Land Charges Register. The question arises, therefore, as to what is required in order to establish that a purchaser should have been put on enquiry, and this has given rise to some difficulty, particularly in respect of a beneficial owner's occupation of the property which, in most cases, will be the sole or main factor relied on as constituting constructive notice.

In *Caunce v Caunce* [1969] 1 WLR 286, it was held that occupation by a wife would not constitute constructive notice since her occupation was consistent with her right at common law to be provided with a roof over her head and did not point unequivocally to the possession by her of a beneficial interest inconsistent with the title offered by the husband. A cohabitant, of course, does not possess such a personal right to be housed and her occupation is thus not explicable on such a basis. However, there were further observations in *Caunce v Caunce* to the effect that occupation by other relatives, guests or lodgers would likewise be insufficient to put a purchaser on enquiry, notwithstanding that the occupier might have contributed money towards the purchase of the property.

Caunce v Caunce was disapproved in *Williams & Glyn's Bank v Boland* [1981] AC 487, but not overruled. However, the House of Lords in *Boland* effectively extended an invitation to lower courts not to follow *Caunce*: an invitation taken up in the High Court in *Kingsnorth Finance Co Ltd v Tizard* [1986] 1 WLR 783, where a wife, by virtue of her contributions, had a beneficial interest in unregistered land on which the husband, as sole legal owner, had secured a mortgage. The marriage had broken down and the wife normally did not sleep in the house though she returned there each day to provide meals for the children who resided there continuously. She kept most of her clothes there and stayed overnight on the frequent occasions when the husband was away. It was held that the wife was in occupation of the property: to amount to actual occupation physical presence in the house does not have to be either exclusive or continuous and uninterrupted, and is not negatived by regular and repeated absence. Thus, in *Kingsnorth Finance Co Ltd v Tizard*, the wife had not ceased to be in occupation merely because she had changed her habits, significant though that change was. Counsel for the wife had submitted that the fact of occupation itself fixed the mortgagees with constructive notice of such rights as she had, but (at 794) the judge accepted the mortgagees' submission that the mortgagee has notice only where he *finds* the claimant in occupation, subject to the 'significant qualification' that the mortgagee has carried out such inspections as ought reasonably to be made and either does not find the claimant in occupation or does not find evidence of that occupation reasonably sufficient to give notice of it. It was held that, in the circumstances of the *Tizard* case (which included the husband's disclosure of the existence of a wife from whom he said he was separated), the mortgagees through their surveyor agent had information which should have alerted them that the full facts were not in their possession. He further found that, in the circumstances, a single pre-arranged inspection of the property by the surveyor (on which occasion the husband had contrived to eliminate signs of the wife's occupation) did not constitute 'such . . . inspections . . . as ought reasonably to have been made', as required by s 199(1) of the Law of Property Act 1925.

In sum then, the interest in the property of a cohabitant who is a beneficial owner is relatively secure so long as that owner is in occupation of the property. Where the beneficially entitled cohabitant has moved out, however, it will be necessary to take the steps outlined above to secure the appointment of a second trustee if the beneficial owner is not to be left with a (possibly illusory) right to recover her share of the proceeds of sale from the vendor. It may be desirable to take these steps in any event, in order to ensure that the parties to any application for an order for sale under the Law of Property Act 1925, s 30 are the cohabitants themselves, and not the beneficial owner and the purchaser who has taken his interest from the sole legal owner for, in proceedings between the beneficial owner and the purchaser, considerations will be relevant which would not arise in a dispute between the cohabitants themselves and these considerations may affect the outcome in a manner unfavourable to the beneficial owner (for a discussion of the Law of Property Act 1925, s 30, see further §2.1.3 below).

Registered land

A beneficial interest in registered land is a minor interest which may be protected by entry on the title by way of restriction, notice or caution. However, entry by way of restriction and notice both require the co-operation of the legal owner as registered proprietor since production of the land certificate is required. Entry by way of caution does not require the cooperation of the proprietor, and will ensure that the beneficial owner is warned of any prospective dealing with the land so as to have an opportunity to object to the dealing. However, the primary function of cautions is to afford temporary protection to a claim, not permanent protection of an established right.

The Law of Property Act 1925, s 59(6) provides that 'a purchaser acquiring title under a registered disposition shall not be concerned with any . . . document, matter or claim (not being an overriding interest . . .) which is not protected by a caution, or other entry on the register, whether he has or has not notice thereof, express, implied or constructive'. (See also Law of Property Act 1925, s 20(1).) Thus, as a general rule, minor interests such as equitable interests under trusts for sale will not bind a purchaser, even a purchaser with notice, unless protected by an entry on the register.

However, an equitable interest not protected by an entry on the register can constitute an overriding interest, by which a transferee will be bound. The Land Registration Act 1925, s 70(1) provides a list of overriding interests, which includes:

'(g) The rights of every person in actual occupation of the land . . . save where inquiry is made of such person and the rights are not disclosed.'

In *Williams & Glyn's Bank v Boland*, above, the House of Lords held that the fact that the vendor is in occupation does not preclude occupation by others. In that case, the interest of a beneficially entitled wife was an overriding interest: her interest was an interest subsisting in reference to the land itself and not merely an interest in the proceeds of sale; she was in actual occupation, and no enquiry had been made of her so that there had been no failure on her part to disclose her rights. It cannot be doubted that the *Boland* decision is equally applicable to beneficially entitled cohabitants who are in actual occupation.

As to what constitutes actual occupation, it may be noted that in *Kingsnorth Finance Co Ltd v Tizard*, the facts of which have been set out above, the judge opined that, had the case concerned registered title, the wife would have been in actual occupation for the purpose of s 70(1)(g) (and see also *Chhokar v Chhokar and Another* [1984] FLR 313, and *Abbey National Building Society v Cann* [1990] 2 FLR 122).

Where the transaction concerned is one under which a legal charge is created, the overriding interest protected by s 70(1)(g) is the interest of a person in actual occupation when the legal charge is executed, rather than merely when it is registered (*Abbey National Building Society v Cann*, above).

Finally, it must be noted that equitable interests in either registered or unregistered land bind only those purchasers whose own interest comes into being after the creation of the equitable interest, which might tend to suggest that when a property is purchased with the aid of a mortgage the mortgagees will be bound by the interest of a beneficial owner interested under a resulting trust since that interest arises from the purchase itself whereas, technically, the mortgage takes effect *after* the transfer of ownership of the property. This result was, in practice, avoided by holding that the beneficial owner has, in effect, conceded priority to a mortgage where the beneficial owner is fully aware of the transaction (see *Paddington Building Society v Mendelsohn* (1985) 50 P&CR 244 – registered land; *Bristol & West Building Society v Henning* [1985] 2 All ER 606 – unregistered land). However, in *Abbey National Building Society v Cann*, above, the House of Lords went further, rejecting as 'no more than a legal artifice' the notion of a *scintilla temporis* between the purchase and the mortgagee's charge, and acknowledging the reality that the acquisition of the legal estate and the creation of the charge constitute a single transaction, the two events being 'not only precisely simultaneous but indissolubly bound together' (per Lord Oliver at 140). Thus, the interest of a beneficial owner will be postponed to the rights of the mortgagees.

The postponement of a beneficial owner's interest may apply to any subsequent mortgage even where the later mortgage is substituted for the original mortgage in circumstances which would normally result in the beneficial owner's interest being protected. In such a case, to the extent that the new mortgage replaces the original mortgage on no less favourable terms, the mortgagees' interest will have priority but the beneficial owner's interest will not be encumbered by any *increased* indebtedness (*Equity and Law Ltd v Prestidge* [1992] 1 FLR 485).

1.6   Realisation of interests

Co-ownership of a family home necessarily involves a trust for sale. The Law of Property Act 1925, s 30 provides:

> 'If the trustees for sale refuse to sell . . . , or any requisite consent cannot be obtained, any person interested may apply to the court [for an order for sale], and the court may make such order as it thinks fit.'

In the majority of cases in which a dispute arises as to whether a sale should take place, one party will be in occupation of the property and will thus be deprived of that accommodation if an order for sale is made. Therefore, the considerations to which the court will have regard in deciding whether to order a sale are considered, in the context of occupation rights, at §2.1.3 below.

1.7   Proprietary estoppel

A claim of proprietary estoppel invokes the power of the court to interfere in cases where it would be unconscionable to permit the assertion of strict legal rights (*Taylors Fashions Ltd v Liverpool Victoria Trustees Co Ltd* [1982] QB 133). Thus, an owner will be prevented from insisting on his strict legal rights where another person, with the owner's knowledge and acquiescence, has changed his position in reliance on a belief known to and encouraged by the owner that he already has or is to be given a right in relation to the owner's property and where, by virtue of that change of position, that other person will suffer detriment if the owner is permitted to resile from the assurance which he has expressly or impliedly given.

There are three prerequisites to establishing an estoppel:

(i) An *assurance*, which must create the expectation of an interest *in the land*: a vague promise of 'financial security' will not suffice (*Layton v Martin* [1986] 2 FLR 227; but see also *Re Basham* [1986] 1 WLR 1498).

(ii) *Reliance*: the change of position must take place on the faith of the belief that the assurance has induced. This reliance requirement can create difficulties in the context of disputes involving a family home. For example, if the making of improvements to the property is pleaded, the court may take the view that they would have been made in any case simply for reasons of domestic convenience (see eg *Stilwell v Simpson* (1983) 133 NLJ 894; and see *Layton v Martin*, above). Likewise, contributions to joint household expenses may be attributable to nothing more than a contributor's readiness to 'pay her way'.

(iii) The *detriment* incurred need not relate to money or labour expended on the property: it could comprise, for instance, deliberately refraining from purchasing other property (see *Re Basham*, above).

A constructive trust is commonly described in terms of a frustrated *bargain*, whereas estoppel is more clearly founded upon a concept of frustrated *expectation*. In practice, claims under both heads often go hand in hand. However, the concept of the constructive trust is clearly available for use as a sword whereas there are indications that a claim of proprietary estoppel will be most readily accepted where it is used as a shield, as in *Pascoe v Turner* [1979] 1 WLR 431, where estoppel was raised as a defence to an action for possession. In that case, the unmarried couple lived together in the man's house for eight years. On the breakdown of the relationship, the man moved out and repeatedly assured the woman that the house and its contents were hers, but he never executed the requisite deeds. In reliance on his assurances, and to the man's knowledge, the woman spent a substantial part of her savings on redecoration, improvements and repairs. The contents were held to have passed to her by gift, but the trial judge's finding of a constructive trust was rejected by the Court of Appeal. There was thus merely a purported gift of the house which was imperfect for lack of writing. Nevertheless, an equity had arisen in the woman's favour and the Court concluded that it must be satisfied by perfecting the gift and ordering the conveyance of the property to the woman. It rejected the alternative of an order declaring that she had a licence to occupy the house for her lifetime.

1.7.1　Range of remedies

Where an estoppel is raised, the resulting order will depend on what the court considers necessary to satisfy the equity. In *Pascoe v Turner*, above, the court was faced with a 'ruthless' plaintiff who was determined to get the defendant out of the property, and concluded that nothing less than an outright transfer to the woman would sufficiently secure her continued occupation, quiet enjoyment and freedom of action; eg with respect to charging the property to secure a loan. (An alternative means of securing the desired autonomy would have been to declare her a tenant for life under the Settled Land Act 1925, so as to entitle her to call for the property to be vested in her with a power to sell; see *Ungurian v Lesnoff and Others* [1990] 2 FLR 299.) Often, however, the equity will be satisfied by some lesser order, such as an order conferring the right to occupy the property for life, either rent-free or at a nominal rent (see eg *Jones (AE) v Jones (FW)* [1977] 1 WLR 438; *Greasley v Cooke* [1980] 1 WLR 1306; *Griffiths v Williams* (1977) 248 Estates Gazette 947). Alternatively, there is no reason why the court should not order the payment of monetary compensation where such a course will suffice to satisfy the equity.

1.7.2   Protecting the 'inchoate' equity

There is general agreement that an estoppel claimant has no interest in the land unless and until the court makes an order in a form which confers such a right. Once conferred, the right can be enforced against third parties in whatever manner is appropriate to the type of right awarded but, while inchoate, an equity in respect of unregistered land is neither an equitable interest capable of being overreached, nor a land charge susceptible to registration. On the other hand, such an equity can 'run with the land' so as to bind the proprietor's trustee in bankruptcy or the trustees of his will (see *In re Sharpe* [1980] 1 WLR 219; *Inwards v Baker* [1965] 2 QB 29; *Jones (AE) v Jones (FW)*, above; but see also *Bristol & West Building Society v Henning* [1985] 2 All ER 606, specifically leaving open whether the decision in *Re Sharpe* was correct). Moreover, it is enforceable against a purchaser who has actual notice of the circumstances which gave rise to the equity (*ER Ives Investment Ltd v High* [1967] 2 QB 379), but the law is unclear as to the effect of constructive notice.

2 OCCUPATION

2.1 Owner-occupied property

2.1.1 Sole legal and beneficial ownership

Where one cohabitant alone holds the legal and beneficial title to property then, as against the person living with him, his right to occupy the property is absolute and indefeasible save by an order under the Domestic Violence and Matrimonial Proceedings Act 1976 excluding him from the property (see §2.4 below).

As a general proposition, a cohabitant not having any legal or beneficial interest in the property (a 'bare' cohabitant) has no right to remain there and may be excluded by the owner at any time. This general proposition must be qualified by reference to four situations in which a bare cohabitant may have some protection.

(i) A bare cohabitant who has been excluded from the home may apply to the court under the Domestic Violence Act 1976 for an order requiring the other cohabitant to permit the applicant to enter and remain in the home (see §2.4 below).

(ii) A cohabitant may have a contractual licence to remain in occupation of the property (see §2.1.4 below).

(iii) A cohabitant may be able to establish a licence by estoppel, also giving a right to remain in occupation (see §2.1.4 below).

(iv) A cohabitant who is caring for a child born of the relationship will be able to remain in occupation if an order is made under the Children Act 1989, Sch 1, requiring the settlement or transfer of the property for the benefit of the child (see §2.1.5 below).

2.1.2 Joint ownership

Joint legal owners

As noted above, a legal owner of property has a right to occupy the property by virtue of his proprietorship, and cannot be excluded from the property by any joint owner except by a court order. For rights as against third parties, see §1.5.1 above.

Joint beneficial owners

Where there is only one legal owner but both cohabitants have a beneficial interest (eg under a resulting or constructive trust), again, each beneficial owner has a right as against the other not to be excluded from the property save under a court order (*Bull v Bull* [1955] 1 QB 234). For rights as against third parties, see §1.5.2 above.

2.1.3   Orders for sale

As noted at §1.5 above, where the beneficial interest is shared, it is open to a beneficial owner to seek an order for sale of the property under the Law of Property Act 1925, s 30. Applications involving property purchased to serve as a matrimonial or family home should be dealt with by the Family Division rather than the Chancery Division (*Williams v Williams* [1976] Ch 278; and see *Bernard v Josephs* (1983) FLR 178 at 185).

As a matter of theory, a trust for sale is a trust which imposes a duty to sell unless there is agreement to exercise the power to postpone sale. Thus, on an application under s 30, the court will normally expect to assist the party who wishes to compel execution of the trust. Nevertheless, the court has the power to make 'such order as it thinks fit', and it is clear that there is a discretion to refuse immediate enforcement of the trust. The courts have evolved a flexible approach towards applications in respect of a family home.

Underlying purpose and other factors

Where the property was purchased to serve as a family home, the court will be slow to order a sale where that underlying purpose is still capable of fulfilment. However, where the parties' relationship has foundered, the court will have to give careful consideration, among other factors, to whether it would be right to prevent a beneficially entitled party from realising that part of his capital which is locked up in the home. Nevertheless, it has been pointed out (in *Browne v Pritchard* [1975] 1 WLR 1366 – a case concerning property adjustment on divorce) that the argument that a person is being 'kept out of his money' is not apt to describe the position in respect of property purchased as a family home: if the relationship had not broken down neither party would have touched a penny of the value of the house: 'investment in a home is the least liquid investment that one can possibly make' (per Ormrod LJ at 1371). Likewise, in *Williams v Williams*, above, at 285, Lord Denning stressed that the courts:

> 'nowadays have great regard to the fact that the house is bought as a home in which the family is brought up. It is not treated as property to be sold or as an investment to be realized for cash . . . The court, in executing the trust, should regard the primary object as being to provide a home and not a sale. Steps should be taken to preserve it as a home for the remaining partner and children, but giving the outgoing partner such compensation, by way of a charge or being bought out, as is reasonable in the circumstances.'

In practice, therefore, the court is likely to hold that the underlying purpose is still subsisting if, despite the breakdown of the relationship, the property is still serving as a home for the 'remnant family'; that is to say, for the remaining cohabitant and the parties' children. Indeed, the presence in the home of minor children will often be of crucial importance. In *Re Evers' Trust* [1980] 1 WLR 1327, for example, the parties had lived together for several years in a house purchased in their joint names. When they separated, the woman remained in occupation with the couple's own child, and her two other children from a previous union. The Court of Appeal refused the man's application for an order for sale and specific reference was made to the fact that the underlying purpose of the trust had been to provide a home for the couple and the children 'for the indefinite future'. The Court noted also that the woman had provided more capital than the man; that she was prepared to accept full responsibility for future repayments of the joint mortgage; that she would have found it extremely difficult to rehouse herself if the property were sold; and that the man had a secure home with his mother and had no immediate need to realise his investment. Thus, the 'subsisting underlying purpose' test was applied here in a context where the balance of the parties' competing needs also indicated postponement. The Court rejected that part of the trial judge's order in which he postponed sale until the parties' own child attained the age of 16. The Court observed that it was inappropriate to specify an arbitrary date for a sale in the relatively distant future: there should be freedom to reapply in the intervening period in the light of a change of circumstances, such as the woman's re-marriage or if she became capable of buying out the man's interest. All the court can do is decide whether, in the present case, at the present moment, and in the existing circumstances, it would be wrong to order a sale. (However, postponement of sale to a speci-fied, though distant, date in the future is a more likely outcome where the court exercises its power under the Children Act 1989 to order the settlement of property for the benefit of a child; see §2.1.5 below.)

According to Lord Denning MR in *Bernard v Josephs*, above (at 184), even where there are no children in occupation, the court can refuse to order a sale at the instance of the outgoing party if it would be unduly harsh to require the remaining party to vacate, but it is submitted that this will normally be dependent upon it being practicable to compensate the party seeking a sale for depriving him of the immediate benefit of his capital (see Kerr LJ at 194).

As noted above, in *Re Evers' Trust*, the court adverted to the fact that the occupying party had provided the major share of the pur-chase price. This is a relevant consideration whether the proceeds of sale are to be equally or unequally divided. Where they are to be unequally divided, the court may legitimately have regard to the wishes of the person with the major interest and, where the proceeds are to be equally divided, the fact that sale is resisted by a party who in reality furnished most of the purchase price will again carry some weight, as in *Bedson v Bedson* [1965] 2 QB 666, where the property in question had been bought in the spouses' joint names out of the husband's savings. In that case, the nature of the property also militated against a sale since it comprised a draper's shop with flat above. The wife had deserted the husband and had applied for an order for sale. The shop constituted the husband's sole livelihood and therefore his sole means of supporting not only himself but also the wife. (Since the wife was not in reality seeking to deprive the husband of the home it was possible to compromise the proceed-ings on the basis of an agreement that the husband would pay the wife an occupation rent during his continued occupation.)

In *Jackson v Jackson* [1971] 1 WLR 1539, the parties were entitled to share equally in the proceeds but the husband had contributed much more to the purchase than the wife. On his application for an order for sale, significance was attached to the fact that the house was considerably larger than was necessary to meet the wife's reasonable needs. Moreover, her share in the proceeds of sale would be sufficient to enable her to obtain alternative accommodation.

If the court accedes to the request for an order for sale, it may postpone sale for a period sufficient to allow the occupying party to make other arrangements with respect to accommodation, or it may suspend the sale on terms. In *Bernard v Josephs*, above, the court found that the underlying purpose of the trust was exhausted following the breakdown of childless cohabitation and that there would have been no legitimate ground for refusing a sale. However, the applicant for sale was prepared not to insist on a sale if the defendant bought out her share. The order for sale contained a condition that it should not be enforced if, within four months, the defendant did so buy out her interest. The court noted that such an outcome may also be advantageous where, for example, a forced sale at short notice would adversely affect the price that could be obtained.

Where the party out of occupation is not necessarily anxious to achieve a sale, it may be possible to reach an agreement that the property shall not be sold, but that the occupying party shall pay an occupation rent, as occurred in *Bedson*, above. However, although the court has powers to make orders ancillary to an order for sale which are necessary to implement the sale, if it makes *no* order for sale it lacks the power to make other orders and thus cannot *impose* payments of an occupation rent. Moreover, although the court may use the threat of an order for sale to induce an occupier to reach an equitable agreement with a non-occupying party who is not insisting on a sale, it cannot use the threat of *withholding* an order for sale in order to induce the non-occupier to reach an equitable agreement (see *Bernard v Josephs*, above, per Kerr LJ at 194).

Applications by third parties

The above discussion has been concerned with the attitude of the court in s 30 proceedings as between the parties to the original relationship. However, such proceedings may be mounted by a third party. Where a sale is sought by a third party in what may be described as a 'commercial' context there is likely to be more emphasis on 'the purely property aspect of the matter' (*In re Bailey* [1977] 1 WLR 278, at 283). In *re Bailey*, an application by the husband's trustee in bankruptcy succeeded despite occupation of the home by the ex-wife and children. The later case of *Re Holliday* [1981] Ch 405, where the remnant family were protected, was subsequently described as representing a 'high-water mark', 'very much against the run of recent authorities' (see *Harman v Glencross* [1986] 2 FLR 241, per Balcombe LJ at 253), and is distinguishable on the basis that there was in that case a realistic prospect that the creditors would be paid in full, the husband having himself filed the petition for bankruptcy as a tactical move.

The position with respect to spouses of persons who become bankrupt is now governed by the Insolvency Act 1986, s 366 which expresses the statutory intention that protection for spouses should not exceed one year from the date of bankruptcy 'unless the circumstances of the case are exceptional' (s 336(5)). *Re Citro* [1991] 1 FLR 71 establishes that the voice of the creditors will normally prevail over the voice of the other spouse so that a sale will be ordered within a short period. Exceptional circumstances which might be relied upon to justify a postponement of sale do not include the hardship of having to move to a poorer area or disrupting the children's education since these are the melancholy but routine consequences of debt and improvidence (see per Nourse LJ at 82). The 'underlying purpose' argument will be of no avail: where the interest of one spouse has vested in his trustee in bankruptcy, the secondary purpose of the trust for sale falls with the change in ownership (contrast *Stott v Ratcliffe* (1982) 126 SJ 310, where, on an application for sale by the personal representatives of a deceased tenant in common, the court concluded that the underlying purpose of the trust encompassed the continued provision of a home for the survivor). The specific framework provided by the Insolvency Act 1986, s 336 is not directly applicable to cohabitants, but the court is unlikely to allow cohabitants of bankrupts to fare better than bankrupts' spouses.

It may be noted that the Insolvency Act also provides some indirect protection for cohabitants (whether beneficially entitled or not) by preserving the bankrupt's own right of occupation where he has a child or children under 18 living with him. Section 337 requires the trustee in bankruptcy to seek an order under the Matrimonial Homes Act 1983, s 1 before effecting a sale. Again, however, the protection is clearly intended to be limited to an adjustment period of one year following the bankruptcy since, if an immediate sale is not ordered, when one year has elapsed from the date of bankruptcy the court must assume 'unless the circumstances of the case are exceptional' that the interests of the bankrupt's creditors outweigh all other considerations (s 337(6)).

Finally, special mention should be made of the somewhat remarkable case of *Chhokar v Chhokar and Another* [1984] FLR 313, where the person seeking an order for sale had purchased the property from the husband in a collusive transaction designed to defeat the wife's interest. The sale (at an undervalue) was deliberately timed to coincide with the wife's absence from the home (she was in hospital for the birth of the couple's child). Following the sale the husband had disappeared but, the wife having returned to the property, they were subsequently reconciled and occupied the property together. On the purchaser's application for an order for sale the court referred to the traditionally strict approach to bankruptcy cases where the trustee speaks for the innocent creditors, but emphasised that in the instant case the applicant's role in the transaction had been 'from first to last . . . stamped with immoral stigma'. In the context of his 'monstrous fraud' he could not be regarded as being truly a stranger to the marriage and, since the underlying purpose of the trust was still capable of being performed, a sale was refused.

2.1.4 Licences

Contractual licence

A contractual licence comprises a permission to occupy property which derives its force from some contract, express or implied. The distinguishing feature of a contractual licence is that the occupier furnishes consideration for the permission to remain in the property, whereas a bare licence is granted gratuitously. A contractual licence differs from a bare licence in so far as a bare licence is revocable at will whereas a contractual licence is revocable only according to the express or implied terms of the contract. Furthermore, a bare licence cannot survive the licensor's death or the assignment by him of the property whereas a contractual licence may do so. The right of occupation under a contractual licence may be protected by way of injunction (see *Crabb v Arun District Council* [1976] Ch 179 at 198).

In *Tanner v Tanner* [1975] 1 WLR 1346, the defendant had been the plaintiff's mistress for two years and they had two children. At a time when the relationship was already breaking down the parties decided that it would be best to purchase a house for occupation by the defendant and the children. The plaintiff made it clear that he did not intend to marry the defendant, but he provided the house and the defendant gave up her rent-controlled flat to move into it with the children. The parties never cohabited there. The plaintiff sought a possession order which was granted by the judge at first instance. The Court of Appeal reversed that decision and held that, in the circumstances, a contract could be inferred under which the plaintiff had granted the defendant a licence to have accommodation in the house for herself and the children so long as they were of school age and the accommodation was reasonably required for them. The defendant had given good consideration by giving up her rent-controlled flat and by looking after the plaintiff's children at the house. Since the defendant had vacated the premises in pursuance of the trial judge's order and had been rehoused by the local authority, the Court of Appeal awarded her a money sum to compensate her for the breach of contract.

There are few indications that the courts are favourably disposed towards the contractual licence as a device for securing occupation by bare cohabitants. Indeed, in cases subsequent to *Tanner v Tanner*, claims to contractual licences have met with little success. In *Horrocks v Foray* [1976] 1 WLR 230, there had been no cohabitation but the relationship between a married man and his mistress had continued over a period of 17 years until the man died, leaving an estate which would probably have been insolvent if there was not a sale of the property in which he had installed the mistress. There was one child of the relationship, and the woman had another child born of a different union. In possession proceedings brought by the man's executors the mistress claimed a contractual licence to remain in the property either for her life, or while the man's child was in full-time education, or for so long as she and the child reasonably required the accommodation. She alleged that she had provided consideration by relinquishing her previous accommodation, and by agreeing to the man's proposals with respect to their child's support and accordingly refraining from taking any proceedings with respect thereto. Stressing the need for a meeting of the minds of the parties on contractual terms reasonably clearly made out, with an intention to affect the legal relationship, the court was unable to find any basis for inferring the existence of any promise such as had been alleged. It rested its decision on that ground, but appears also to have doubted whether the facts disclosed any sufficient consideration for the alleged contract.

In *Chandler v Kerley* [1978] 1 WLR 693, the plaintiff had purchased the home from the defendant and her husband at an undervalue on the understanding that the defendant and the children of her marriage would continue to live there and that the plaintiff would join them there when the defendant obtained a divorce so that she and the plaintiff could marry. In answer to a possession action the defendant claimed, in the alternative, licences of various durations. In the absence of an express promise, the court could not infer that the plaintiff had assumed the burden of another man's wife and children indefinitely even after his relationship with them had ceased. The court concluded that there was a contractual licence terminable on reasonable notice and held that, in the circumstances, 12 months was a reasonable period to allow.

There are clearly significant difficulties in establishing a contractual licence, chief among which will be establishing an understanding based on sufficiently clear terms, and proving the required consideration (see further *Coombes v Smith* [1987] 1 FLR 352, the facts of which are outlined below).

Licence by estoppel

A licence by estoppel arises in the same way as proprietary estoppel; that is, by virtue of an assurance, reliance and detriment (see §1.7 above), save that in this instance the assurance will relate to continued occupation of the property rather than the conferring of an interest in the land. In *Maharaj v Chand* [1986] AC 898, a Privy Council case on appeal from Fiji, the plaintiff had cohabited with the defendant in the defendant's flat. They decided to build a house for themselves and the plaintiff's application for building land held the defendant out as his wife. In reliance on the plaintiff's representation that the new house would be a permanent home for her and her children, one of whom was the plaintiff's child, the defendant supported his application and eventually gave up her flat to move into the house. It was held that the plaintiff could not evict the defendant after their relationship broke down, and that the expectation which the plaintiff had encouraged could only be made good by safeguarding her right to remain permanently in occupation.

In *Maharaj v Chand*, the Privy Council followed *Greasley v Cooke* [1980] 1 WLR 1306, where the defendant, originally engaged as a maid, subsequently cohabited with a son of the family for almost 30 years, and performed domestic services for other family members resident in the property including, in particular, a daughter who was mentally ill. She neither received nor asked for any payment, but the family members had led her to believe that she would be entitled to remain in the property for as long as she wished. In an action for possession, the court held that the burden of proof was on the plaintiffs to establish that the defendant had not acted to her detriment on the faith of the assurances given to her and, since they had failed to discharge that burden, an equity had been raised which could only be satisfied by allowing her to remain in the house for as long as she wished.

This case may be contrasted with *Coombes v Smith*, above, where a man had maintained his mistress and their daughter in a separate establishment and, when requested by the mistress to put the house into joint names, had replied to the effect: 'Don't worry. I have told you I'll always look after you'. Her claim to a contractual licence failed due to uncertainty of terms and lack of consideration. Her claim to an estoppel-based licence also failed since there was no evidence that she had acted to her detriment in reliance on the assurance: her actions in leaving her husband, becoming pregnant, bringing up her child and refraining from getting any job could not be said to have stemmed from any belief as to her legal position. Moreover, the defendant had done nothing to encourage her to act to her detriment. (In fact, the defendant conceded her a right to occupy the property until the daughter became 17.)

The Settled Land Act 1925

The right to remain in rent-free occupation for life may constitute the occupier a life tenant under the Settled Land Act 1925, which confers on the tenant for life a power to sell the property (see *Ungurian v Lesnoff and Others* [1990] 2 FLR 299). In *Griffiths v Williams* (1978) 248 EG 947, the case was taken outside the ambit of both the Settled Land Act 1925 and the Rent Act 1977 by the grant to the occupier of a non-assignable long lease at a nominal rent.

2.1.5 Settlement for the benefit of a child

Under the Children Act 1989, Sch 1, para 2(d) the High Court or a county court has the power on an application by a parent or

.ardian of a child, or by any person in whose favour a residence order is in force, to make an order requiring the settlement for the benefit of the child of property to which either parent is entitled. This power is appropriate to cover orders similar in type to certain orders which have long been common in the divorce court, the effect of which is to preserve the family home for occupation by the remnant family while the child is a minor. Such an order may be particularly indicated where cohabitation has been of considerable duration, with older children at a crucial stage in their education or children with special needs for whom a move would be especially disruptive.

Schedule 1, para 2(e) confers the power to order the transfer of property to the child or to the applicant for the benefit of the child. It is submitted that it will rarely be appropriate for this power to be exercised in relation to an owner-occupied home unless the net equity is small.

These powers are considered further at §4.3.2 below.

2.2   Rented accommodation

2.2.1   Private sector accommodation

The Housing Act 1988

The Housing Act (HA) 1988 made radical changes to the law of landlord and tenant as it affects dwelling-house tenancies created after 15 January 1989. As part of an attempt to revitalise private sector provision of rented accommodation, the HA 1988 in many respects reduced the protection previously accorded to tenants, both as regards rent control and in relation to security and transmission of tenancies. It introduced a new regime of 'assured' tenancies and, as a general rule, prevented the creation after 15 January 1989 of any new protected tenancies under the Rent Act (RA) 1977. (The HA 1988 also made significant changes to the rules governing Rent Act tenancies already in existence on 15 January 1989, see below.) The new assured tenancy has little in common with the assured tenancy under the Housing Act 1980, and as a general rule existing assured tenancies under that Act were automatically converted into the new form of assured tenancy on 15 January 1989.

The new form of assured tenancy is closely modelled on the

public sector 'secure' tenancy. It is not within the scope of this book to offer a comprehensive guide to the HA 1988. In particular, no consideration is given to assured shorthold tenancies which attract considerably less protection than assured tenancies. Rather, attention is focussed on assured tenancies and on provisions particularly affecting cohabitants.

An assured tenancy can only exist if three conditions are satisfied:

(i) the dwelling house must be let as a separate dwelling;

(ii) the sole tenant, or each of the joint tenants, must be an individual;

(iii) The tenant or at least one of the joint tenants must occupy the premises as his or her only or principal home (HA 1988, s 1(1)).

Moreover, by s 1(2), a tenancy cannot be an assured tenancy if any of the exceptions listed in Sch 1 applies.

Security of tenure: The basic position governing security of tenure in respect of an assured tenancy is set out in s 5, which provides that an assured tenancy cannot be brought to an end by the landlord except by obtaining a court order under the Act (as to which, see s 7 and Sch 2), or by the exercise of an express power contained in a fixed-term tenancy.

Where there has been a fixed-term tenancy then, provided that a tenant is occupying the property as his only or principal home, when the tenancy expires, either by effluxion of time or because the landlord exercises a right to terminate it, that tenancy will (unless it is expressly renewed) be replaced by a periodic tenancy on the same terms as the fixed term tenancy (s 5(2)), and this 'statutory periodic tenancy' will be protected insofar as the landlord will not be able to bring that tenancy to an end save by obtaining a possession order from the court under the HA 1988, s 7, having satisfied the court of the existence of a sufficient ground. The grounds are set out in Sch 2 of the Act, and are less restrictive than their Rent Act counterparts and, like the RA provisions, comprise both mandatory and discretionary grounds.

The primary concern here is the situation which arises on relationship breakdown; ie, when parties who are joint tenants cease to cohabit so that only one of them remains in occupation. Mere cessation of occupation by one joint tenant will not cause a tenancy to cease to be assured if the other joint tenant remains in occupation. Moreover, a statutory periodic tenancy will not be prevented from arising on the termination of a fixed-term tenancy by effluxion of time. However, the statutory periodic tenancy will nevertheless be a *joint* tenancy, and not a tenancy vested only in the occupying tenant (see s 5(3)(b)). This renders the occupier potentially very vulnerable since, by analogy with the position in respect of secure tenancies, a periodic joint tenancy may be determined by notice to quit given by only one of the joint tenants (see *Greenwich London Borough Council v McGrady* (1982) 42 P&CR 223; *Hammersmith & Fulham London Borough Council v Monk* [1992] 1 FLR 465). The position is different in respect of fixed-term tenancies, which cannot be surrendered by one tenant without the agreement of the other joint tenant (see *Leek & Moorlands Building Society v Clark* [1952] QB 788).

Thus, where a periodic tenancy is vested in the parties jointly and one party remains in occupation of the property after separation, the absent tenant may determine the tenancy by giving notice to quit. It seems therefore that when an absent tenant gives notice to quit, the landlord may simply seek an order for possession in 'ordinary' possession proceedings (ie without being required to establish a Sch 2 ground). In essence then – and in contrast to the position under the RA 1977 – by serving notice to quit one joint tenant may render the other joint tenant homeless. Moreover, it will not be open to the occupying tenant to use a notice to quit as a means of ensuring the other tenant's exclusion from the property, since this will no longer leave her with residual protection.

Where there is a tenancy in the sole name of a cohabitant who leaves the property on the breakdown of the relationship, there is little scope for protection of the remaining occupier's position. On the authority of *Colin Smith v Ridge* [1975] 1 All ER 290, the absent tenant will not be regarded as being in occupation through the cohabitant who remains in the property so that where an assured tenant moves out permanently, the tenancy ceases to be assured by reason of failure of the 'tenant condition'. Likewise, no statutory periodic tenancy will arise if the tenant is not occupying the property as his home when a fixed-term tenancy comes to an end.

It may also be noted that, by contrast with the provisions affecting spouses under the Matrimonial Homes Act 1983, there is nothing to compel a landlord to accept payments of rent from a deserted cohabitant as if they were payments made by the tenant himself.

Succession to tenancies: Where cohabitants are joint tenants, the death of one of them should not create problems for the other since the tenancy will remain vested in the survivor. The position is obviously less simple on the death of a cohabitant who was the sole tenant. For the purposes of succession to tenancies, the HA 1988, s 17(4) provides that a person living with the tenant as his or her wife or husband is to be treated as the tenant's spouse. The Act provides for succession to an assured tenancy by a spouse where the sole tenant under an assured periodic tenancy dies and, immediately before the death, the tenant's spouse was occupying the dwelling house as his or her only or principal home (s 17(1)). However, where the deceased tenant was himself a successor, there can be no further succession. A deceased tenant is a successor for this purpose if the tenancy became vested in him by virtue of s 17(1), or under the will or intestacy of a previous tenant; or where the tenancy was originally a joint tenancy and the deceased tenant became sole tenant by survivorship on the death of the other joint tenant; or where certain transitional provisions apply under which, with the aim of phasing out Rent Act tenancies, certain successions to *assured* tenancies will occur on the death of a protected or statutory tenant under the RA 1977. Thus, for example, there can be no further succession where a husband and wife have occupied property together (either as joint tenants or under a sole tenancy in the wife's name) until the wife's death, and when the widower takes in a cohabitant who is left in occupation where the widower himself dies. The landlord will be able to seek a possession order free from the need to establish a Sch 2 ground.

The Rent Act 1977

As noted above, no new protected tenancies can have been created since 15 January 1989 save in the narrowly defined exceptional circumstances set out in the HA 1988, s 34.

Security of tenure: Existing protected and statutory tenants under the Rent Act continue to enjoy security of tenure. A statutory tenancy can arise either on the termination of a 'protected' tenancy (ie the contractual tenancy) or by succession (as to which, see below). Thus, for present purposes, the most important occasions when a statutory tenancy will come into existence are when a fixed-term tenancy expires by effluxion of time, or when a periodic tenancy is terminated by notice to quit given either by the landlord or by the tenant. A statutory tenancy can be determined on the application of the landlord only on proof of one of the grounds set out in the RA 1977, Sch 15, Part 1.

Where a protected tenancy is vested in the joint names of a cohabiting couple and a deserted cohabitant remains in occupation, the occupying tenant will be entitled to remain in occupation as a statutory tenant (*Lloyd v Sadler* [1978] 2 All ER 529), and this will apply whether or not the absent tenant serves notice to quit. Moreover, the occupying tenant may serve notice to quit in order to defeat the other tenant's right to return and, again, the occupying tenant will become a statutory tenant.

If there is a *sole* tenancy vested in the deserting cohabitant, the tenant is not regarded as being in occupation of the property by virtue of occupation by the deserted partner, and the 'tenant condition' is thus no longer satisfied so that a deserted partner will be vulnerable irrespective of any notice to quit.

Succession to tenancies: The HA 1988 made significant changes to the rules governing succession to tenancies under the RA 1977. In particular, the qualifications for succession as a member of the tenant's family are made more stringent, and any succession *in that capacity* will be to an assured tenancy, not to the RA statutory tenancy. However, whereas a cohabitant could formerly be eligible to succeed to a statutory tenancy only by qualifying as a 'member of the tenant's family', it is now provided that a person who was living with the original tenant as his or her wife or husband shall be treated as the spouse of the original tenant (RA 1977, Sch 1, para 2, as amended by the HA 1988, Sch 4). A surviving cohabitant succeeding to the tenancy on the death of the original tenant will take a RA statutory tenancy rather than an assured tenancy. However, where a first successor dies after the commencement of the HA 1988, a surviving cohabitant will be required to establish eligibility as a member of the first successor's family. This qualifying ground (as amended) requires the potential second successor to have been residing in the dwelling house with the first successor at the time of his death and for the period of two years immediately before the first successor's death. Moreover, the potential second successor must not only have been a member of the first successor's family, but also of the original tenant's family. Thus, where a cohabitant moves in with a first successor who was the widow or widower of an original tenant, the cohabitant will be unable to succeed on the death of the first successor.

In *Dyson Holdings v Fox* [1976] 1 QB 503, there had been 20 years' cohabitation without marriage and the woman had taken the man's name. The Court of Appeal held that although relationships of a casual and intermittent character could not qualify, a stable cohabitation relationship could do so, having regard to the changing meaning of the word 'family'. By contrast, in *Helby v Rafferty* [1979] 1 WLR 13, the Court of Appeal referred to earlier cases in which cohabitants' claims had been rejected on the basis that cohabitation did not create a 'family', asserting that 'family' had to be given the meaning it bore when first used by Parliament.

However, in *Watson v Lucas* [1980] 1 WLR 1493, the Court of Appeal considered itself bound by *Dyson v Fox*, and allowed succession by a man who had lived with the deceased tenant for nearly 20 years, even though he had never been divorced from his wife, and the woman cohabitant had never taken his name or he hers. A much shorter period of life in the same household may suffice if there is evidence of a sufficient state of permanence and stability (*Chios Property Investment Income Co v Lopes* (1987) 29 HLR 120). If the couple have had children, this strengthens the presumption that they are a family (see *Helby v Rafferty*, above).

If the conditions for succession are satisfied and a second succession occurs, it will be to an assured tenancy under the HA 1988, and not to a statutory tenancy under the RA 1977.

2.2.2   Public sector housing

As noted above, the new assured tenancy under the HA 1988 is derived from the public sector secure tenancy regime contained in the Housing Act (HA) 1985. Accordingly, it is not proposed here to repeat at length the discussion given earlier with respect to the 1988 Act.

A tenancy under which a dwelling house is let as a separate dwelling is a secure tenancy at any time when the 'landlord condition' and the 'tenant condition' are satisfied (HA 1985, s 79). The landlord condition is that the interest of the landlord belongs to one of the bodies listed in s 80. The tenant condition is that the tenant or each of the joint tenants is an individual and that the tenant or at least one of them occupies the dwelling house as his only or principal home (s 81).

As with assured tenancies, a secure periodic tenancy cannot be brought to an end by the landlord except by obtaining an order of the court (s 82). Grounds for possession are set out in Sch 2.

Where cohabitants are joint tenants, the security of tenure enjoyed by a deserted secure tenant is essentially as described at §2.2.1 above. Thus, if a joint tenant who has left the property gives notice to quit (a step which may be required by the local authority before agreeing to rehouse him), the remaining tenant becomes vulnerable to an action for possession (see *Hammersmith & Fulham London Borough Council v Monk* [1992] 1 FLR 465). Equally, notice to quit given by the occupying joint tenant will defeat the absent tenant's interest and, where the local authority is sympathetic to the remaining occupier, may be the preliminary to the granting of a new tenancy in the sole name of the deserted tenant.

Where the tenancy is in the sole name of the cohabitant who has permanently left the home, the 'tenant condition' ceases to be satisfied and the secure tenancy will cease, enabling the local authority either to obtain possession or to grant a sole tenancy to the cohabitant who has remained in occupation.

Succession to tenancies on death is governed by rules resembling those for assured tenancies (see §2.2.1 above). Only one succession is possible. A succession will be treated as having occurred where an original joint tenancy becomes a sole tenancy on the death of one of the joint tenants (but not where a joint tenancy is determined and a new tenancy of the same property is granted to one of the former joint tenants; see *Bassetlaw District Council v Renshaw* [1992] 1 All ER 925). Succession is possible by a spouse of the deceased tenant or by a person who is a member of the tenant's family and who has resided with the tenant throughout the period of 12 months ending with the tenant's death (whether or not they have resided together for that period in the premises of which the tenant was the secure tenant at the time of his death; see *Waltham Forest London Borough Council v Thomas* [1992] 3 All ER 244). By s 113, a person is a member of another's family if *inter alia* he and that person were living together as husband and wife.

2.2.3 Transfer of tenancies

It has already been noted (at §2.1.5 above) that the court has power under the Children Act 1989, Sch 1 to order a transfer of property to or for the benefit of a child. The situation here envisaged is that which arises where one parent has left the home not intending to return and a transfer is sought in favour of the other parent, in whose care the child is. The considerations which might lead a court to make such an order are examined elsewhere (see §4.3.2), but it should be noted that the exercise of this power in respect of tenancies of rented accommodation raises a number of potential difficulties and pitfalls.

First, and potentially most important, the power is exercisable only in respect of property which is in existence. Where a tenancy is a joint tenancy in respect of which no notice to quit has been given, this will not create any difficulty since the tenancy subsists while the other joint tenant remains in occupation and an order can accordingly be made requiring the absent joint tenant to transfer to the occupier his interest under the joint tenancy. However, where a sole tenant leaves and it is clear that the property has ceased to be his only or principal home, the assured or secure tenancy (as the case may be) will cease to exist for failure of the tenant condition and will no longer be available to be transferred. In principle, therefore, the power to order a transfer will be exercisable only where both parties are still living in the property or where, although the tenant has left, the property has not yet ceased to be his 'only or principal home' (eg where he has not yet obtained alternative *permanent* accommodation) (see also *Thompson v Elmbridge Borough Council* [1987] 1 WLR 1425: nothing to transfer following secure tenant's breach of terms of suspended possession order).

Secondly, the power is exercisable only in respect of property which the tenant has the power to transfer (see *Hale v Hale* [1975] 2 All ER 1090; *Thompson v Thompson* [1975] 2 All ER 208).

Assured tenancies

In the case of assured tenancies, the tenancy agreement itself may make provision for assignment, either by way of prohibition or by granting general or limited permission. Where no such provision is made, it is an implied term of every assured tenancy agreement that the tenant shall not assign the tenancy except with the consent of the landlord, and the HA 1988 expressly provides that there is *no* requirement in respect of this implied term that the landlord's consent is not to be unreasonably withheld (see s 15(2)). In any given case, therefore, it will be important to provide the court with evidence that the landlord concerned would be willing to consent to the particular transfer that is proposed (for a statement of that principle, see *Thompson v Thompson*, above).

Secure tenancies

The HA 1985, s 91 provides that a secure tenancy, though not normally capable of being assigned, may be assigned by the tenant (*inter alia*) if the assignment is to a person who would be qualified to succeed to the tenancy if the tenant died immediately before the assignment (as to which, see above). According to the principle in *Thompson v Thompson* above, the court would in most cases be precluded from making an order for transfer since, presumably, the parties will not still be living together as husband and wife.

Finally, it may be noted that there is no provision in the CA 1989, Sch 1 equivalent to the Matrimonial Homes Act 1983, Sch 1 para 3, which empowers the court to make an order that a tenant's spouse shall be *deemed* to be the tenant. Thus, when an order for the transfer of a tenancy is made, that order does not by itself achieve the ultimate desired result, and care must be taken to ensure that the tenant who is ordered to effect the transfer does in fact execute the required formal assignment (see *Crago v Julian* [1992] 1 FLR 478).

2.2.4 Bankrupt tenants

By the HA 1988, s 117 assured tenancies under that Act, protected tenancies under the RA 1977, and secure tenancies under the HA 1985 (where not assignable other than to a person who would be eligible to succeed on the tenant's death) are all excluded from a bankrupt's estate. By preventing such tenancies from vesting in the trustee in bankruptcy, the section makes it possible for the bankrupt's continued occupation to be occupation as 'the tenant', as is required for the continued application to the tenancy of the relevant statutory protective scheme.

2.3 Homelessness

2.3.1 Introduction

It is not the intention here to give an exhaustive account of the law relating to the housing of homeless persons: the following account gives only a brief general introduction to the law before examining aspects of particular potential relevance to cohabitants.

The duties of local authorities towards homeless persons are contained in the Housing Act 1985, Part III. Unless a homeless person has a 'priority need' (see below), the duty of the local authority extends no further than an obligation to provide him with advice and assistance in his attempts to secure that accommodation becomes available for his occupation (s 65(4)).

Where the local authority is satisfied that a person has a priority need and is not satisfied that he became homeless intentionally (see below), the authority must secure that suitable accommodation becomes available for his (permanent) occupation, but where the authority is satisfied that a person with a priority need has become homeless intentionally, the duty is limited to the provision of accommodation for such period as they consider will give him a reasonable opportunity to secure accommodation for himself, together with a duty to provide advice and assistance in his attempts to secure accommodation (s 65(2), (3)). Comparable duties apply in respect of those threatened with homelessness (s 66).

The local authority has a duty to enquire into cases of apparent homelessness when an application is made to it for accommodation or advice or assistance, and will be under an interim duty to accommodate the applicant pending its enquiries if it has reason to believe that he may be homeless and have a priority need (s 62). On the completion of its enquiries, the local authority must notify the applicant of its decision and, if it has made a finding adverse to the applicant's case for rehousing, must notify the applicant of the reasons for the decision (s 64).

If the local authority is satisfied that the applicant is homeless, and has a priority need, and has not become homeless intentionally, it may nevertheless refer the applicant to another local authority on the basis that neither the applicant nor any person who might reasonably be expected to reside with him has a local connection with the district of the authority to which the application has been made, but that the applicant or a person who might reasonably be expected to reside with him has a local connection with the district of that other authority (s 67; and on the meaning of 'local connection' see s 61, and *R v Eastleigh Borough Council, ex parte Betts* [1984] FLR 156).

An application cannot be referred to another local authority if the applicant or a person who might reasonably be expected to reside with him will run the risk of domestic violence in that other authority's district, and a person runs the risk of domestic violence if he runs the risk of violence from or threats of violence likely to be carried out by a person with whom, but for the risk of violence, he might reasonably be expected to reside, or from a person with whom he formerly resided (s 61).

A decision of a local authority may be challenged by means of an application for judicial review of the authority's decision (see *Ali v Tower Hamlets London Borough Council* [1992] 3 All ER 512).

2.3.2 Is the applicant homeless?

By s 58, a person is homeless if he has no accommodation, and he has no accommodation if there is no accommodation available for his occupation which he is entitled or permitted to occupy together with any other persons who normally resides with him as a member of his family or in circumstances in which it would be reasonable for that person to reside with him. The Code of Guidance advises that the phrase 'member of his family' should be taken to cover 'not only established households where there is a blood or marriage relationship but also other circumstances where people are living together as if they were members of a family, eg cohabiting couples'.

A person is threatened with homelessness if it is likely that he will become homeless within 28 days.

By s 75, accommodation is to be regarded as available for a person's occupation if it is available for occupation both by him and by any other person who might reasonably be expected to reside with him. In *R v Wimbourne District Council, ex parte Curtis* [1986] 1 FLR 486, the applicant was occupying her former matrimonial home under a separation agreement which contained a clause to the effect that if she remarried or cohabited the property was to be sold. When the applicant started to cohabit, her former husband called for a sale. The authority's finding that she was intentionally homeless was quashed by the court since the authority had failed properly to consider the primary question whether the accommodation which the applicant had been occupying was accommodation which was 'available for her occupation'. Given that the accommodation was not available for occupation by herself *together with the cohabitant*, the authority should have considered whether it was reasonable in all the circumstances for the applicant to have the cohabitant living with her.

A person is homeless unless it is reasonable for him to continue to occupy the accommodation which is available for his occupation.

Thus, in *R v South Herefordshire District Council, ex parte Miles* (1984) 17 HLR 82, on the birth of a third child it was not reasonable for a family to continue to occupy a rat-infested hut measuring 20 feet by 10 feet, with no mains services (see also *R v Medina Borough Council, ex parte Dee* (1992) 24 HLR 562: beach chalet to which applicant did not return, on medical advice, following birth of child; and see *R v Eastleigh Borough Council, ex parte Beattie (No 1)* (1983) 10 HLR 134: not intentional homelessness where it ceases to be reasonable for an applicant to occupy accommodation by reason of pregnancy).

A person is also homeless notwithstanding that accommodation is available for his occupation if in fact he cannot secure entry to it (eg because a cohabitant has changed the locks) or it is probable that occupation of it will lead to violence from or threats of violence likely to be carried out by some other person residing in it.

Moreover, a local authority will be failing in its statutory duty if its enquiries and decision-making do not give proper consideration to the reasonableness of an applicant continuing to reside in accommodation where there has been violence against her even though that violence did not occur in the accommodation concerned and was not committed by a person who resides there (see *R v Kensington and Chelsea Royal London Borough Council, ex parte Hammell* [1989] 2 FLR 223: tenant of council flat the victim of violence from ex-husband who lived nearby, violence having occurred outside the flat; see also *R v Broxbourne Borough Council, ex parte Willmoth* (1989) 22 HLR 118).

A person may be homeless even though he has a roof over his head. Thus, a person who resorts to temporary crisis accommodation such as a refuge for battered women will still be homeless (*R v Ealing LBC, ex parte Sidhu* [1982] FLR 438), as will a person who is residing with a relative on a temporary basis and the relative wants that person to leave (*R v Ealing London Borough Council, ex parte McBain* [1986] 1 FLR 479).

The involuntary loss of temporary accommodation will not necessarily render a person unintentionally homeless if that person left his *previous* accommodation voluntarily (*R v Purbeck District Council, ex parte Cadney* [1986] 2 FLR 158). Likewise, an intentional act causing eviction from temporary accommodation will not affect an applicant who originally became homeless unintentionally (see *R v East Herefordshire District Council, ex parte Hunt* [1986] 1 FLR 431).

2.3.3 Intentional homelessness

A person becomes homeless intentionally if he deliberately does or fails to do anything in consequence of which he ceases to occupy accommodation which is available for his occupation and which it would have been reasonable for him to continue to occupy (see s 60). A person may become intentionally homeless by leaving accommodation voluntarily even though he would probably have lost the right to occupy that accommodation within a short time had he remained there (*Din v Wandsworth London Borough Council* [1983] 1 AC 657). On the other hand, the fact that a person would probably soon, by some default, have lost the right to occupy accommodation does not prevent that person being involuntarily homeless if she left in circumstances which justified her leaving (see eg *Gloucester County Council v Miles* [1985] FLR 1043: substantial rent arrears, but house rendered uninhabitable by husband's vandalism). Similarly, a person becomes *threatened* with homelessness intentionally if he deliberately does or fails to do anything the likely result of which is that he will be forced to leave accommodation which is available for his occupation and which it would have been reasonable for him to continue to occupy.

When cohabitation breaks down

The concept of intentional homelessness may cause problems for a cohabitant wishing to sever the relationship since a cohabitant who is pregnant or who has a dependent child will have a priority need but may find herself regarded as intentionally homeless if she moves out of the accommodation which is available for the couple's joint occupation. However, she will not be intentionally homeless if there has been a history of violence, or if she has been locked out of the home or excluded from it by a court order, or if she leaves and is likely to be subjected to violence or to serious threat of violence if she returns.

Although the Code of Guidance states that: 'A battered woman who has fled the marital home should never be regarded as having become homeless intentionally because it would clearly not be reasonable for her to remain . . .', many local authorities will apply pressure on women to take ouster proceedings in respect of the violence since, if successful, these proceedings will often result in a priority need applicant being replaced by someone who has no priority need. Moreover, some authorities will not regard a woman as homeless (or not as *unintentionally* homeless) while such proceedings are available. As a matter of principle, a local authority would be acting unlawfully if it adopted a blanket policy in this respect and would be susceptible to proceedings for judicial review. However, it is not possible to say that a reasonable authority could *never* require a woman to use her private remedies (see *R v Eastleigh BC, ex parte Evans* [1986] 2 FLR 195; *R v Purbeck DC, ex parte Cadney*, above).

While the relationship subsists

It should be noted that where a homeless applicant establishes a priority need, the local authority's duty to rehouse extends not only to that person, but also to any person who might reasonably be expected to reside with him. Clearly, there is scope here for the consequences of the intentional homelessness of one member of a family group to be circumvented by the making of an application by another member, with the intention of joint residence. In *R v North Devon District Council, ex parte Lewis* [1981] 1 WLR 328, it was held that a local authority is not entitled to treat all members of the family unit as automatically tainted by the actions of one member of it which resulted in the homelessness. However, it was found in that case that the woman cohabitant had acquiesced in the man's decision to give up the job on which the family's tied accommodation depended (see also *R v Swansea City Council, ex parte John* (1982) 9 HLR 56: council tenant evicted because of nuisance caused by alcoholic partner. Held, that by failing to sever her relationship with him she had effectively acquiesced in his conduct). However, if the applicant dissociated herself from the conduct and remonstrated with the family member responsible, the applicant may succeed in showing unintentional homelessness and have a right to be rehoused even though that other family member might benefit indirectly from her eligibility (see *R v North Devon District Council, ex parte Lewis*, above; *R v West Dorset District Council, ex parte Phillips* (1985) 17 HLR 336; *R v Penrith District Council, ex parte Trevena* (1984) 17 HLR 526).

The restriction on local authorities' duties in respect of persons who are intentionally homeless cannot be circumvented by the making of an application by a dependent child (see *R v Bexley London Borough Council, ex parte B; R v Oldham Metropolitan Borough Council, ex parte G* [1992] *The Times*, 26 August).

2.3.4   Priority need

Among those recognised as having a priority need are: a pregnant woman or a person with whom a pregnant woman resides or might reasonably be expected to reside, and a person with whom dependent children reside or might reasonably be expected to reside (s 59). A person may have a priority need even though the dependent children do not reside wholly and exclusively with him (see *R v London Borough of Lambeth, ex parte Vagliviello* (1990) 22 HLR 392: children with applicant three and a half days each week). It is not necessary for a person with whom dependent children reside to have a residence order in his or her favour in order to establish a priority need (*R v Ealing London Borough Council, ex parte Sidhu*, above). However, a residence order would be relevant where children are not currently residing with the applicant but might reasonably be expected to do so; as where the applicant has a residence order but cannot assume actual custody for want of accommodation.

Vulnerability as a result of old age, mental illness or handicap, physical disability or other special reason also constitutes a priority need (but see also *R v Bexley London Borough Council, ex parte B; R v Oldham Metropolitan Borough Council, ex parte G*, above).

2.3.5   Relevance to ouster applications

The extent of local authorities' duties towards different categories of homeless persons is relevant to the deliberations of a court which is asked to exclude a cohabitant from the home. The manner in which the court has regard to such duties towards the homeless is considered at §2.4 below.

2.4   The Domestic Violence and Matrimonial Proceedings Act 1976

The Domestic Violence and Matrimonial Proceedings Act (DVA) 1976 empowers the county court to grant non-molestation injunctions and ouster injunctions. Such relief by way of injunction may be sought under the DVA 1976 irrespective of whether any other relief is sought in the proceedings.

2.4.1   The orders available

An injunction under the DVA 1976 may contain any one or more
of the following:

(a) a provision restraining the respondent from molesting the
applicant;

(b) a provision restraining the respondent from molesting a child
living with the applicant;

(c) a provision excluding the respondent from the matrimonial
home or a part of the matrimonial home or from a specified area
in which the matrimonial home is included;

(d) a provision requiring the respondent to permit the applicant
to enter and remain in the matrimonial home or part of the matrimonial home (s 1(1)).

2.4.2   Who may apply?

Section 1(1) of the Act sets out the court's powers by reference to
an application by one party to a marriage for injunctive relief against
the other spouse and, in the case of ouster injunctions, by reference
to the 'matrimonial home'. However, by s 1(2), the court's jurisdiction under the Act is extended to cover 'a man and a woman who
are living with each other in the same household as husband and
wife', and any reference in the Act to the 'matrimonial home' is to
be construed accordingly.

In determining whether a man and a woman are living with each
other in the same household as husband and wife, the court will
not deprive itself of jurisdiction by a strict application of the cases
concerning separate households in the context of desertion. Thus,
in *Adeoso v Adeoso* [1980] 1 WLR 1535 the Court of Appeal rejected
the argument that the parties were living in separate households
under the same roof, notwithstanding that sexual relations had
ceased, that the woman applicant had ceased to cook or provide
other services for the respondent, that they slept apart, and that
they communicated by notes. Ormrod LJ did not rule out a finding
of separation of households in a case involving the division of large
premises, but the parties in *Adeoso* were living in a council flat
consisting of one bedroom, a sitting-room, kitchen and bathroom.
Ormrod LJ observed (at 1539):

> 'In practical terms one cannot live in a two-roomed flat with
> another person without living in the same household. One has

to . . . take great care not to fall over one another in most of these cases; and it would be quite artificial to suggest that two people living at arm's length in such a situation, from which they cannot escape by reason of the housing difficulties, are to be said to be living in two separate households.'

Their relationship was said to be 'exactly comparable' to a marriage in the last stages of break-up.

The court will likewise not deprive itself of jurisdiction by a literal application of the reference in s 1(2) to parties who '*are* living together . . .'. Recognising that the applicant will often have already left the house by the time the application is made, it has been held that the statutory words are used to denote the relationship between the parties immediately before the incident which gave rise to the application. If they were then living together in the same household as husband and wife, that is enough (*Davis v Johnson* [1979] AC 264; *White v White* (1983) FLR 696; *Adeoso v Adeoso*, above).

Thus, the court's jurisdiction to hear an application for an order under the DVA 1976 survives the ending of cohabitation, and in *O'Neill v Williams* [1984] FLR 1, the Court of Appeal held that there was jurisdiction to entertain an application where cohabitation had ceased six months prior to the making of the application (see also *McLean v Nugent* (1979) 123 Sol Jo 521: cohabitation for three months, injunction obtained two months after cessation of cohabitation).

On the other hand:

'the longer the time that elapses the less and less likely it will become that any judge would, or could, find it right to grant the remedy . . . because [the 1976] Act deals with short term relief, not with long term solution of conflicts in matters of property.' (*O'Neill v Williams* [1984] FLR 1, per Balcombe LJ at 10).

Where the complaint is that, having given cause for complaint during the subsistence of the relationship, the respondent persists in attending at and entering without permission the property in which the applicant now lives, but which is not the former 'matrimonial' home, there is no power under the DVA to restrain the respondent specifically from attending at that property but such conduct will generally fall within the range of conduct prohibited by a non-molestation injunction (see §2.4.3 below).

2.4.3 Non-molestation

The precise form of a prohibition on molestation is at the discretion of the court. It is now considered that the prohibition on molestation is best expressed as two distinct provisions: first, a provision whereby the respondent is forbidden to use any violence against the applicant or (if necessary) against any named child(ren) living with the applicant; and secondly, a provision whereby the respondent is forbidden to threaten, harass or pester the respondent or the children. In each case the prohibition extends to instructing or encouraging any other person to commit the forbidden acts. Where appropriate, the injunction may further particularise the nature of the conduct that is prohibited (see [1991] Fam Law 192 for specimen clauses).

The DVA 1976 does not itself specify any pre-conditions for the granting of a non-molestation injunction. However, the cases establish that an applicant will need to show that there has already been 'molestation'. The following summary encapsulates the import of that term:

> ' "Molestation" for the purposes of the [DVA] 1976 is deliberate conduct which substantially interferes with the applicant or a child, whether by violence or by intimidation, harassment, pestering or interference that is sufficiently serious to warrant intervention by the court. "Molestation" includes the forcing by the other party of his or her society on the unwilling suffering party, whether the purpose of the molester is seeking to resume affectionate relations or to harm or annoy the suffering party.' (*F v F (Protection from Violence: Continuing Cohabitation)* [1989] 2 FLR 451, per Judge Fricker QC, citing *Vaughan v Vaughan* [1973] 3 All ER 449; *Davis v Johnson* [1979] AC 264; *Horner v Horner* [1983] FLR 50.)

Incidents following relationship breakdown

It often happens that the conduct complained of occurs only after, and in reaction to, the applicant's withdrawal from the relationship and the cessation of cohabitation (see *Pidduck v Molloy* [1992] 2 FLR 202, per Lord Donaldson MR at 206). It must be stressed that the jurisdiction to hear an application after the cessation of cohabitation is dependent upon there having been incidents *during the cohabitation* which have given rise to the complaint. Where the cause for complaint arises only after the ending of the relationship, the only recourse is to the law of tort as it applies between any other fellow citizens and the injunction may be made only in support of some identifiable and protectable legal interest. Thus where there has been a battery (ie the application of unlawful personal violence) or an assault (ie a threat to apply immediate and unlawful personal violence), the appropriate course will be to commence proceedings in tort seeking an injunction (which may now be sought without the need to claim other relief; see County Courts Act 1984, s 38, as substituted by the Courts and Legal Services Act 1990, s 3).

With respect to the terms in which the injunction should be couched in such cases, in *Burnett v George* [1992] 1 FLR 525 the Court of Appeal acknowledged the general proposition that molestation and interference are not in themselves actionable wrongs. However, the Court held that, where there is evidence that the health of the plaintiff is being impaired by molestation or interference *which is calculated to create such impairment*, the relief granted may extend as far as is necessary to avoid that impairment of health (describing that exception as 'validly grounded' in *Wilkinson v Downton* [1897] 2 QB 57). In *Burnett v George*, the Court disallowed a general prohibition of molestation and interference, but was prepared to substitute a prohibition against the narrower form of wrong which involved an impairment of the plaintiff's health. In *Pidduck v Molloy*, above, there had been violence during the subsistence of the relationship but it seems that protection against the continuing threats and molestation was sought in tort proceedings rather than under the DVA 1976 (possibly because it was considered that too long a period had elapsed since the ending of the relationship). In that case, an injunction was made which (*inter alia*) forbade the defendant speaking to the plaintiff. It was made on the express basis that speaking to her against her will constituted a nuisance. The Court of Appeal rejected that provision of the injunction (which was itself made in substitution for an earlier injunction which was held to be too widely framed) but since the evidence was that when the defendant did speak to the plaintiff it was usually for the purpose of intimidating, threatening or abusing her ('all of which are capable of amounting to crimes or torts'), it was replaced by an injunction 'not to speak to the plaintiff in an intimidatory, threatening or abusive manner'.

A non-molestation injunction may also be made, in the exercise of the court's inherent jurisdiction, in proceedings under the

Children Act 1989 where such an order is necessary to protect the child or the person having care of the child (see *M v M (Ouster: Children Act)* [1992] Fam Law 504. For other recorded instances, see *S v C* (1992) Legal Action, March 18; noted at [1992] Fam Law 134, and *J v W* (1992) Legal Action, March 21).

Where the ex-cohabitant persists in entering without permission premises where the other party is now living, the appropriate course will be an action in trespass.

Effect of continuing cohabitation

In *F v F*, above, Judge Fricker QC held that, while a non-molestation injunction can be granted to an applicant whose continuing cohabitation is an empty shell or vestigial, such an injunction cannot be granted to an applicant who is still in 'full cohabitation' with the respondent and intends to continue in full cohabitation: where parties are still living together an injunction can be granted only to protect the applicant so as to enable her to free herself from cohabitation and thereafter to keep free from cohabitation with the respondent.

Availability of non-molestation injunctions

In summary, the position is as follows:

(i) Where cohabitation has ended and the conduct complained of occurs only after the separation, injunctive relief can be sought in accordance with the ordinary law of tort (see §2.4.2 above) or through the court's exercise of its inherent jurisdiction in proceedings under the Children Act 1989.

(ii) Where cohabitation has ended and there was conduct prior to the separation which gave cause for complaint, and there has been or is likely to be a recurrence of such behaviour subsequent to the separation, a non-molestation injunction may be granted under the DVA 1976 but a long delay in seeking relief may render tort proceedings a more reliable route to relief.

(iii) Where cohabitation has not ended and there has been conduct giving cause for complaint but the applicant seeks protection in order to break free from the relationship, a non-molestation injunction may be granted under the DVA 1976.

(iv) If *F v F*, above, is correct, where cohabitation has not ended and the applicant is willing to continue in cohabitation, a non-molestation injunction will not be available even if the applicant is only willing to continue in cohabitation if the violence or molestation ceases. On the other hand, the express intention of the 1976 Act was to enable the court to grant injunctions in cases of domestic violence without any requirement that the injunction be sought ancillary to any other relief, provided that the parties are cohabitants who fall within s 1(2) (see s 1(1)). Thus where, as in *F v F*, reference is made to the inappropriateness of an order which, under pain of imprisonment, seeks to regulate the extent to which one party 'forces his society' on the other, it may nevertheless be argued that there is nothing to prevent the court exercising its discretion under the DVA 1976 by granting an injunction limited to a prohibition on any repeated *assault*.

2.4.4 Ouster

It is clearly established that a court may make an ouster order on the application of a cohabitant notwithstanding that the cohabitant has no legal or beneficial interest in the property, nor any contractual right on her own behalf to occupy it (*Davis v Johnson*, above). Moreover, although the DVA 1976 itself provides no express guidance on the matter, it is also clearly established that, whether an application under the DVA 1976 involves spouses or cohabitants, the court is bound to apply the criteria set out in the Matrimonial Homes Act (MHA) 1983, s 1(3) (see *Richards v Richards* [1984] FLR 11; *Wiseman v Simpson* [1988] 1 FLR 490). Section 1(3) provides that:

'the court may make such order as it thinks just and reasonable having regard to the conduct of the spouses in relation to each other and otherwise, to their respective needs and financial resources, to the needs of any children and to all the circumstances of the case.'

In *Wiseman v Simpson* (above, at 497), in a most important passage Ralph Gibson LJ observed:

'it can only be "just and reasonable" to make an ouster order if the case of the party claiming the order is not only stronger on those matters than the other party's case but is such as to justify making an order that a man or woman be ousted from his or her home.'

Children's needs

In *Richards v Richards*, above, the House of Lords resolved a conflict of authorities by making clear that the needs of any children involved are not, as a matter of law, the determining factor on an application for an exclusion order: the Guardianship of Minors Act 1971, s 1(1) had no application to ouster proceedings since these are not proceedings in which the custody or upbringing of a minor is directly 'in issue', even though the interests of the child are directly or indirectly affected by the outcome. It has been held that *Richards* has not been overruled on that point by the Children Act 1989 (See *Gibson v Austin* [1992] 2 FLR 437, at 443).

Thus, under the MHA 1983 (and, consequently, under the DVA 1976), the needs of the children are an important consideration to which the court must specifically have regard, but they are not in every case the first or paramount consideration. Nevertheless, in *Richards v Richards*, above (at 22), Lord Hailsham expressly adverted to the possibility that, in a given case, it might be just and reasonable that the needs of the children should prevail, either owing to the urgency of those needs or to the seriousness of denying them.

In *Lee v Lee* [1984] FLR 243, a woman cohabitant sought to oust her partner from the home – a council house of which they were joint tenants. She did not allege violence against him (though he did against her), but there were frequent quarrels. While she was hospitalised after taking a drugs overdose, her daughter (by a former marriage) made allegations of sexual indecency towards her by the man, and she was taken into interim care. After the woman left hospital, she and the couple's son went to accommodation which was unsatisfactory, and in which the daughter would not be permitted to join her. It was held that in the circumstances greater weight should be placed on the needs of the children than on any other matters listed in the MHA 1983, s 1(3), and that their needs required them to be re-established as a family unit in the council house.

Violence not essential

In *Davis v Johnson*, above, Lord Salmon observed (at 341–2):

'I do not think that a county court judge could properly exclude the paramour from his home or its environs under s 1(1)(c) unless he had been guilty of serious molestation likely to expose the common law wife or her children to serious danger or intolerable conditions whilst he remained there'

while in *Richards v Richards*, above, Lord Scarman observed (at 25) that:

'it must be unlikely that the section, though it offers no express guidance, can be applicable unless there be shown violence, or the threat of it, or a reasonable apprehension that the presence of the man (or woman) in the house constitutes a danger to the physical or emotional health or well-being of the woman (or man) and the children.'

Although ouster is normally only a temporary remedy (see §2.4.5 below), it is nevertheless a remedy of last resort, and it is clear that the existence of a 'disagreeable state of affairs', without more, will not suffice (see, eg *Wiseman v Simpson*, above: no injunction where there was nothing in the man's conduct that could amount to reasonable grounds for refusing to live in the flat if he were there). On the other hand, physical violence will generally be sufficient to justify an order (but see *Lacey v Lacey* (1980) FLR 1: two incidents of violence, unpremeditated and 'not serious'; children not at risk; non-molestation order adequate). In the absence of violence, the Draconian nature of an order ousting a person from his or her home may lead the court to doubt whether it would be just and reasonable to do so. Nevertheless, in *Wiseman v Simpson*, above, the Court of Appeal reiterated the view that it is not necessary to prove violence in order to justify the making of an ouster order (The observation in *K v K (Minors: Property Transfer)* [1992] 2 FLR 220, at 226, that an ouster injunction was not appropriate in that case may have been sufficiently supported by the particular facts, but should not be construed as suggesting that no such injunction could be granted in the absence of violence).

In *Wiseman v Simpson*, Ralph Gibson LJ referred (at 496) to *Summers v Summers* [1986] 1 FLR 343, where there was no violence but repeated loud quarrels between a young couple who were equally to blame for those quarrels, to which the children were witnesses. Although the Court of Appeal quashed the injunction in *Summers*, it did so because it appeared that the judge might have misdirected himself with respect to the approach which the MHA 1983 requires the court to take (order made to allow dust to settle in the hope that the break might facilitate a reconciliation). The

Court did not dismiss the application on the ground that there was no power to grant the injunction on the facts, but directed a new trial on the basis that there was a *prima facie* case to be considered. In *Phillips v Phillips* [1973] 1 WLR 615, there had been no violence, but there was evidence from the family doctor that the ex-husband's hostile attitude to the ex-wife and to their 14-year-old son was imposing very great strain on both mother and boy, and that they would become 'psychiatric invalids' if they were not enabled to live separately from the ex-husband. *Phillips* seems to fall squarely within the category of a 'no violence' case which Ralph Gibson LJ was contemplating in *Wiseman v Simpson*, above, but note that, as a general rule, cases decided prior to *Richards v Richards*, above, must be approached with caution since, although an injunction may have been justified on the facts, the reasoning employed may not accord with the *Richards* approach.

Applicant's unreasonable attitude or behaviour

Where there is nothing in the respondent's conduct towards the applicant that would amount to reasonable grounds for the applicant to refuse to live in the home if the respondent continues to be present, then the adopting of such an attitude by the applicant will itself constitute relevant conduct within the meaning of the MHA 1983, s 1(3) (*Wiseman v Simpson*, above: woman's conduct in excluding cohabitant by changing the locks regarded as a serious matter from which she ought not to gain advantage). Moreover, in *Richards v Richards*, above, although he had disposed of the argument that the children's needs were paramount, Lord Hailsham commented (at 22) that, in any event, 'it is not necessarily for the interests of children that either parent should be allowed to get away with capricious, arbitrary, autocratic, or merely eccentric behaviour'.

Prospects of being rehoused

The court will have regard to the availability or otherwise of alternative accommodation for each party. Thus, an injunction may be refused to a cohabitant who has the financial means to go elsewhere (*Freedman v Freedman* [1967] 1 WLR 1102). Similarly, the court may be more easily persuaded to grant an ouster if the party to be ousted can readily find other accommodation with members of his family, or by paying rent (*Baggott v Baggott* [1986] 1 FLR 377).

In practice, the question of alternative accommodation will commonly involve an examination of the position with respect to local authority housing and, in particular, to the duties owed by local authorities towards persons who are homeless (see generally 2.3 above).

On the one hand, the court is not willing to allow its processes to be used merely 'to play the obscure housing policy game of the local authority' where the local authority requires an ouster order against a husband before rehousing an applicant from a woman's refuge. In *Warwick v Warwick* (1982) FLR 393, the wife had no desire to return to the particular house but had been advised that, before the local authority would rehouse her and her children elsewhere, she needed an order ousting the husband so that the tenancy of their home would lapse for non-compliance with the 'tenant condition' (see §2.2.2 above; but see further below). Ormrod LJ described the situation as 'a deplorable, paradoxical, absurd state of affairs' and observed that the local authority ought to be prepared to treat the case as a 'welfare decision'. The same phrase was used in *Eade v Eade* [1983] FLR 573, where the wife had left the home and she and the children were living with another man in overcrowded conditions. The husband remained in the council house, of which he was sole tenant, but since the wife's departure he had been joined there by a lady-friend and her children. The wife's application was refused: although the position of the children of the marriage was important it would have been wrong to have made an order which would have had the effect of turning out the husband's friend and her children. Ormrod LJ observed that local authorities should secure the housing of wives and children without resort to ouster: even where there is no *duty* to rehouse under (now) the Housing Act 1985 local authorities nevertheless have a *power* to do what is reasonable and necessary.

The granting of an injunction will not be prevented by the fact that, for the purpose of the homelessness legislation, the applicant but not the respondent would have a priority need (as to which, see §2.3.4 above).

In *Wooton v Wooton* [1984] FLR 871, the parties' relationship had lasted for 18 years and they had four children. The man was prone to epileptic fits during which he became violent. He was admitted to hospital and, during his long stay there, he informed the woman that she and the children should leave the house. On his discharge from hospital, the woman sought to have him excluded from the home, a council house of which the man was the tenant. The court approached the case on the basis that, if ousted, the man would have no priority need for rehousing as a homeless person (though that assumption is open to question; see Housing Act 1985, s 59(1)(b)), whereas the woman and children would have a priority need. The court stressed that the DVA 1976 is designed to provide an emergency procedure for short-term remedies whereas in the instant case the situation had existed for many years, and there was no need for *urgent* protection. In contrast, the man was ousted in *Thurley v Smith* [1984] FLR 875, where the woman and her son would have had a priority need while the man would not, and where the court was told that it was not the local authority's normal policy to rehouse single men with no dependants. The court considered that, whatever might have been the rights and wrongs in relation to conduct in respect of the compulsive epileptic in *Wooton v Wooton*, above, the instant case (involving an alcoholic) was different. The wife was faced with an indefinite stay in wholly unsatisfactory refuge accommodation until the local authority could eventually rehouse her permanently and, on weighing the respective needs of the parties, and placing the man's conduct in the balance, it was right to oust the man from the home, a council house of which the parties were joint tenants.

Exclusion from area

The court has the power to restrain a party from entering a specified area in which the home is included. Such orders are likely to be uncommon but may be appropriate, for example, where an excluded party has been in the habit of sitting in his car outside the house keeping watch on the premises at all hours, or where an excluded party who has broken past non-molestation injunctions persistently follows the other on regular journeys to and from the children's school, especially where this is done in an intimidatory manner with the intention of deterring that other party from remaining in occupation of the home. The excluding provision may be expressed by reference to distance (eg 'not to approach within 100 yards of the home') or to a named street or part of a street (eg 'not to enter that part of South Street which lies between the junctions with East Street and West Street'). It may be that the respondent's workplace or the homes of his close relatives are in the immediate vicinity of the home, or can only be reached either by passing the home or by an unreasonably lengthy or impractical detour from the normal route. Special care must be taken in such cases to ensure that the respondent is in no doubt as to what is required of him and has no excuse for asserting that he 'didn't think it meant I couldn't visit my sister', and consideration should be given to attaching exceptions to the prohibition (for clauses suitable for use in cases where exceptions to the exclusion are considered appropriate, see [1991] Fam Law 192).

The area from which the ousted party is excluded should be the minimum necessary for the applicant's protection and will normally be no greater than one or two hundred yards: the fact that a chance encounter in the town's shopping centre may be the occasion of a violent incident is not a sufficient justification for imposing extensive limitations on the respondent's freedom of movement. (In practice, if the respondent faces criminal charges arising from earlier incidents, a court which grants him bail may impose bail conditions involving more extensive restrictions on his movements.)

Applicant no longer living in the former joint home

Where the complaint is that, having given cause for complaint during the subsistence of the relationship, the respondent persists in attending at or watching and besetting the property in which the applicant now lives, but which is not the former matrimonial home, there is no power under the DVA 1976 to restrain the respondent specifically from entering or approaching that property, but such conduct will generally fall within the range of conduct prohibited by a non-molestation injunction (see §2.4.3 above).

2.4.5 Duration and commencement of ouster injunctions

Duration

It has been stressed that the DVA 1976 is not designed to provide long-term solutions to housing disputes (see *Hopper v Hopper* [1978] 1 WLR 1342; *Thurley v Smith*, above; *Freeman v Collins* (1984) 12 HLR 68). It is designed to provide the party in occupation with a breathing-space in which to make other arrangements for accommodation and to set in train any other proceedings that may be available (eg petition for divorce with a request for a property adjustment order). In *Davis v Johnson*, above, Lord Salmon observed (at 343): 'I find it difficult to believe that it could ever be fair, save in the most exceptional circumstances, to keep a man out of his own flat or house for more than a few months'. Accordingly, the protection given by an injunction should normally be of limited duration: the aim is to provide 'first aid, not intensive care' (*Davis v Johnson*, above).

The general rule is that, in the first instance, exclusion limited to three months is likely to be appropriate (see *Practice Direction* [1978] 1 WLR 1123), but this is not a rule to be slavishly applied. Thus, for instance, to take a comparatively trivial example, where the behaviour complained of is usually committed when the respondent is drunk, and the normal three-month period would expire in mid-December, it may be appropriate to invite the court to stipulate that the injunction shall last over the 'festive' season. In any event, if difficulties continue, it will always be open to the applicant to apply for an extension. Often, a court dealing with a respondent who is in breach of an injunction will extend the duration of the injunction, whether or not it imposes any punishment for the breach. It is also open to a respondent to apply to be discharged from the prohibition before the date specified in the order.

Examples can be found of indefinite orders where the home involved has been a council house or flat. In *Spencer v Camacho* (1983) FLR 662, there was again a joint tenancy of council housing which was being occupied by the woman and the couple's young son. The man had repeatedly put himself in breach of previous non-molestation and ouster injunctions and the ouster had already been extended for six months. The court granted a renewal of ouster until further order. Sir David Cairns quoted the passage from Lord Salmon's judgment in *Davis v Johnson* (quoted above) but (at 665) he stressed the fact that in *Spencer v Camacho* there was a *joint* tenancy rather than a tenancy in the man's name alone. Moreover, he seemed (at 666–7) to attach considerable significance to the fact that, unlike a wife, a cohabitant has no other proceedings to which she could have resort during the 'breathing-space'.

That point is no longer valid where there is a child of the relationship since it is open to a parent to apply for an order requiring the respondent to transfer the tenancy to the parent with care of the child (see Children Act 1989, Sch 1; and see further §4.3.2 below).

Commencement

Since an ouster injunction is a Draconian order which, in essence, is only likely to be made where the court finds that the situation in the home is intolerable, there is an obvious inconsistency in holding that such an injunction is justified, but postponing its operation for anything more than a very short period designed to allow the person ousted a reasonable opportunity to vacate the home. In *Chadda v Chadda* (1981) Fam Law 142, the judge ordered that the ouster should take effect three and a half months after the date of the hearing, having found that the atmosphere in the home was intolerable, especially for the children. That provision of the injunction was quashed on appeal and it was said that once a judge finds that the situation is so intolerable that it is fair and just to make an order, the sooner the order is made effective the better for everyone, including the children. In that case, the man had a good wage and was likely to be able to make other arrangements in a comparatively short time. (*Chadda v Chadda* was decided before *Richards v Richards* and the language used would be different today, but it remains an appropriate authority on the particular point regarding commencement of the injunction.)

The same critical approach to delayed commencement is demonstrated by *Burke v Burke* [1987] 2 FLR 71, where the judge had granted an order but, to enable the parties to readjust and to consider their position, had ordered that it should take effect after eight weeks. On appeal it was held that it is 'inherently undesirable' to postpone operation for eight weeks save in unusual and compelling circumstances: where an ouster is justified, the order should take effect within one week or two weeks. In *Dunsire v Dunsire* [1992] Fam Law 266, commencement was deferred for 11 weeks in the expectation that in the interim the long-term issues would have been resolved at the hearing of the ancillary relief application. The injunction had been made as a 'longstop', with delayed commencement in view of the husband's disability. The Court of Appeal observed that such a disability might be a reason for not making an order at all but, once the court concluded that it was right to make the order notwithstanding that special circumstance, the *Burke* and *Chadda* approach obliged the court to make the order effective without undue delay.

2.4.6   Oral evidence required in cases of disputed facts

On an application for an ouster injunction, where relevant matters are in dispute the court should not grant an order on affidavit evidence alone: the Draconian nature of the order requires that there be a proper investigation of the evidence by examination and cross-examination of the parties (*Shipp v Shipp* [1988] 1 FLR 345; *Tuck v Nicholls* [1989] 1 FLR 283; *Whitlock v Whitlock* [1989] 1 FLR 208).

2.4.7   *Ex parte* relief

Although in *Shipp v Shipp*, above, the court expressly observed that there might well be circumstances where it would be right to make an ouster order on an *ex parte* application, it follows from what has been said in the preceding section that *ex parte* applications for ouster will not be favourably received save in the most compelling circumstances (not least because an application under the DVA 1976 requires only two clear days' notice to the respondent). Where there is no justification for proceeding *ex parte*, such applications are an abuse of the process of the court and the solicitors responsible for them may find themselves ordered to pay the costs (*Masich v Masich* (1977) Fam Law 245).

Likewise, an *ex parte* application for a non-molestation injunction should not be made or granted unless there is real immediate danger of serious injury (see *Practice Note* [1978] 1 WLR 925). However, such an application would be appropriate where, for example, it is not possible to effect service because the whereabouts of the other party are unknown, or where there is a particularly urgent need for protection, as where a respondent is likely to react with violence to the service of proceedings.

2.4.8   Powers of arrest

When the court grants an injunction which restrains the use of violence against the applicant or a child living with the applicant, or which excludes the other party from the home or its surrounding area, the judge may attach a power of arrest to the injunction if he is satisfied that the other party has caused actual bodily harm to the applicant, or to the child concerned, and considers that he is likely to do so again (DVA 1976, s 2(1)). A copy of the power of arrest must be delivered to the police station for the area in which the applicant resides. 'Actual bodily harm' means 'any hurt or injury calculated to interfere with the health and comfort of the [victim]' (*R v Miller* [1954] 2 QB 282, per Lynskey J at 292). In the absence of any evident injury (eg bruising), actual bodily harm may be found to have occurred where the act of violence has induced in the victim a hysterical or nervous condition (as in *R v Miller*, above), but for this purpose there has to be 'real psychological damage as a result of physical battery . . . there must be some clear evidence of a real change in the psychological condition of the person assaulted' (*Kendrick v Kendrick* [1990] 2 FLR 107, per Glidewell LJ at 110). In *Kendrick v Kendrick* it was held to be insufficient that the wife was so afraid that the husband would return home that she was too afraid to return there herself.

A power of arrest makes it possible for a constable to arrest without a warrant a person whom he has reasonable cause to suspect of being in breach of such an injunctive provision by reason of that person's use of violence or his entry into the home or a prohibited area (DVA 1976, s 2(3); and see *Bowen v Bowen* [1990] 2 FLR 93). A person arrested in reliance on a power of arrest must be brought before a judge within the period of 24 hours beginning at the time of his arrest, that period to be reckoned taking no account of Sundays, Good Friday and Christmas Day. Moreover, he is not to be released in that period except on the direction of the judge, thus, in effect, providing for a 'cooling-off' period (see s 2(4)). The judge before whom he is brought will deal with him for the contempt without any necessity for service of notice to show cause why a committal order should not be made against him. However, as illustrated by *Bowen v Bowen* above, if the respondent commits a breach of the wider provisions of the injunction but does not use violence, enter the home or go into a prohibited area, any arrest without warrant in purported exercise of the power of arrest will be invalid and the judge before whom the respondent is brought will have no power to deal with him in relation to that particular breach unless notice to show cause is served (a matter of some difficulty given the timescale involved) or the judge expressly exercises his power to dispense with service of the notice to show cause.

A power of arrest is not to be routinely attached to injunctions, but is to be used in exceptional circumstances only (*Widdowson v Widdowson* [1983] FLR 121; *Lewis v Lewis* [1978] Fam 60). When a power of arrest is to be sought, notice should be given to the other party that this is to occur (*Lewis v Lewis*, above). When a power of arrest is attached to an injunction, the judge should state his reasons for considering it necessary to do so (*Widdowson v Widdowson*, above). A power of arrest should not normally be attached for more than three months (*Widdowson v Widdowson*, above). Save as conferred by the DVA 1976, s 2, there is no inherent power to attach a power of arrest to an injunction (see *Re G (Wardship) (Jurisdiction: Power of Arrest)* (1982) FLR 538).

2.4.9   Committal

When no power of arrest is attached to an injunction, the remedy for breach lies in an application for the party in breach to be committed to prison for contempt. In family cases, committal should be regarded as the very last resort (*Ansah v Ansah* [1977] Fam 138). Hearing of an application to commit may proceed even though criminal proceedings are pending arising out of the same facts: committal proceedings should be dealt with swiftly and decisively (*Szczepanski v Szczepanski* [1985] FLR 468), but this does not take away the discretion of the judge to decide whether or not there is 'a real risk of serious prejudice which might lead to injustice' if committal proceedings are heard prior to the conclusion of the criminal proceedings (*H v C (Contempt and Criminal Proceedings)* [1993] 1 FCR 1).

Contempt of court is an offence of a criminal character and must be proved beyond reasonable doubt (*Dean v Dean* [1987] 1 FLR 517). Committal to prison for contempt must be for a fixed term. Imprisonment will not be appropriate where the breach was minor (*Smith v Smith* [1988] 1 FLR 179). The maximum term of imprisonment that can be imposed on any occasion is two years (Contempt of Court Act 1981, s 14(1)). Each case must be dealt with on its own facts, and the following are merely examples.

In *Wright v Jess* [1987] 2 FLR 373, the contemnor appeared before the court on four occasions for numerous acts of molestation which included, in various combinations, breaking into the applicant's home (including break-ins at night), assaulting the applicant, and removal of the children. On successive occasions, sentences were imposed of imprisonment for 14 days; three months, and six months. On the last of these occasions the contemnor was warned that a further breach might incur the maximum penalty. On his fourth appearance, a sentence of two years was imposed and the

Court of Appeal held that this sentence could not be regarded as wrong in principle on the facts as known at the time it was imposed.

In *G v G (Contempt: Committal)* [1992] Fam Law 130, the husband had been committed to prison for four months for breaches of a non-molestation injunction. On his release, he had continued a campaign of threats against the wife and was sentenced to 16 months imprisonment for contempt. On appeal, that sentence was upheld, despite the absence of actual violence.

The court has power to suspend a committal order conditional upon compliance with certain conditions (*Lee v Walker* [1985] QB 1191; but see further *Ansah v Ansah*, above).

The Court of Appeal has repeatedly stressed the need for care in ensuring strict compliance with the procedural rules applicable to committals (*Nguyen v Phung* [1984] FLR 773; *Clarke v Clarke* [1990] 2 FLR 115; *Bowen v Bowen* [1990] 2 FLR 93). However, it has been said that there is a sharp distinction between an error invalidating the committal order itself, and a procedural impropriety following the making of an impeccable committal order. An error in the latter category, if it has in fact resulted in no injustice to the contemnor, may not require the quashing of the sentence of imprisonment (*Re M (Minors) (Contempt: Committal)* (1992) 142 NLJ 1339). It is beyond the scope of this book to set out the relevant rules. For a comprehensive account, the reader is referred to Fricker and Bean: *Enforcement of Injunctions and Undertakings* (Jordans, 1991).

2.4.10 Undertakings

The court may accept an undertaking from the respondent. The giving of an undertaking does not imply any admission as to the matters relied on in support of the application for an injunction but is a quick and convenient way of disposing of cases where, notwithstanding that he does not admit the acts alleged, the respondent is willing to give assurances as to his future behaviour. An undertaking is a promise made to the court, and has all the force of an injunction (*Roberts v Roberts* [1990] 2 FLR 111). However, no power of arrest can be attached to an undertaking (*Carpenter v Carpenter* [1988] 1 FLR 121).

An undertaking should not be accepted where it is intended that there should be an injunction. Thus, it is not proper for the judge to accept an undertaking while at the same time purporting to declare that the applicant is entitled to an injunction in the terms of the undertaking (*McConnell v McConnell* (1980) Fam Law 214).

Where an undertaking is accepted it operates until it is quashed on appeal or discharged, and must be obeyed whether or not it should have been accepted (*Johnson v Walton* [1990] 1 FLR 350. (See also *Holtom v Holtom* (1981) Fam Law 249: in proceedings to exclude the husband, the court ought not to have accepted a wife's cross-undertaking not to cohabit in the home with another man.)

2.4.11   Orders to prevent removal of children

It may be that an applicant for an injunction fears not only physical violence or harassment by the respondent, but is also concerned at what she regards as the likelihood of an attempt by the respondent to remove their child(ren) from her care. That is a matter to be dealt with by the making of an appropriate order under the Children Act 1989, and a court which is hearing an application for an injunction has the power in those proceedings to make an order under the Children Act 1989, s 8, either on the application of a party or of its own motion (Children Act 1989, s 8(3), (4); s 10(1)). Such orders may be made enforceable by committal (see §8.5 below).

2.4.12   Frustrating an injunction

It must be noted that cohabitants will often remain vulnerable even when an ouster injunction is granted. A cohabitant acquires no proprietary right in the property by virtue of an ouster injunction and since a cohabitant has no statutory right of occupation comparable to that conferred on spouses by the MHA 1983, there is nothing to prevent an ousted cohabitant from selling or letting property which is in his sole name, nor can the injunction affect the rights of a third party who has an interest in the property. However, it was noted in *Davis v Johnson*, above (at 243), that the steps necessary to exclude the occupying cohabitant would take a little while so that the occupier would still have the breathing-space which it is the main object of ouster orders to provide. There is also nothing to prevent the ousted party removing such contents from the home as are his.

Where the home consists of rented accommodation, there is a potential problem with respect to termination of the tenancy. The position where a tenancy is deliberately terminated by one joint tenant has been considered above (at §2.2), but a question arises as to whether the injunctive exclusion from the property of a sole tenant will itself bring about a failure to satisfy the tenant condition (ie of occupation by the tenant as his only or principal home). Mere temporary absence will not by itself necessarily involve a failure of the tenant condition, provided that the tenant intends to return and has the right to return whenever he chooses, but it seems that a tenant whose right to occupy has been suspended and who can be lawfully prevented from entering the property cannot be regarded as occupying it. This may be a desirable result in many cases involving the tenancy of a local authority house or flat, since it would leave the local authority free to grant a sole tenancy to the party remaining in occupation; thereby achieving, albeit indirectly, a long-term resolution of the housing issue which the court itself is unable to achieve directly given the insistence that ouster is a short-term remedy.

With respect to private sector accommodation, the same consequences would apply to ouster of a sole tenant. However, a result which may create desirable flexibility in respect of council housing may have wholly different implications in cases involving private landlords not subject to any statutory duties with respect to the provision of housing. The landlord will be free to grant a new tenancy to the remaining cohabitant on wholly different terms (eg at a higher rent) or, indeed, to refuse to grant a new tenancy at all.

Part II
MONEY

3 THE ADULT PARTIES

It is a fundamental principle that parties who cohabit do not acquire any right, by virtue of that cohabitation, to financial support from each other during the subsistence of their relationship or on its breakdown. In practice, however, that principle remains inviolate only in respect of couples who have no children: the children of unmarried parents possess a right to financial support which is enforceable against each parent and enforcement of this right (whether by the Child Support Agency or, where available, by private proceedings) can involve an indirect contribution to the support of the parent with whom the child has his home (see Chapter 4). Moreover, even in the absence of any enforceable right to maintenance during the lifetimes of the parties, if the relationship is ended by the death of one cohabitant, the other may be able to seek provision for his or her maintenance from the deceased party's estate, or from a tortfeasor whose wrongful act resulted in the death (see Chapter 5).

Conversely, notwithstanding the absence of an enforceable right to be supported, cohabitants may be treated for a number of purposes as if they were married to each other, most notably in the context of state welfare benefits (see §3.2 below).

3.1 Ownership of and agreements concerning money and property

3.1.1 Agreements

'Cohabitation contracts'

The term 'cohabitation contract' is used here to denote an agreement entered into at the commencement of cohabitation and intended to regulate the financial relationship of the parties either during the subsistence of cohabitation or at its termination, or both. Used in this sense, it is to be distinguished from an agreement entered into at the termination of the relationship.

It is often suggested that it is feasible for those intending to cohabit to make a cohabitation contract spelling out the rights and obligations each party is to have with respect to the discharge of household expenses, the acquisition of property, its division on the termination of the relationship, and any rights of support which the parties agree should survive the ending of cohabitation. Certainly, it would be a comparatively simple matter to ensure that the agreement clearly disclosed an intention to enter into legal relations, thereby avoiding the pitfall which lies in wait for certain agreements between husbands and wives (see, eg *Balfour v Balfour* [1919] 2 KB 571).

On the other hand, even where the agreement clearly discloses an intention to be legally bound, there is no guarantee that a court will be willing to give effect to it. A long shadow is cast by older cases in which the courts have declined, on grounds of public policy, to enforce agreements which tended to promote sexual immorality (see, eg *Benyon v Nettlefold* (1850) 3 M & G 94; *Ayerst v Jenkins* (1873) LR 16 Eq 275). Notwithstanding changes in social attitudes, it has still to be settled that the courts will enforce agreements where cohabitation is the *sole* consideration for a promise to confer some benefit. Moreover, if such an agreement contains terms purporting to allocate responsibility for the care and maintenance of any (as yet unborn) children of the union, making the operation of those terms contingent upon the termination of cohabitation, the agreement can offer little certainty. As far as maintenance is concerned, no provision of the agreement will be effective if it purports to restrict the right to request an assessment under the Child Support Act 1991. Where (exceptionally) the matter remains within the court's jurisdiction the agreement may have some evidential value, but it cannot displace the court's duty to inquire into the level of provision necessary to meet the child's needs, and the means available for that purpose. Where the Child Support Agency is involved, the absence of any substantial discretion to depart from the statutory formula for assessing the maintenance payable will effectively render the agreement irrelevant.

Where the agreement embodies provisions concerning the future residence of any children born to the couple, it would at first sight appear to be consistent with the philosophy underlying the Children Act 1989, which places the emphasis on the desirability of parents arranging matters by agreement wherever possible. On the other hand, to the extent that the agreement seeks to anticipate future events and to deal in advance with their consequences, it runs counter to the court's insistence that matters such as a child's residence must be decided by reference to the child's interests at the time that the issue arises (and see eg *Re W (A Minor) (Residence Order)* [1992] 2 FLR 332). Even a property law-based provision that the parties' jointly owned home be sold on termination of their relationship may offer only illusory security if the case is one where the court can be persuaded that the home should be preserved for occupation by the children.

Finally, children apart, there exists the very real difficulty of drafting an agreement in terms flexible enough to cater for the many unforeseen and sometimes unforeseeable changes of circumstances that can occur during the lifetime of a relationship which can, for example, render unjust or onerous an undertaking given or accepted in all good faith and in complete (but misguided) confidence as to its ability to produce a fair result.

There are, therefore, many reasons for expressing caution before undertaking the arduous task of drafting a cohabitation contract as that term has been used here. That is not to say, however, that there is no place for formally expressed agreements in the context of cohabitation. For example, the manifestation of an agreement in the form of conveyance of the home into the parties' joint names with a declaration of their beneficial entitlements is an eminently sensible means of avoiding costly litigation (see §1.3.1 above).

Even where an agreement about interests in the home is not made manifest in the terms of the conveyance and is not binding in itself because, for some reason, it fails to satisfy formal requirements, if it is reliably recorded it will nevertheless be invaluable evidence from which the court may draw conclusions as to the parties' intentions at the relevant time for the purposes of the rules governing constructive trusts (see §1.3.4 above). This consideration applies with equal force to other forms of property, and some further examples are considered at §3.1.2 below.

Maintenance agreements

When cohabitation ceases and it is felt that there is a moral obligation on the part of one partner to continue to provide for the maintenance of the other, there is no objection to such provision being made by agreement. Where the intended recipient has the responsibility of caring for a child of the union, there will be no difficulty in finding consideration for the other party's undertaking to provide maintenance not only for the child but also for the parent in whose care the child is (see *Horrocks v Foray* [1976] 1 WLR 230; and see also *Ward v Byham* [1956] 1 WLR 496), but the agreement will be ineffective in preventing that parent requesting an assessment under the Child Support Act 1991 (see Chapter 4). However, where there are no children for whom the recipient of the payments is to provide care, a simple agreement may be insufficient to ensure that the undertaking becomes enforceable: an agreement following the cessation of cohabitation may face the objection that it is unenforceable as a contract by reason of the rules affecting past consideration (see *R v Bernhard* [1938] 2 KB 264). Such maintenance should therefore be provided for by deed (see *Nye v Moseley* (1826) 6 B & C 133).

3.1.2   Chattels

The fundamental rule is that the court has no power to intervene in order to adjust the property rights of parties to a failed cohabitation relationship, but that those parties may take from the relationship what they have brought into it. Thus, the broad principles outlined in Chapter 1 apply similarly to personal property as to real property and, with respect to the contents of the home and other personal property, the basic rule is the same as that which applies to the matrimonial home itself: he who pays owns. Thus, in the absence of evidence of a contrary intention (such as an intention to make a gift), each item of property may be owned, on the basis of contributions to its purchase, by one of the parties as sole owner, or by them jointly (or indeed by either or both of them jointly with a third party).

If it is alleged that items of personal property were given by one party to the other, the normal requirements for gifts must be established. Thus, unless a deed of gift is executed, it will first be necessary to prove an intention to transfer ownership (as opposed to an intention to allow the other party the use and enjoyment of the item; see *Windeler v Whitehall* [1990] 2 FLR 505: dressing-table purchased for cohabitant's use, but intended to be available for use by any successor). It will then be necessary to prove actual delivery (see *Re Cole* [1964] Ch 175), though this may be achieved by symbolic delivery of one item (see *Lock v Heath* (1892) 8 TLR 152: one chair representing all furniture). Except in the case of small personal items, the act of delivery may be hard to prove but it would, for instance, be of crucial importance if the donor died and a claim were made to the property by his personal representatives, or if he became bankrupt and his partner sought to retain property as against the trustee in bankruptcy.

As far as disputes between the cohabitants are concerned, since most chattels are depreciating assets, it will usually be unrealistic to contemplate proceedings for the purpose of ascertaining or enforcing proprietary rights. The court is unenthusiastic about hearing such claims (see eg *Windeler v Whitehall*, above, at 516; *H v M (Property: Beneficial Interest)* [1992] 1 FLR 229 at 240) and will generally be forced to take a very broad approach. Indeed, in *H v M*, Waite J observed (at 242) that in respect of household goods 'the parties must expect the court, in ordinary cases, to adopt a robust allegiance to the maxim that "equality is equity", if only in the interests of fulfilling the equally salutary maxim *sit finis litis*' (but see also *Richards v Dove* [1974] 1 All ER 888 and *Windeler v Whitehall*, above).

In *Windeler v Whitehall* the claim was made by way of an action for conversion, but in *H v M*, above, in the course of useful observations with respect to the procedural conduct of proceedings between former cohabitants, actions for detinue and conversion were said not to be normally appropriate: where ownership of chattels is in issue the proper way of bringing the matter before a court is by a claim to a declaration or enquiry along similar lines to a claim under the Married Women's Property Act 1882, s 17 (per Waite J at 242).

Overall, however, the division of household goods is considered to be a matter which the parties should be expected to achieve by agreement between themselves and it will often be appropriate for a fair balance to be struck according to considerations of common sense and comparative needs rather than by reference to strict legal rights in relation to individual items. Clearly, however, the professional adviser may need to be able to resolve the question of ownership in his own mind in order to assist in the attainment of a fair result. Even where parties have apparently arrived at a mutually acceptable division of their chattels it would be wise to enquire, at least in general terms, as to the manner in which assets were acquired, since there may be a danger that one party is agreeing to a division of property under the influence of a misapprehension as to the strict legal position with respect to its ownership.

3.1.3 Joint accounts

The principles which govern bank and building society accounts held in the joint names of spouses are, it is submitted, equally applicable to the joint accounts of cohabitants. In *Jones v Maynard* [1951] Ch 572, Vaisey J gave the classic explanation of the principles applicable to a joint account which has been operated as a 'common pool'. He said (at 575):

> 'In my judgment, when there is a joint account between husband and wife, a common pool into which they put all their resources, it is not consistent with that conception that the account should thereafter . . . be picked apart, and divided up proportionately to the respective contributions of husband and wife . . . [T]he idea that . . . the contents of the pool can be dissected by taking an elaborate account as to how much was paid in by the husband and wife is quite inconsistent with the original fundamental idea of a joint purse or common pool.'

Where an account is opened in their joint names but only one party is responsible for the provision of funds, the basic equitable rule is to presume a resulting trust in favour of the contributor, but the court will in general readily infer an intention to benefit the other party from any evidence which obviates the need to rely on presumptions (see generally *Pettitt v Pettitt* [1970] AC 777, per Lord Diplock at 824). There may, however, be an alternative explanation other than an intention to benefit the other party. There are older cases in which it was asserted that the joint account was opened for reasons of convenience (as where the contributor finds it difficult to administer the account or deal with household bills himself). In view of the flexibility of modern banking arrangements and the advent of 24-hour automated services, it will be rare to encounter a case where the court is satisfied that a current account was placed in joint names purely for reasons of convenience. However, such a case presented itself in *Simpson v Simpson* [1992] 1 FLR 601, where the parties, from the start of their marriage, had a joint current account, but where numerous assets (including deposit accounts formerly in the husband's sole name) were put into their joint names at a later stage when the husband was terminally ill. It was held that these transfers had been for convenience only, to facilitate the management of the husband's affairs by his wife during his final illness.

Joint account holders are joint tenants of the contents of the account. Thus, on the death of one party, the entire fund will pass to the survivor by virtue of the right of survivorship. During the joint lives of the parties, the joint tenancy may be severed, with the effect that each party will become entitled to one half of the balance in the account at the date of severance. However, unless and until there has been an effective severance of the joint tenancy, either party is entitled to make use of the entire contents of the account for his or her sole benefit. Indeed, when one party withdraws funds from the account to make a purchase, the presumption is that the property so purchased belongs solely to that party, be it clothes, a car, or stocks and shares. However, where the property purchased is not of a personal nature, it may be possible to establish that the property purchased was intended by the parties to retain the investment character of the original fund and that, despite its purchase in the name of one party only, it was in fact intended to be held on trust for them both.

This situation arose in *Jones v Maynard*, above, in which the wife's claim concerned an account which the parties had treated as a joint account. She claimed a one half share in the credit balance on the day the husband closed the account and a one half share also in investments which the husband had previously made in his sole name using funds from the account. The husband's contributions to the account had been greater than the wife's but the parties had regarded the fund as their joint savings to be invested from time to time. The wife succeeded in establishing, first, that there was a common pool and, secondly, that there was an intention that the investments be held on trust for them both (but compare *Re Bishop* [1965] Ch 450). Given the recent spread of share ownership, such questions may well start to arise more frequently than in the past.

Many couples regard the opening of a joint account as both a practical and a symbolic acknowledgement of their partnership. The fact remains, however, that a joint account carries vulnerability as well as benefits. As noted above, upon severance of the joint interest, the parties become tenants in common of the fund, and each is entitled to one half of the balance. However, up to the moment of severance, either party is entitled to withdraw and dispose of the entire fund and it is not uncommon for this to occur when a relationship is in the final stages of breakdown. Such action may be forestalled by notifying the bank that the mandate for sole-signature operation of the account is cancelled with immediate effect. In divorce cases involving the court's discretionary powers to reallocate spouses' assets, the behaviour of one spouse in dissipating any particular fund can be taken into account in deciding upon a just division of the remaining property. In cases involving cohabitants, there is no scope for such compensatory provision and it will be essential to act quickly to preserve the fund.

3.1.4   Other savings

It may be possible to establish that funds or other personal property held in the name of one party only are nevertheless to be regarded as held on trust for them both. Again, it is the intention of the parties which is the determining factor, as in *Paul v Constance* [1977] 1 WLR 527, where a cohabitant successfully claimed an interest in the contents of a deposit account opened in the sole name of her deceased partner who, during his lifetime, had frequently said that the money was as much hers as his. In that case it was held that there had been an express declaration of trust with respect to the account under which the parties were entitled in equal shares. The cohabitant therefore received one half of the closing balance.

Housekeeping allowances

In cases involving cohabitants, there is nothing corresponding to the Married Women's Property Act 1964, which provides that, in the absence of agreement to the contrary, savings derived from a housekeeping allowance paid by a husband to a wife are to be treated as belonging to them both in equal shares. Thus, where one cohabitant pays the other a housekeeping allowance, *prima facie* any surplus funds revert to the provider under a resulting trust. However, this presumption may be rebutted by evidence of a contrary intention. Thus, for example, there may be evidence of an intention in relation to the entire period during which the allowance was paid that any sums accumulated from it as the result of efficient household management should belong to the recipient of the allowance. Alternatively, there may be an agreement in relation to individual purchases made from an accumulated surplus. (For passing reference to this possibility, see *Windeler v Whitehall* [1990] 2 FLR 505 at 516–517.)

3.2 Cohabitation and welfare benefits

It is not intended within the confines of this book to offer an extensive account of the present social security system, which came into being in April 1988. This account confines itself to a consideration of the impact of cohabitation on the right to and quantification of welfare benefits: for certain purposes the system treats persons living together as husband and wife as if they were married, thus perpetuating the old 'cohabitation rule' (see Social Security Contributions and Benefits Act 1992, s 137).

3.2.1 Income-related benefits and the cohabitation rule

The three main income-related (means-tested) benefits are: *Income Support*, which is payable to claimants who are without employment and who satisfy the relevant conditions with respect to availability for employment; *Family Credit*, which is payable where a claimant is in work but receiving a low income, and is a member of a family unit containing at least one dependent child; and *Housing Benefit*, which is available where a claimant is liable to make payment in respect of residential accommodation which he occupies as his home.

In broad terms, the cohabitation rule has its most important impact in relation to ineligibility for separate assessment of benefit, and the aggregation of resources.

The unit of claim for means-tested benefits is the 'family' which, for this purpose, essentially means a married or unmarried couple (with or without children), or a lone-parent family. If one member of a family is entitled to a means-tested benefit, any other member of the family is excluded from being a claimant for that benefit during the same period of entitlement. Likewise, in applying the means test, the income and capital of any member of the family is normally to be treated as the income and capital of the claimant. Where children are involved, the cohabitation rule will prevent payment of the *lone-parent premium* to a recipient of Income Support, whether or not the children living with the unmarried couple are the children of both parties.

In the case of Income Support, the claim may be made by whichever member of a married or unmarried couple the parties agree should make it. In the case of Family Credit, the claim is normally to be made by the woman. In the case of Housing Benefit, if both parties are liable to make the payments in respect of their accommodation, the claim may again be made by whichever of them they agree should make it.

Clearly, therefore, in respect of Income Support and Family Credit, notwithstanding the absence of any legally enforceable mutual right of support as between cohabitants, the welfare benefits system presumes: (a) that the existing resources of one partner are available for the support of them both; and (b) that the sums paid to the claimant in benefit will be expended for the benefit of them both and of any child or children living with them, whether the child is the child of them both or is the child of the non-claimant partner only and is thus not a child in respect of whom the parent's cohabitant has any enforceable obligation.

3.2.2   Cohabitation indicators

The legislation itself offers no further guidance on the meaning of the phrase 'living together as husband and wife', but guidelines produced by the DSS have been described as 'admirable signposts' (see *Crake v Supplementary Benefits Commission* [1981] FLR 264, per Waite J at 270–271. These 'signposts' are as follows.

The man is normally living in the same household as the woman and has no other home

Occasional and casual cohabitation for a matter of only a few days at a time while the visiting party retains a home of his or her own ought not to be regarded as satisfying this criterion (and see further *R(SB) 8/85*, where the Commissioner held that a person cannot simultaneously be a member of more than one couple/household). Conversely, where the underlying basis is one of stable co-residence, periodic absences connected, for example, with work commitments will not take the case outside the scope of the cohabitation rule (see *R(SB) 30/83*; but see also *R(SB) 19/35*). The co-residence must not only be under the same roof, but also in the same household, and it will in some cases be possible to present an argument that the parties are separate households under the same roof, where there is no genuine sharing of daily life and no significant provision of services by one for the other. Living together in the same household is clearly a prerequisite to the application of the cohabitation rule, but it is not sufficient by itself: the parties must be living in the same household *as husband and wife* (see *Crake v Supplementary Benefits Commission*; *Butterworth v Supplementary Benefits Commission* (1981) FLR 264; where, in the *Butterworth* case, the man had moved into the woman's home to look after her during her recovery from serious injuries; see also *Kingsley v Secretary of State for Social Services* (1983) FLR 143; and *R(SB) 35/85*). It is in respect of this *qualitative* aspect of the rule that the remaining criteria come into play. The weight to be attached to any one or more of these criteria may vary from case to case.

The man and woman are living together in a stable marriage-like relationship

This may be indicated by the existence of children of the union, the use by the woman of the man's surname or their pursuit of a joint lifestyle, for example, by going out together socially and going on holiday together.

There is some mutual financial support or sharing of household expenses

On the one hand, payment by a man for his board and lodging may support a woman's assertion that his place in the household is as a lodger and that they are not living together as husband and wife, but the existence of a 'common purse' is likely to be regarded as strong evidence of quasi-marital cohabitation (and see *Kaur v Secretary of State for Social Services* (1982) FLR 237). Conversely, however, if other indicators of a quasi-marital relationship are present, the *absence* of any financial contribution will not by itself be sufficient to displace the application of the cohabitation rule since this would operate as an incentive not to support a partner for the sake of increasing benefit entitlements.

The couple have a sexual relationship

Since sexual intercourse is a normal feature of marriage, the fact that a couple have a sexual relationship is regarded as significant in determining whether two persons are living together as man and wife. However, in theory at least, casual and infrequent intercourse with a lodger ought not to result in the application of the cohabitation rule. The absence of a sexual relationship will greatly reduce the likelihood of a finding that a couple are living together as husband and wife (see further *Robson v Secretary of State for Social Services* (1982) FLR 232; see also *Kaur v Secretary of State for Social Services*, above).

The presence of children

As noted above, the birth of a child of the union will generally be a strong indication that the parties are living together as husband and wife, as will evidence that they are engaged *jointly* in the care of children of either of them (but see *Kingsley v Secretary of State for Social Services*, above).

They hold themselves out publicly as being man and wife

This will cover a couple's dealings with third parties generally. More specifically, as noted above, the woman's use of the man's surname may be relied on as very significant evidence that they are living together as husband and wife (see *R(G) 5/68*), but the use of different surnames will not by itself prevent such a finding. Similarly, in *Campbell v Secretary of State for Social Services* (1983) FLR 138, where the woman alleged that the relationship was one of housekeeper and master, an intention to apply for a joint tenancy of the home was regarded as not the kind of step that would be taken by a mere lodger or housekeeper.

3.2.3   Commencement and breakdown of cohabitation

Commencement of cohabitation

Where a person already in receipt of Income Support has a dependent child or children and begins to cohabit with a person whose means are such as to disentitle the new family unit to benefits, benefits in respect of the children will continue to be payable for a period of adjustment of four weeks (which may be extended for a further six weeks), if it is considered that the reduction in income resulting from the withdrawal of benefit would be disproportionate.

Breakdown of cohabitation

Where the cohabitation rule has been applied and the relationship subsequently breaks down, separate entitlement to benefit will arise, but the breakdown must be (or be intended to be) permanent, and the parties must not be living together in the same household. Clearly, separation will provide evidence of such breakdown, but where circumstances compel the parties to remain under the same roof for the time being, it will be necessary to mount an argument based on the existence of two separate households under one roof.

Although the effect of the cohabitation rule is to treat cohabitants as liable for each other's maintenance while their relationship subsists, once the relationship has broken down, neither is to be treated as a 'liable relative' for the purpose of recovering sums paid by way of benefit to the other following the breakdown.

Community Care Grants

Community Care Grants may be payable, among other purposes, to ease the stress immediately following the breakdown of established family relationships. In the case of couples with children, the parties must have been living with each other for at least three months before the cohabitation ended. In the case of couples without children, the relationship must have been long-standing (normally for two years or more).

3.2.4 Other benefits

Social Fund loans

Where a loan has been made from the Social Fund, it may be recovered from the person to whom it was made, or from the other member of a married or unmarried couple of which that person is a member.

Maternity payments

The scheme under which these payments are made treats unmarried and married couples alike, and a payment in respect of a child is made where the claimant or the claimant's partner has been awarded either Income Support or Family Credit.

Funeral payments

The scheme under which these payments are made also treats unmarried and married couples alike. Thus, where the couple has been in receipt of an income-related benefit, a surviving cohabitant is eligible for a payment to meet the funeral expenses of the deceased partner.

Pensioners' Christmas bonus

When a Christmas bonus has been paid to pensioners the cohabitation rule has been applied so that cohabiting pensioners received the payment at the rate applicable to couples, and not at the rate payable to single pensioners.

Child Benefit

If a child is living with cohabitants, both of whom are his parents, the mother is entitled to receive Child Benefit. If a child is living with cohabitants and only one of them is his parent, that parent is entitled to Child Benefit.

Where a person entitled to Child Benefit has sole responsibility for bringing up a child or children, an additional benefit known as One-Parent Benefit is payable. This additional benefit is affected by cohabitation insofar as it is not payable where the person entitled to the Child Benefit is living with a spouse or is living with someone as his spouse.

Contributory benefits

For the purpose of contributory benefits, cohabitants are treated as single persons and entitlement is based on the claimant's own contributions (or those of a spouse). Thus, for example, no entitlement to a Retirement Pension can arise by virtue of a cohabitant's contribution, and there can be no entitlement to Widow's Pension on the death of a male cohabitant. On the other hand, cohabitation by a recipient of Widow's Pension or Widowed Mother's Allowance or Child's Special Allowance (payable in certain circumstances to a divorced mother on the death of her former husband) will suspend her right to receive that benefit and, if she was cohabiting at the date of her husband's death, no Widow's Pension becomes payable.

3.3 Cohabitation and divorce

3.3.1 Introduction

This section is concerned with the impact of cohabitation on the financial relationships of those who are parties to a marriage which is dissolved. Briefly, the divorce court has the power to make financial provision orders and property adjustment orders in favour of the parties to the dissolved marriage and in favour or for the benefit of any children of the marriage, save that the power to make periodical payments orders in respect of children is greatly circumscribed by the Child Support Act 1991 (see Chapter 4).

Financial provision orders comprise secured and unsecured periodical payments orders and orders for the payment of a lump sum. Property adjustment orders comprise orders for the transfer or settlement of property, and orders varying existing settlements, or extinguishing the interest of either spouse under an existing settlement (see Matrimonial Causes Act 1973, ss 23 and 24). Where the court makes a secured periodical payments order, or a lump sum order or a property transfer order, it has the additional power to order the sale of property (s 24A).

Matters to which the court must have regard in deciding whether and in what manner to exercise these powers are set out in s 25 and s 25A. Section 25(1) requires the court to give first consideration to the welfare, while a minor, of any child of the family who has not attained the age of 18. Section 25A gives the court the power to impose a 'clean break' (s 25A(3)), and requires the court to give consideration to whether it would be appropriate so to exercise its powers as to terminate the financial obligations of each party towards the other (s 25A(1)). It also obliges the court to consider whether it would be appropriate to require periodical payments to be made only for such limited period as would enable the recipient to adjust without undue hardship to the termination of his or her financial dependence on the other party (the so-called 'deferred clean break'; s 25A(2)). The existence of children of the family may preclude the imposition of a clean break which, in the view of the courts, is only realistic where the wife is capable of being (or becoming) self-supporting. In practice, however, there has arisen a widespread practice of achieving settlements of claims to financial relief on a clean break basis even where the wife is not capable of supporting herself without assistance from the State (see §3.3.8 below).

Section 25 sets out a list of matters to which the court must have regard and which relate to the circumstances and needs of the parties and of any children of the family to whom the Act applies. (It may be noted that, during the subsistence of a marriage which has broken down, periodical payments orders and lump sum orders limited to £1000 may be sought from the magistrates' ('family proceedings') court under the Domestic Proceedings and Magistrates' Courts Act (DPMCA) 1978. The relevant guidance to the family proceedings court (DPMCA 1978, s 3) substantially replicates the MCA 1973, s 25. There are no express provisions corresponding to s 25A, but a power to make limited duration orders for periodical payments is contained in s 4(1)).

The following discussion will draw attention to those matters in relation to which the court's consideration may be affected by cohabitation. Save where otherwise indicated, the discussion assumes the most common factual situation; that is, that an order is sought (or has been made) which imposes on the husband obligations towards his wife and any children of the family, that prior to the breakdown of the marriage the wife and children (if any) were wholly or substantially dependent upon the husband, and that any children are living with the wife.

3.2.2   Cohabitation and periodical payments

The formula laid down by the Child Support Act (CSA) 1991 for assessing a child's 'maintenance requirement' includes a significant element to represent the basic support cost of the child's mother. It is likely that in many cases the available means of the father will be exhausted by the enforcement against him of an assessment under the CSA 1991 and that there will therefore be little purpose to be served in pursuing him independently of that Act for an order in favour of the wife. Much of the following discussion is therefore likely to be of relevance primarily to cases where there are no children (or no children to whom the CSA 1991 is applicable). But, it should be borne in mind that if there are no children the court is particularly likely to take the view that a clean break (immediate or deferred) is appropriate, at least where the wife is still young or otherwise has a realistic prospect of employment which will enable her to be self-sufficient.

Cohabitation at the time of the divorce

It has been said that, when asked to exercise its powers to order financial provision, the court 'is faced with essentially a financial and not a moral exercise' (*Duxbury v Duxbury* [1987] 1 FLR 7, per Ackner LJ at 14). Thus, responsibility for the breakdown of the marriage will not normally be regarded as relevant in determining the extent to which each party should provide or receive financial support: conduct is to be taken into account only 'if that conduct is such that it would in the opinion of the court be inequitable to disregard it' (MCA 1973, s 25(2)(g)). Thus, in the absence of aggravating circumstances, mere adultery by a wife will not operate to debar her from financial support, nor will a husband's adultery be a justification for increasing the payments he must make above the level indicated by the other factors listed in s 25(2).

Wife's cohabitation

Where the ex-wife is cohabiting at the time when financial provision is sought, the question arises as to whether she is being wholly and adequately supported by her new partner. Where this is in fact the case, she runs the risk that the court will dismiss her claim for periodical payments and impose a 'clean break', the result of which will be that the question of continued support by way of periodical payments cannot be reopened at a later stage, whatever the fate of the relationship with her new partner (see s 25A(1), (3)).

Where there is some partial support from her new partner, either by way of direct payment of household expenses or by contributions in kind, the effect of the cohabitation will be to reduce the financial needs in respect of which she seeks the husband's assistance and, in the context of periodical payments, financial needs (viewed in relation to the other spouse's financial resources) are in practice the most important of the considerations to which the court's attention is directed by s 25. (*Inter alia*, s 25(2) lists the following matters for consideration: '(a) the income, earning capacity, property and other financial resources which each of the parties to the marriage has or is likely to have in the foreseeable future . . . ; (b) the financial needs, obligations and responsibilities which each of the parties to the marriage has or is likely to have in the foreseeable future'.)

Where an ex-wife's cohabitant has the means to make a contribution to the joint household expenses but fails to do so, the court may take the view that he could and should so contribute, and this view may be reflected in its treatment of the ex-wife's claim to be maintained. In *Suter v Suter and Another* [1987] 2 FLR 232, a clean break was imposed and the husband's continuing liability limited to maintenance for the children where the ex-wife's behaviour in inviting her lover to share the former matrimonial home for the foreseeable future without making any contribution was held to be conduct which it would be inequitable to disregard.

Conversely, where the ex-wife is cohabiting with a man who is wholly or partly dependent upon her for support, or whose means are modest by comparison with the resources available to the husband, it will not be open to the husband to resist the ex-wife's application for periodical payments by arguing that her new partner will benefit from the payments the husband may be ordered to make (*Duxbury v Duxbury*, above, at 13; and see *Atkinson v Atkinson* [1988] 2 FLR 353, at 364; *Hepburn v Hepburn* [1989] 1 FLR 373).

Husband's cohabitation

It follows from what has been said above that where a husband is cohabiting at the date of the hearing of the ex-wife's application for financial provision, the extent of the responsibility which he has undertaken towards his cohabitant and any children will be relevant in determining the resources which he has available to meet any order for periodical payments which is made against him. The Act does not require the court to have regard only to legally enforceable obligations (see *Roberts v Roberts* [1970] P 1). Thus, where a husband's means are modest, any award in favour of his ex-wife may have to be lower than would otherwise be appropriate in order that the income which remains available to the new family unit of which he is a member is not so depleted as to reduce that family's income below subsistence level (see *Allen v Allen* [1986] 2 FLR 265; *Shallow v Shallow* [1979] Fam 1). Where this is the situation, the court will have regard to the availability to the wife of welfare benefits (see, eg *Williams v Williams* [1974] 3 All ER 377; *Allen v Allen*, above; *Chase v Chase* (1983) Fam Law 21; and see also *Delaney v Delaney* [1990] 2 FLR 457 at 461: 'there is a life after divorce').

Where the husband is cohabiting with a woman who has her own income and is contributing to their joint living expenses, or to the husband's support (eg by providing him with rent-free accommodation, as in *Ette v Ette* [1964] 1 WLR 1433), the effect is to relieve the husband of expenses which he would otherwise have to bear, thereby freeing more of his resources to meet his obligations to his former wife.

Cohabitation after divorce

As will be seen, property transfer orders and lump sum orders are closed transactions. However, periodical payments orders impose continuing obligations and are susceptible to applications for variation (see MCA 1973, s 31).

Wife's cohabitation

An ex-wife's remarriage automatically terminates any existing periodical payments order in her favour. Remarriage, of course, creates a new matrimonial status whereby the wife acquires rights enforceable against her new husband. If she cohabits she acquires no such enforceable rights with respect to her cohabitant, and there is no automatic effect on a periodical payments order, but her cohabitation may prompt an application by the husband to vary the order by reducing or possibly extinguishing his obligation to make further payments. A court hearing a variation application will have regard to all the circumstances and not merely any financial changes (see MCA 1973, s 31(7); and see *Lewis v Lewis* [1977] 3 All ER 992). Much of what has been said in the preceding paragraphs applies equally to variation applications and, in particular, it may be noted that the Court of Appeal has expressly refused to equate cohabitation with remarriage. Nevertheless, the overall circumstances may justify a reduction in her maintenance (see *Atkinson v Atkinson*, above; *MH v MH* (1982) FLR 429) and, where the ex-wife has come to a deliberate decision not to remarry and her decision is financially motivated, this can amount to conduct which it would be inequitable for the court to disregard (*Atkinson v Atkinson*, above) but this does not necessarily mean that a punitive approach will be adopted and her entitlement to maintenance from her husband altogether forfeited.

Husband's cohabitation

In the same way that cohabitation by a recipient may affect her needs and resources, cohabitation by the payer may also affect the resources available to him. Cohabitation by a husband may thus provide grounds for a variation application by himself, seeking a reduction in his maintenance obligations in view of his new responsibilities, or by his ex-wife seeking an increase in payments where the circumstances of his new relationship are such as to free additional resources.

3.3.3 Cohabitation and capital provision

As noted above, the divorce court has extensive powers to reallocate spouses' capital and property. In considering what effect cohabitation may have on the exercise of these powers, it is important to distinguish the different purposes which capital orders may serve, albeit that the distinction is not always clearly articulated by the courts. First, orders by way of capital may be based on an assessment of *needs*, as where the husband has the resources to make a substantial lump sum payment and the wife requires such a sum in order to purchase a new home. Secondly, a lump sum order may represent capitalised periodical payments in a case where the court considers that there should be a clean break. Thirdly, a capital award may be based on *deserts*, in recognition of the contribution that the ex-wife has made over the years of the marriage (including any contribution which she has made by looking after the home or caring for the family (see MCA 1973, s 25(2)(f)).

Clearly, where the court is asked to make provision by way of capital on the basis of *needs*, the presence in the wife's life of a cohabitant will be relevant along lines similar to those already considered in connection with periodical payments. Likewise where the capital award is intended to replace future payments of income. Thus, in *Ibbetson v Ibbetson* [1984] FLR 545, the ex-wife's cohabitant was proposing to re-convey his house into the joint names of himself and the ex-wife, and it was held that her expectation of a one half share in the house was to be taken into account in the award made by the divorce court since it constituted a resource likely to be available to her in the foreseeable future.

Where the assertion is that capital or assets should be awarded to the wife in recognition of the duration of the marriage and her services and efforts during its subsistence, it is submitted that the fact that the ex-wife has formed a new relationship is irrelevant. By way of analogy, the unexpected death of the ex-wife within months of the making of a substantial capital award in her favour may lead the court to grant leave to appeal out of time against the making of the order (see §3.3.4 below), but it does not mean that her estate should get nothing because she no longer had any 'needs' if the order also reflected 'deserts' (see *Smith v Smith* [1991] 2 FLR 432; *Barber v Barber* [1992] Fam Law 436; and see *Amey v Amey* [1992] 2 FLR 89: death of wife before agreement embodied in consent order; agreement stood).

Nevertheless, in any given case there may be special factors which justify a reduced award, as in *Ibbetson v Ibbetson*, above, where the ex-wife's conduct was taken into account in determining the award where, after 15 years of marriage and having no complaint of any kind against the husband, she had left him to live with his best friend (but compare: *Trippas v Trippas* [1973] 2 All ER 1).

3.3.4   Appeals and variation

The position with respect to variation of periodical payments orders in the light of subsequent cohabitation has been considered above (at §3.3.2). It is not possible to seek variation of orders imposing a clean break, or orders for the transfer of property, or orders for the payment of a lump sum (save where provision is made for payment by instalments). However, in certain circumstances, leave may be given to appeal out of time against the *making* of the order, and such leave may be sought where circumstances have changed so fundamentally that justice requires the matter to be reopened. In *Livesey v Jenkins* [1985] FLR 813, Lord Brandon observed (at 830) that a case for setting aside will be considered only where there has been a change of circumstances which renders the order made substantially different from the order which the court would have made if the true circumstances had been known. In *Barder v Barder (Caluori Intervening)* [1987] 2 FLR 480, Lord Brandon set out the circumstances in which a court could exercise its discretion to grant leave to appeal out of time. Lord Brandon said (at 495):

'A court may properly exercise its discretion to grant leave to appeal out of time from an order for financial provision or property transfer made after divorce on the ground of new events, provided that certain conditions are satisfied. The first condition is that new events have occurred since the making of the order which invalidate the basis, or fundamental assumption, on which the order was made, so that, if leave to appeal out of time were to be given, the appeal would be certain, or very likely, to succeed. The second condition is that the new events should have occurred within a relatively short time of the order having been made. While the length of time cannot be laid down precisely, I should regard it as extremely unlikely that it could be as much as a year, and that in most cases it will be no more than a few months. The third condition is that the application for leave to appeal out of time should be made reasonably promptly in the circumstances of the case. To these three conditions I would add a fourth . . . The fourth condition is that the grant of leave to appeal out of time should not prejudice third parties who have acquired, in good faith and for valuable consideration, interests in property which is the subject matter of the relevant order.' (For examples, see *Chaudhuri v Chaudhuri* [1992] Fam Law 385: ex-wife remarrying 14 months after order: leave refused; *Wells v Wells* [1992] Fam Law 386: ex-wife remarrying six months after order: leave granted.)

3.3.5   Consent orders

Costly litigation can be avoided if the parties to a divorce are able to reach an agreement with respect to the division of their property and their future financial obligations to each other. Such an agreement can then be incorporated in a *consent order* and the court has power to make such an order, without attendance by the parties, on the basis of documents containing the information prescribed by the Family Proceedings Rules 1991, r 2.61.

Non-disclosure

The Rules require the details supplied with the application to include information as to whether either party has remarried, or has any present intention to marry or cohabit with another person. Failure to make full and frank disclosure may lead to the order being set aside. The duty to make full and frank disclosure applies at the time when the statement of information is prepared and continues throughout the period up to the making of the order, so that notice must be given of any material change of circumstances. Thus, in *Livesey v Jenkins*, above, a consent order was set aside where, between the making of the application and the making of the order (which provided, *inter alia* for the transfer to the ex-wife of the husband's interest in the home) the ex-wife became engaged to be married, but failed to disclose this fact to the husband or to the court.

Failure to make full and frank disclosure in the prescribed form will not necessarily result in a consent order being set aside. In *Cook v Cook* [1988] 1 FLR 521, the ex-wife had given inaccurate information with respect to her intention to cohabit. The court made reference to the remarks of Lord Brandon in *Barder v Barder*, above, to the effect that the facts must be such as to suggest that a substantially different order would have been made if the true circumstances had been known, and it was held that, although the non-disclosure constituted a change of circumstances, it would have made no substantial difference if the matter were reopened and reconsidered since the case was not one where there was a complete change of circumstances but rather only a development in an existing relationship of which the husband was aware.

Variation

Like the order in *Livesey v Jenkins*, the consent order in *Cook v Cook* provided for the transfer to the wife of the husband's interest in the home and, as noted above, property transfer orders are not susceptible to variation. Thus, the only available courses are an application to set aside the order or an application for leave to appeal out of time. However, where the terms of the consent order are such as to give the court power to vary (eg provision for periodical payments), the fact that an order was made by consent does not oust the court's power to hear an application for variation (see *Jessel v Jessel* [1979] 3 All ER 645), and a failure to disclose at the time of the order may provide the basis for a variation application in the same way as a subsequent change of circumstances. The court is generally reluctant to interfere with agreed provisions since this might tend to discourage parties from attempting to reach agreements. Nevertheless, it will intervene if persuaded that the circumstances which actually exist would merit a substantially different order (see *B(GC) v B(BA)* [1970] 1 All ER 913).

In *Prow (Formerly Brown) v Brown* (1983) FLR 352, no consent order had been made, but the parties had reached an agreement under which the husband transferred the matrimonial home to the ex-wife in full and final settlement of her claim to financial relief. Shortly after the transfer, the ex-wife reconveyed the house so as to confer on her future husband a 25 per cent share in the property. At the same time, a mortgage was entered into on the security of the property. At the time of the agreement, the wife had not disclosed her intention to remarry. It was held that the agreement was tainted by the wife's misrepresentation of her intentions. The husband's application for rescission of the agreement could not succeed owing to the acquisition by third parties of an interest in the property, but his application for rescission was converted into an application for financial provision on his own behalf under the MCA 1973, ss 23 and 24 (a course which would not have been open to the court if the husband had remarried). On that application, the court ordered the ex-wife to pay the husband a lump sum (see further §3.3.8 below).

3.3.6   Ascertaining a cohabitant's means

Where it is sought to argue that an award to or against a divorced spouse should take account of the support which he or she is receiving or could receive from a cohabitant, it is desirable to ascertain the cohabitant's means. The cohabiting spouse may be ordered to file an affidavit disclosing the cohabitant's means in so far as they are known to the spouse, but there is no provision in the rules for obtaining a statement of means directly from a cohabitant (see *Wynne v Wynne* [1980] 3 All ER 659; but see also *W v W* (1981) FLR 291; and FPR 1991, r 2.62).

Where no information is forthcoming as to a cohabitant's means or the degree of support being provided, the court is free to draw adverse inferences on the matter as appropriate having regard to evidence as to the cohabiting spouse's general standard of living (see, eg *Ette v Ette* [1964] 1 WLR 1433: inferences could be drawn from cohabiting husband's whole way of life and 'circumstances of comparative affluence').

3.3.7   Avoidance of dispositions

The MCA 1973, s 37 contains provisions which enable the court to set aside or forbid dispositions made or about to be made with the intention of defeating a claim to financial relief or reducing the amount of any financial relief which might be granted. Briefly, a disposition is a 'reviewable disposition' for this purpose unless it has already been made and was made for full valuable consideration to a person who, at the time of the transaction, acted in good faith and without notice of an intention to prevent or reduce an award of financial relief. Where an application is made under s 37 in respect of a disposition which took place less than three years before the date of the application or which is about to take place, and the court is satisfied that the disposition concerned has had or would have the effect of defeating the applicant's claim for financial relief, an intention to defeat the applicant's claim will be presumed and the onus will be on the respondent to show that no such intention existed at the relevant time. Otherwise, the onus of proving the requisite intent lies on the applicant.

Clearly, gifts to a cohabitant and purported sales to a cohabitant with notice of the disponor's intention to defeat a spouse's claim will be vulnerable to an application under s 37.

3.3.8 Cohabitation and the former matrimonial home

Introduction

Where a divorcing couple have children, the divorce court will, wherever possible, make an order which will safeguard the children's occupation of the matrimonial home. In the majority of divorce cases, the children will be in the care of the wife so that she too will remain in occupation. Such preservation of the home for occupation by the children will commonly have the effect of preventing the husband from realising the capital which he has tied up in the matrimonial home: his claim to realise his interest is being postponed to the needs of the children. It should be borne in mind that, as noted at §3.3.1 above, in exercising its powers under the MCA 1973 the court is directed to give first consideration to the need to safeguard and promote the welfare of any children of the family throughout their childhood, though it should be noted that the statute does not make the children's needs the paramount or overriding consideration (see *Suter v Suter and Another* [1987] 2 FLR 232).

An obvious solution to the problems posed by the desire to preserve the home for the children would be to order the wife to buy out the husband's interest. This, however, is in most cases unrealistic due to the wife's lack of capital or an income sufficient to enable her to buy out the husband's share with the aid of a mortgage.

In the early 1970s, a common solution to the problem of securing the home for the children was the *Mesher* order (from *Mesher v Mesher* (1973), reported at [1980] 1 All ER 126). This form of order gives the wife and children exclusive possession of the property, but provides that the spouses shall retain such interests in it as the court directs, with sale postponed until some specified future date, commonly on the youngest child attaining the age of 18 (or 16 or 17) or ceasing to be in full-time education. This type of order has the effect of ensuring the preservation of the home for the children during their minority while preserving the husband's interest in the capital with the prospect of eventual realisation. A number of variations on this theme were developed.

The *Mesher* order has come under heavy criticism. For example, in *Hanlon v Hanlon* [1978] 2 All ER 889, it was pointed out that a family does not simply 'magically dissolve' on the youngest child's eighteenth birthday, and the mother will usually have to continue to provide a home for the children for some years after that date until they marry or otherwise leave home (and see, eg *Grimshaw v Grimshaw* (1981) Fam Law 75). Moreover, such orders are likely to compel a sale at a time in the ex-wife's life when she will find it difficult, if not impossible, to re-enter the housing market on the basis of her own income and resources. Hence, it has been said that such orders 'are likely to produce harsh and unsatisfactory results' (*Mortimer v Mortimer-Griffin* [1986] 2 FLR 315; and see *Clutton v Clutton* [1991] 1 FLR 242: *Mesher* order likely to be appropriate only where ex-wife's share of the eventual proceeds of sale is likely to be sufficient for the purchase of new accommodation).

In consequence of these disadvantages of the *Mesher* order, a preference has arisen for the *Martin* order (see *Martin v Martin* [1978] Fam 12). This order enables the ex-wife to remain in the property until her death or remarriage (or, perhaps, cohabitation, see below) and usually involves a transfer of the entire legal and beneficial interest to the ex-wife, but with a requirement that she execute a charge in the husband's favour in respect of a specified proportion of the value of the property: a form which has the advantage that husband and the ex-wife will not be required to co-operate in effecting the eventual sale but which offers the husband only a distant and uncertain prospect of receiving any capital in respect of his interest in the home.

A limited compromise can be achieved by means of an order where sale is postponed beyond the children attaining the age of majority but with provision for the wife to pay to the husband an 'occupation rent' (based on a reasonable market figure) from the date when the youngest child reaches the age of 18 (see, eg *Harvey v Harvey* (1982) FLR 141; *Brown v Brown* (1982) FLR 161). Such an order protects the ex-wife against becoming homeless at a vulnerable age while ensuring not only that the husband retains a right to receive a capital sum, but also that he receives some return on his investment once the children reach adulthood.

In some cases, the husband may be ordered to transfer his interest in the home to the ex-wife without any compensatory payment. This may be appropriate, for example, where there are sufficient other capital assets to be apportioned so that the house may be treated as representing the ex-wife's share of the whole. There are also cases in which such a transfer may appropriately be ordered in lieu of future periodical payments for the ex-wife. In *Hanlon v Hanlon* [1978] 2 All ER 889, for example, the husband was living rent-free in a police house and the former matrimonial home was required for occupation by his wife and four children, two of whom were under 18, in respect of whom the ex-wife was willing to forgo further periodical payments (see also *Bryant v Bryant* (1976) 120 Sol Jo 165; *S v S* [1976] Fam 18). It has been noted above that the court is unlikely to order a clean break where the ex-wife's immediate prospects of self-sufficiency are seriously affected by her commitment to caring for children. However, the court may be prepared to sanction a consent order which has that effect and the practice has become widespread of settling applications for financial provision on the basis that the husband will transfer to the ex-wife his entire interest in the former matrimonial home in return for the dismissal of her claim to periodical payments for herself (and possibly maintenance at a lower level than normal in respect of the children), in recognition of his sacrifice of what is usually his sole capital asset. Where the home is likely to be preserved for occupation by the children in any event, the husband loses only a right to receive capital where its receipt may be long-delayed, and is relieved of demands on his income so that he is free to re-establish himself: the wife acquires freedom of action and, if the existing property ceases to be appropriate for her needs, can move without losing any part of the net proceeds (unless there is a deferred charge in favour of the Legal Aid Board which cannot be transferred to the substituted property).

Impact of the Child Support Act (CSA) 1991

Outright transfer of the home in return for a clean break became a common basis of consent orders, particularly attractive in cases where the wife and any children were reliant on state benefits and where the wife's total income from all sources would not be significantly affected by maintenance payments from a husband who could not afford to pay sufficient to lift the family out of the benefits system altogether. (Normally, where the home is subject to a mortgage, the interest payable on the capital debt will be paid by the DSS as long as the wife remains dependent upon state benefits.) Such orders have lost all attraction for husbands in consequence of the CSA 1991. While the family remains reliant on state benefits for support, the ex-wife will (in effect) be incompetent to sign away her right to be supported by her former husband: the assessment of the maintenance requirement of the parties' children will include an element for the mother's support and the Child Support Agency will not normally concern itself with the terms of any capital settlement that may have been embodied in an order of the divorce court (even if the District Judge did describe the consent order as 'eminently sensible and fair!') (but see further §4.2.4 below). Moreover if, as is not uncommonly the case, the husband has returned to his parents' home following the breakdown of the marriage, his own low housing cost will serve only to increase the proportion of his income which is deemed to be available to meet the support needs of the ex-wife and children (see §4.2.4 below).

It is therefore inevitable that settlements will be harder to achieve in many cases, and that there will be a significant revival of attempts to secure *Martin* and *Mesher* orders, or even an immediate sale in the expectation that an ex-wife with dependent children will be rehoused by the local authority.

Cohabitation and its impact on orders in respect of the home

Where the court makes an order (other than an outright transfer) to preserve the home for occupation by the wife and children, the order will invariably provide for a sale on the wife's death or remarriage. As noted above, it may also provide for a sale on the youngest child attaining a specified age. The question arises, however, as to whether it is appropriate to include provision for a sale if the ex-wife cohabits in the property. It must be stated at the outset that it is not easy to discern consistency in the courts' approach. (It may be noted, in passing, that in *Suter v Suter and Another*, above, the wife was already cohabiting in the home at the time of the ancillary proceedings, but the home was nevertheless preserved for the children's occupation, and that in *Mesher v Mesher*, above, the ex-wife planned shortly to remarry, with the expectation that her new husband would join her in the home, his own property being required by his previous spouse and their children).

The court may be prepared to include a term in the order in respect of the house which would result in a sale if the ex-wife were to cohabit there. For example, in *Chadwick v Chadwick* [1985] FLR 606, where there were no children but where the wife was disabled and unable to work, sale was postponed until the wife remarried, cohabited or died. A sale would be triggered by the *commencement* of cohabitation. To do justice to the husband, the court felt it necessary to impose on the wife the burden of ensuring that any new partner she selected was in a position to provide her with suitable alternative accommodation. If he could not, this was to be viewed as a grave misfortune that the wife had brought upon herself.

Grimshaw v Grimshaw, above, provides an example of a slightly less rigid approach. In *Grimshaw*, where the only child still living at home was a son aged 24 who was in work, the husband's charge would become enforceable if the wife cohabited for six months. Although the court was 'not enthusiastic' about this provision, the qualifying period of six months at least offered the assurance that mere casual cohabitation would not suffice to trigger a sale.

A variation on the same theme is illustrated by *Harvey v Harvey*, above, where the husband was securely housed in council accommodation, and sale was expressed to be enforceable upon the wife 'becoming dependent on another man'. The court had in mind that 'if she begins to cohabit with another man in the premises, then obviously that man ought to take over the responsibility of providing accommodation for her'. A provision couched in these terms is clearly likely to give rise to hotly contested issues of fact, but it ensures that, if the cohabitant is in fact unable or unwilling to provide for the ex-wife, her occupation remains protected.

By contrast, in *Eagle v Eagle* (referred to at (1983) Fam Law 101), the Court of Appeal lifted a provision that a sale should take place if the wife cohabited in the property for more than 28 days in any six months. The inclusion of a term referring to cohabitation may encourage constant supervision or the use of enquiry agents by the husband but, in *Clutton v Clutton*, above, the court appeared to accept that this was an inevitable consequence of seeking to achieve a just result.

Clearly, a term which provides for a sale in the event of cohabitation may precipitate a sale while the children are still minors. Clearly too, an ex-wife's cohabitant has no obligation to house either the wife or the children. It can be argued that a court which makes an order that can result in automatic enforcement of a sale in the event of cohabitation is neglecting its duty to have first regard to the children's welfare but, as was pointed out in *Suter v Suter and Another*, above, the statute makes the children's needs the *first* consideration: it does not make them paramount. Nevertheless, it can be argued that, in the absence of compelling evidence to suggest that the husband's circumstances at the relevant time will render his need to realise his interest particularly compelling, the order should avoid triggering an *automatic* sale (see *Greenham v Greenham* [1989] 1 FLR 105). It may be noted that, in *Prow v Brown*, outlined at §3.3.5 above, the original order provided for payment of a lump sum to the husband on the expiry of nine months from the date of the order, which would have had the effect of forcing a sale by the wife and her new partner. On appeal, and having regard to the needs of the child of the family, the order was varied so as to defer payment until the child ceased to be in full-time education.

If cohabitation is to be included as an event which puts the preservation of the home at hazard, it is arguable that this should be done by conferring on the husband a limited right to come back to the court in specified circumstances to apply for a sale at an earlier date than is specified by other provisions of the order. This would preserve the court's discretion to order a sale if justice so requires at that future stage, or to postpone a sale if the circumstances which then exist are such that the children's needs must continue to have priority.

Where an order is made in respect of the home which provides that the property is *not* to be sold until the happening of certain events, that order is not itself an order for sale. Thus, where any of the triggering events occur and the party in occupation obstructs a sale, the way is open to apply to the court for an order for sale under s 24A (see *Dinch v Dinch* [1987] 2 FLR 162) and, if necessary, to invoke the court's further powers (see s 24(2)(1) and (b)), which now include the power to require the party in occupation of the home to leave the property in advance of a sale (see FPR 1991, r 2.64(3), applying RSC Ord 31, r 1).

3.3.9 Cohabitation before marriage

The preceding sections have been concerned with the impact on the outcome of ancillary proceedings of cohabitation with a third party since the marital breakdown. For the sake of completeness, it remains to consider how far cohabitation with each other will be taken into account in determining applications for financial provision by divorcing parties.

In *Kokosinski v Kokosinski* (1980) 1 FLR 205, it was said that there are likely to be few occasions on which a court will feel that justice requires the parties' pre-marital cohabitation to be taken into account. Certainly, in *Campbell v Campbell* [1977] 1 All ER 1, the court refused to take into account the period of three years' cohabitation prior to a marriage which lasted less than two and a half years: the period of cohabitation was not to be treated as extending the duration of the marriage (this being a factor to which the court must have regard under s 25), nor was the wife's performance of 'wifely duties' to be considered as relevant conduct.

Nevertheless, in *Kokosinski*, it was noted that while 'conduct' is usually associated with grounds for *reducing* awards, conduct could also be relied upon as justifying an increased award in appropriate cases. Moreover, the list of considerations to which the court is directed to have regard by s 25 is prefaced by an instruction to have regard to 'all the circumstances of the case', and for this purpose relevant circumstances are not limited to those applying during the existence of the marriage itself. Accordingly, in *Kokosinski*, the faithful, loving and hard-working wife who had 'given the best years of her life' to the husband during 24 years of pre-marital cohabitation (during most of which they had not been free to marry each other) was entitled to an award which recognised her contribution to the family's well-being and material success, notwithstanding that the marriage itself had lasted only a few months.

In the normal run of cases, however, where there has been a relatively short period of pre-marital cohabitation, it will commonly be legitimate for the court to conclude either that the cohabitation is of no significance (see *Hayes v Hayes* (1981) Fam Law 208), or at least that it is not entitled to be given the same weight as cohabitation within marriage (see *Foley v Foley* (1981) FLR 215).

4 CHILDREN

4.1 Introduction

The courts have extensive powers under the Children Act 1989, Sch 1 to make orders in favour of or for the benefit of children of unmarried parents. However, the Child Support Act (CSA) 1991, s 8 provides that, with only limited exceptions, in the case of a child and an absent parent in respect of whom a child support officer would have jurisdiction to make an assessment, no court shall exercise any power which it would otherwise have to make, vary or revive any order which requires the making or securing of periodical payments to or for the benefit of the child (see also s 9(5): similar provisions affecting powers to vary maintenance agreements). Thus, the role of the courts in respect of the maintenance of children becomes residual, and the exercise of the court's powers *apart from* the power to order periodical payments will inevitably be significantly affected by the impact of the CSA 1991 on the absent parent's overall financial position. Accordingly, in this chapter, discussion of the court's powers follows an examination of the system established by the CSA 1991.

4.2 The Child Support Act 1991

4.2.1 Introduction

Within the confines of this book, it is not possible to give an exhaustive account of the system set up by the CSA 1991. Moreover, at the time of writing not all of the relevant Regulations had been promulgated. What is offered here is no more than an introductory guide to the system as it applies to the most common situations, and no attempt is made to explore in detail the provisions affecting special cases. Examples are used to give some indication of the scale of liability involved. These examples are based on 1993 levels of benefits. It should be remembered not only that these levels will change in the ordinary course of events, but also that changes may be made at any time to the component parts of the relevant formulae. Given the radical and innovatory nature of the scheme, it may prove necessary to make a number of early changes in the light of experience of implementation.

In broad terms, the system established by the Act is intended to secure, first, that absent parents (usually, of course, absent fathers) make a proper contribution towards the support of their children and towards the support of the parent with care of the child. Secondly, particularly in cases where the child and the parent with care of him are dependent upon state benefits, it is intended that the recovery of a contribution from an absent parent should not be dependent upon the willingness of the parent with care to bring proceedings, and that the size of that contribution should not be subject to the vagaries and inconsistencies of determination by the courts.

Accordingly, the Child Support Agency has been established, with powers to trace absent parents, to investigate parents' means, and to assess, collect and enforce child support payments. The powers of enquiry are extensive and duties to supply information can be cast on a wide range of persons in addition to the parents themselves.

4.2.2 Jurisdiction

The Agency has jurisdiction to make an assessment only where the person with care of a qualifying child, the child himself, and the absent parent are 'habitually resident' in the United Kingdom (s 44; as to 'habitual residence', see *R v Barnet LBC, ex parte Shah* [1985] 2 AC 309; *Kapur v Kapur* [1984] FLR 920).

Qualifying child

Briefly, by s 55, a 'child' is a child under the age of 16, a person under the age of 19 who is receiving full-time education (other than advanced education), and any other person who is under the age of 18 and in respect of whom prescribed conditions are satisfied. A person is not a child if he is or has been married or has celebrated a marriage which is void (including, it seems, a marriage which is void because either party to it was under the age of 16) or a voidable marriage which has been annulled.

A child is a 'qualifying child' if one of his parents is an absent parent in relation to him, or both of his parents are absent parents in relation to him (s 3(1)).

Person with care

A person is a 'person with care' if he is a person with whom the child has his home; who usually provides day to day care for the child (whether exclusively or in conjunction with any other person); and who does not fall within a category of persons whom the Secretary of State has prescribed as being incapable of being a person with care (s 3(3)). By s 3(4), it is provided that any such Regulations shall not prescribe as a category parents, guardians, and persons in whose favour a residence order is in force. By s 3(5), for the purposes of the Act, there may be more than one person with care in relation to the same qualifying child.

Absent parent

A parent is an 'absent parent' in relation to his child if that parent is not living in the same household with the child and the child has his home with a person who is a person with care in relation to him (s 3(2)).

Parent

'Parent', in relation to any child, means 'any person who is in law the mother or father of the child' and thus includes not only biological parents, but also adoptive parents, and persons who are treated as a child's parents by virtue of the Human Fertilisation and Embryology Act 1990 (see §6.2 below). Where paternity of a child is denied by the person who is alleged to be the child's father, the Agency is not empowered to make a maintenance assessment against that person unless he is the child's parent by adoption, or is treated as such by virtue of the Human Fertilisation and Embryology Act 1990, or a court has made a finding of paternity in the context of any of a range of proceedings. The inclusion of a man's name as the father of a child in the entry of the child's birth in the Register of Births does not by itself give the Agency the right to make a maintenance assessment against him.

In cases where the Agency has no power to make a maintenance assessment because paternity is denied, the Secretary of State or the person with care may apply to the court for a declaration as to whether or not the alleged parent is one of the child's parents (s 27). Until this application is adjudicated the assessment under the CSA 1991 cannot proceed.

4.2.3   The power to make an assessment

The Agency's power to make an assessment is exercisable only on the application of a person with care of the child or an absent parent. The Act contemplates that the 'person with care' may not be an individual (see s 44(2)). Thus, a local authority which is looking after a child may request that a maintenance assessment be made. This account assumes that the child is in the care of a parent. A provision in any agreement which purports to restrict the right of any person to apply for a maintenance assessment is void (s 9(4)).

(a) *Applications by parents in receipt of benefits ('benefit cases')*

Where a parent with care is in receipt of Income Support or Family Credit (or Disability Working Allowance) the Act imposes a duty on that parent to authorise action to recover Child Support if she (*sic* – the Act makes no pretence that the world is other than it is in this respect) is required to do so by the Secretary of State (s 6(1)). Authorisation must be given 'without unreasonable delay' (s 6(5)).

It may be noted that the question is not whether benefit is payable in respect of the qualifying child, but whether it is being paid to or in respect of the parent of the child (see also s 6(8)). It is irrelevant whether the parent is wholly or only partly dependent on benefits.

The Secretary of State must not require a person to give the authorisation referred to above if he considers that there are reasonable grounds for believing that there would be a risk that she or any child living with her would suffer harm or 'undue distress' as a result of giving, or being required to give, that authorisation (s 6(2)). This provision is intended to protect (*inter alia*) those who are likely to suffer violence or harassment at the hands of the absent parent if they are forced to authorise an assessment.

Where a person is under a duty to authorise a maintenance assessment, she must also, so far as she reasonably can, provide information to enable the absent parent to be traced and the amount of child support to be assessed and recovered (s 6(9)).

The exemptions from the requirements that may be imposed on a parent with care under s 6(1) and s 6(9) are of great potential importance. A mother in receipt of benefit who is exempted from them will continue to receive her benefits in full. By contrast, a mother who is not exempted from the duty to comply with any direction or requirement under s 6(1) or s 6(9) may find her benefit reduced as a consequence of a 'reduced benefit direction' under s 46 if she fails to comply.

Following a failure to comply, the parent may be served with a notice requiring her either to comply or to give reasons for her non-compliance, and giving her a period of not less than six weeks within which to do so. At the end of that period, the child support officer must consider whether, having regard to any reasons which the parent has given, there are reasonable grounds for believing that there would be a risk of harm or undue distress being suffered by the parent or any children living with her if she were required to comply. If the child support officer considers that no such reasonable grounds exist, he may give a reduced benefit direction. Such a direction will result in a reduction of the benefits payable to the parent (see s 46(11)).

The penalty for non-cooperation in a standard Income Support case will be a reduction in the personal allowance of the adult concerned and will be a 20 per cent reduction for the first six months and a 10 per cent reduction for the next 52 weeks (representing reductions of £8.80 and £4.40 respectively, at 1993 benefit rates). The effect of the relevant notice provisions is to give her a total period for reflection of eight weeks before the reduction takes effect.

(b) *Applications by other parents with care ('non-benefit cases')*

A parent with care who is not in receipt of benefits *may* apply for a maintenance assessment to be made under the Act (see s 4(1)), but cannot be required to authorise the Agency to make a maintenance assessment. In view of the restrictions imposed on the exercise by the court of its power to make periodical payments orders in respect of children, a parent with care who wishes to seek a contribution from an absent parent to their child's maintenance will generally have no alternative but to apply for a maintenance assessment under the Act if the absent parent is refusing to pay anything, or is offering to pay only an amount which the parent with care considers inadequate.

Once a parent with care has applied for a maintenance assessment, there again arises a duty to comply with the Regulations with respect to the provision of information (s 4(4)), but a person who has applied to the Secretary of State for a maintenance assessment to be made may at any time request the Secretary of State to cease to act (s 4(5), and see s 4(6)).

4.2.4   The elements of the assessment

The maintenance requirement (MR = AG − CB)

The maintenance requirement (MR) is calculated by reference to the benefits which are being paid in respect of the child(ren) and the parent with care, or which would be payable if they were eligible for payment in full of the benefits applicable to their circumstances. Thus, the MR is the aggregate (AG) of the Income Support personal allowance for each child, the Income Support family premium, the Income Support personal allowance for a single adult over 25 and the Income Support lone-parent premium (if payable), *less* the Child Benefit in respect of each child (CB). One-Parent Benefit is not taken into account.

EXAMPLE 1: Mother has care of two children, aged ten and 12. She has no partner living with her.

Allowances for children	
(1 × £15.05; 1 × £22.15)	£37.20
Family premium	£9.65
Lone-parent premium	£4.90
Adult personal allowance	£44.00
Total	£95.75
Less Child Benefit	£18.10
MR =	£77.65

Absent parent's assessable income (A)

The assessable income of the absent parent (A) is the amount of his net income (N) *less* his exempt income (E) (A = N − E). For this purpose, net income (N) means earnings from employment (or self-employment), after tax, NI contributions and 50 per cent of any superannuation contributions. Bonuses, tips, commission, etc are all included. Any income from capital is also included.

Exempt income (E) is determined by reference to the Income Support allowances that would be payable to that parent and to any child *of his* who is living with him. No allowances are included in respect of any new partner that the absent parent has, or any child living with him who is not the absent parent's own child. Also included are any supplements which would have been applicable if the absent parent had been claiming Income Support (eg family premium). To that figure is to be added the absent parent's eligible housing costs; ie, rent or mortgage repayments (of both interest and capital, including loans for improvements, repairs etc, but excluding any remortgage for the purposes of paying off debts not attributable to housing needs). In the case of endowment mortgages, premiums payable in respect of a linked 'with profits' insurance policy are taken into account only to the extent that they are necessary to ensure an eventual sum sufficient to pay off the capital debt. Buildings insurance premiums are not included.

Housing costs are subject to a ceiling of £80 per week or one half of the parent's net income, whichever is the greater, but exceptions to the ceiling apply (*inter alia*) where an absent parent remains in the former joint home, or has the day-to-day care of any child, or where his housing costs are higher than they would otherwise be because of the unavailability of his share of the equity of the former joint home because it is being occupied by his former partner.

A formula exists for the apportionment of housing costs where the absent parent has living with him a person who is irrelevant to the calculation of his exempt income.

EXAMPLE 2: Patrick is in employment, pays no superannuation, and has a gross weekly income of £185 and pays rent of £40 per week. He lives alone.

Net earnings	£144.37 (£185 − £40.63 tax and NI)
Less Exempt income	£84.00 (£44 personal allowance + £40 rent)
A =	£60.37

EXAMPLE 3a: Mark is an absent parent in respect of one child. He is married to Wendy and they have one child, Zoe, aged two. Mark's gross weekly earnings are £185. His net earnings are £152.63. Wendy has no earnings. They pay £50 per week rent.

Mark's exempt income will comprise:

Adult personal allowance	£44.00
Child's personal allowance for Zoe	£15.05
Family premium	£9.65
Housing costs *attributable to Mark and* Zoe	£39.58
Total:	£108.28

Mark's assessable income = (£152.63 − £108.28) = £44.35

EXAMPLE 3b: If the facts are as in Example 3a above, save that Wendy has significant earnings, Mark's exempt income will be reduced by the deduction of one half of the personal allowance in respect of Zoe, and one half of the family premium.

Parent with care's assessable income (C)

The assessable income of the parent with care is ascertained by the same process as the absent parent's assessable income under the formula $C = M - F$, where M and F bear the same definitions as N and E respectively. A parent with care who is dependent on benefits is regarded as having *no* assessable income.

The maintenance assessment

The applicable formula is $(A + C) \times P$, where P is the 'prescribed fraction' (one half). Where the resultant figure is less than MR, the basic principle is that an absent parent is required to contribute one half of his assessable income towards meeting the maintenance requirement.

EXAMPLE 4: Where the MR is £77.65 (as in Example 1) and the absent parent has an assessable income of £60.37 (as in Example 2) and the parent with care has an assessable income of £20, the result of $(A + C) \times P$ will be £40.19; ie less than MR. The absent parent's contribution will be assessed at £30.19 (£60.37 × 50%).

Where the result of $(A + C) \times P$ is a figure greater than MR, the absent parent is expected to continue to contribute to the child's support so that the child may share in the prosperity of the absent parent, but at a lower rate, to reflect the fact that as people become more affluent a smaller proportion of their income is spent on their children. Thus, put very simply, once the MR is met according to the formula $((A + C) \times P)$, the absent parent's contribution rate is 25 per cent of his assessable income. The contribution at 50 per cent is then the 'basic element' (BE) and the further sum required is the 'additional element' (AE).

EXAMPLE 5: Mike is the absent father of two children whose mother has no assessable income and whose MR is £77.65. Mike's assessable income is £210.30. The basic element of the maintenance assessment at the rate of 50 per cent will account for £155.30 of his assessable income to meet the MR of £77.65. The remaining £55 will be subject to the additional element computation which will result in a requirement that he pay a further £13.75, making a total contribution of £91.40 per week.

There is, however, a ceiling to the additional amount payable for each child, equal to three times the amount of the Income Support personal allowance that would be payable for the child and the family premium.

A complex formula exists to make adjustments to the burden imposed on an absent parent where the result of $(A + C) \times P$ exceeds MR because of the caring parent's income. Put simply, the effect of the formula is to recalculate the basic element required from the absent parent so that he and the caring parent contribute *pro rata* at the 50 per cent rate until MR is reached.

Minimum payment

Notwithstanding the 'protected income' provisions outlined below, every absent parent is expected to pay a minimum amount unless he is in an exempted category. The minimum amount is 5 per cent of the adult Income Support personal allowance (£2.20 per week at 1993 rates). The minimum payment is not required from an absent parent on benefit who is sick or disabled or who has children living with him, or who is under 18 and in receipt of Income Support.

Protected income

As has been indicated above, an absent parent's exempt income does not take account of the support needs of other members of his household apart from his own children. However, this would be capable of causing hardship in cases where the absent parent is in fact supporting other dependants. Therefore, a maintenance assessment must be reduced if its effect would be to reduce the absent parent's family's disposable income below the level of the protected income applicable to the family.

Protected income is calculated by aggregating the income support that would be payable in respect of the absent parent's family unit, the family's reasonable housing costs (less any Housing Benefit for which he is eligible), and Council Tax (less any Council Tax Benefit), together with a standard margin of £8 in all cases. This calculation is the 'basic protected income level'. There is then a further margin of 10 per cent of the family's income in excess of the basic protected income level.

EXAMPLE 6: Patrick (from Example 2) is an absent father living alone who pays £40 per week rent and has a Council Tax liability of £5 per week. His Income Support personal allowance would be £44. His basic protected income level, including the £8 margin, is therefore £97. His net earnings are £144.37, which exceeds his basic protected income by £47.37, of which 10 per cent is to be added to produce a total protected income level of £101.74. His assessable income as calculated in Example 2 is £60.37, of which £30.19 would be required as a contribution to the MR. Payment of that amount would leave him an income of £114.18; ie in excess of the protected income level.

EXAMPLE 7: Hugh and Vicky have one child, Sarah, aged two. Hugh is an absent parent in respect of one child aged nine. Hugh's assessable income is £60.98. The family's disposable income comprises his net earnings (£165.68) and Child Benefit (£10), giving a total of £175.68. The basic protected income level is:

Personal allowance for a couple	£69.00
Personal allowance for their child	£15.05
Family premium	£9.65
Mortgage interest (in full but *only* interest, and not including any premiums under a linked insurance policy)	£45.00
Council tax	£8.68
Standard margin	£8.00
Total:	£155.38

The excess of disposable income over the basic protected income is £20.30, so that £2.03 is to be added to give a total protected income of £157.41, which the family must be permitted to retain. A payment at the rate of 50 per cent of Hugh's assessable income would reduce the income of his household to £145.19, ie below the protected income level. The maintenance assessment must therefore be reduced accordingly.

As noted above, the 'protected income' provisions take account of all members of a household and this would, for instance, include step-children. Obviously, if there has been a maintenance assessment against the absent parent of the step-child, the receipt of the relevant sum by the parent with care will increase that family's income and may thus prevent the disposable income of that family falling below its protected level if a member of the family is subject to a maintenance assessment in respect of a child of his own.

4.2.5 Special cases

Among the many special cases dealt with by the Regulations, special note may be made of the following.

Multiple applications relating to the same absent parent

Where two or more applications for a maintenance assessment have been made which relate to the same absent parent (ie where a man has two or more children by different women), the amount which the absent parent is liable to pay is apportioned between the applications in the same ratio that the maintenance requirements of the applications bear to each other.

Person caring for children of more than one absent parent

In this situation, the maintenance requirement as it applies to each absent parent is to be calculated by dividing the aggregate of the adult personal allowance, the family premium and the lone-parent premium by the number of absent parents involved. Thus, if there are two children by two fathers, the total will be halved. Where there are three children, two of whom have the same father, the division will be one-third and two-thirds. (Note, however, that there is no provision for such apportionment where a woman has one child by an absent father, and one child by her husband (or other man), with whom she is living. The element of the maintenance requirement for the first child will still include the full personal allowance for the mother, and her assessable income will not be deemed to include support from her husband.)

Shared care and staying contact arrangements

Where there are shared care arrangements, the parent who provides care to a lesser extent than the other parent is treated as an absent parent, but the formula for assessing the child support payable is adjusted to reflect the division of care. Moreover, where a child spends (on average) at least two nights per week (104 nights per year) with the absent parent, adjustments are made to the exempt and protected income calculations of each parent. Thus, for example, the exempt income of the absent parent whose child stays with him for two nights each week will include two-sevenths of the child's personal allowance, family premium, and lone-parent premium (if payable).

Conversely, where an absent parent himself has day-to-day care of a child of his own who in fact spends at least two nights per week out of his care, his exempt income will be reduced accordingly, and if he has day-to-day care of a child who is not his own, the element of his protected income attributable to that child will also be reduced if the child in fact spends at least two nights per week out of his care.

4.2.6   Interim assessments, reviews and appeals

An interim assessment may be made where it appears to the child support officer that he does not have sufficient information to make an assessment. Clearly, a robust interim assessment may encourage an uncooperative absent parent to be more forthcoming with relevant information.

A complex system of appeals is provided, and the Act also makes provision for reviews, both by way of an appeal and by way of periodic reviews because of the passage of time or some change of circumstances.

4.2.7 Collection and enforcement arrangements

Collection

After an assessment has been made in benefit cases the Agency may arrange for the collection of the sums required from the absent parent. In non-benefit cases the timing and method of payment are a matter for the parties but either party may request the Agency to arrange for the collection of the sums payable (s 29(1)). Where the Agency is arranging for the collection of any payments under a maintenance assessment, it may also arrange for the collection of periodical payments payable under prescribed court orders (eg where the parent with care also has the benefit of an order for spousal maintenance). The Agency may also arrange the collection of periodical payments which are payable for the benefit of a child, whether or not the Agency is arranging the collection of child support maintenance with respect to that child (s 30).

Enforcement

It is beyond the scope of this book to consider in detail the various means of enforcement. However, it should be noted that the Act creates two new methods of enforcement where a person is 'the liable person' in respect of payments of child support, and these are considered below. It may also be noted that interest is payable (at 1 per cent above base rate) on arrears of child support maintenance.

'Deduction from earnings orders' (ss 31 and 32): A deduction from earnings order may be made by the Agency whether or not payments of child support have fallen into arrears (see s 31(3)). It is thus a collection measure as well as an enforcement measure. The order is directed at the liable person's employer, and instructs him to make deductions from the liable person's earnings and to pay the amounts deducted to the Agency. 'Earnings' for this purpose

include not only normal 'Schedule E' earnings from employment, but also, for instance, payments by way of pension.

While a deduction from earnings order is in force, a liable person who changes or leaves his employment is required to notify the Agency and that notification must also contain a statement of his *expected* earnings following the change (s 32(3)). It might thus prompt the making of an increased assessment.

Failure on the part of a liable person or an employer to comply with certain requirements relating to deduction from earnings orders is a criminal offence (s 32(8)). It is, however, a defence for the person charged to show that he took all reasonable steps to comply with the requirement concerned (s 32(10)).

Liability orders (ss 33–40): Liability orders are available only where there has been default on one or more payments of child support maintenance (s 33(1)).

A liability order may be made only where it is inappropriate for a deduction from earnings order to be made (eg because the liable person is not employed) or where a deduction from earnings order has been made against him but has proved ineffective (s 33(1)). Where these conditions are fulfilled, the Agency may apply to a magistrates' court which must make a liability order if it is satisfied that the payments in question have become payable by the liable person and have not been paid. A liability order gives rise to several possible means of enforcing payment of the sums due. Liability orders may be enforced by distress (s 35), by the means available for the enforcement of county court judgments (s 36) and, when all other means of enforcement have failed, by an application to a magistrates' court to commit the liable person to prison (s 40).

Where an application for committal is made the court must enquire (in the liable person's presence) as to his means and as to whether there has been wilful refusal or culpable neglect on his part (s 40(2)). Only if there has been wilful refusal or culpable neglect may the liable person be imprisoned (s 40(3); for an example of comparable provisions in operation, see *R v Luton Magistrates' Court, ex parte Sullivan* [1992] 2 FLR 196). To secure the liable person's presence as required by s 40(2) a summons may be issued and, if he fails to obey the summons, a warrant may be issued for his arrest (s 40(11)).

4.2.8 Commencement of the Act

Phasing-in

The Child Support Agency will take over the primary responsibility for assessing and collecting child support in phases. The Agency will take on all 'new' cases from April 1993, whether or not the parent with care is in receipt of benefits.

In respect of existing 'benefits' cases, the Agency will take over responsibility for the collection and enforcement of child support payments over a period of three years, from 1993–1996. Initially, it is intended that a maintenance assessment will be carried out in such cases as and when there is a change of circumstances.

In existing 'non-benefits' cases where a court order is in force, it will not be possible to request the Agency to carry out an assessment until, at the earliest, April 1996. Thereafter, access to the Agency will become available in stages between April 1996 and April 1997, according to alphabetical order of the surname of the parent with care. Parents may, if they wish, simply retain the existing order, but the court will be unable to vary it once access to the Agency has become available.

From April 1994, the Agency will have the power to collect and enforce 'top-up' orders and other orders made under the court's residual powers (see CSA 1991, s 8; and see §4.3 below).

The power of the Agency (where it is collecting and enforcing child support maintenance) to collect sums payable under other court orders (eg spousal maintenance and maintenance for step-children) will become available in April 1996. In all other cases, the Agency's powers of collection become available in April 1997.

Transitional provisions

Where the result of a maintenance assessment under the Act is that an absent parent will be required to pay a sum greater than that which he is already obliged to pay under existing arrangements for mainten-ance, the absent parent is granted some relief from an immediate large increase in his liability. Three criteria apply. If the maintenance assessment is less than £60 and the absent parent has responsibility for a second family, the increase in the sum payable will be phased in if the difference between the existing liability and the maintenance assessment is more than £20. In such a case the absent parent's liability will be increased by £20 and this limit will apply for one year. Thereafter the absent parent will be required to pay the maintenance assessment in full. Thus, for example, if the maintenance assessment is £57 per week and an existing order requires the absent parent to pay £15 per week, his liability will increase to £35 per week for the first year, rising to £57 per week thereafter.

4.3   The role of the courts

4.3.1   Introduction

There are two situations in which the court may have an important function to perform despite the advent of the Child Support Agency. First, the CSA is concerned with the *income* position of children and those who care for them. The court, however, has powers to deal with parents' *capital* for the benefit of children (see Children Act 1989, Sch 1). Secondly, the court retains its power to make maintenance provision for children in certain cases, for example where, for some reason, the child is not a qualifying child, or where there are funds available which take the case outside even the additional element levels of statutory child support.

4.3.2   Orders relating to capital

The orders available are:

(i) an order requiring either or both parents to pay to the child, or to the applicant for the benefit of the child, a lump sum;

(ii) an order requiring a settlement to be made for the benefit of the child of specified property to which either parent is entitled;

(iii) an order requiring either or both parents to transfer to the child, or to the applicant for the benefit of the child, specified property to which the parent is, or the parents are, entitled (Children Act 1989, Sch 1, para 1(2)).

Application may be made by a parent or guardian of the child, or by any person in whose favour a residence order is in force with respect to the child. Orders may also be made whenever the court makes, varies or discharges a residence order, even though no application has been made under the CA 1989, Sch 1 (Sch 1, para 1(6)).

These powers to make capital orders are exercisable until the child attains the age of 18. Moreover, a lump sum order may be made on the application of a person who has attained the age of 18 provided that he is (or will be if the order is made) undergoing full-time education or training or there are special circumstances which justify the making of an order, but no such application may be made where a periodical payments order was in force with respect to that person immediately before he attained the age of 16 or if the applicant's parents are living together in the same household (Sch 1, para 2).

Orders requiring the settlement or transfer of property may be made only by the High Court or a county court (Sch 1, para 1(1)). The power to require the settlement or transfer of property may not be exercised against the same person more than once (Sch 1, para 1(5)). Lump sum orders are subject to a limit of £1000 if application is made to a magistrates' court. When a lump sum order has been made it is not susceptible to variation save that if it provides for payment by instalments the court may vary the number, amount and due date of the instalments by which the lump sum is to be paid. Although there is power to make more than one lump sum order, this power will be exercised only in unusual circumstances. Indeed, it is relatively uncommon for *any* lump sum order to be made for the benefit of a child (see below).

Relevant factors

In considering whether to exercise its powers to make orders, and if so in what manner, the court is directed to have regard to all the circumstances of the case, including the financial needs and obligations, resources and property of the adults concerned, the financial needs, resources and earning capacity (if any) of the child, and any physical or mental disability which he has, and the manner in which the child was being, or was expected to be, educated or trained (Sch 1, para 4(1); and see also para 4(2)).

When are orders appropriate?

In the vast majority of cases, an order for the payment of a lump sum will be precluded by the lack of any resources from which the lump sum could be paid. There is no limitation on the purposes for which a lump sum may be ordered to be paid. The Act expressly provides that a lump sum may be ordered to meet liabilities already incurred in connection with the birth of the child or his maintenance. A lump sum may therefore be appropriately ordered where a parent has not been maintaining his child and it is sought, in effect, to recover the cost of the child's support retrospectively. (The Child Support Agency is not able to recover child support maintenance in respect of any period prior to the making of an interim assessment in respect of the child.)

Thus, a lump sum order may be made in a 'traditional' unmarried mother case in order to meet expenses connected with the birth, such as the cost of equipment and layette. In the case of cohabiting parents who have separated, a lump sum may be similarly appropriate to cover the expenses incurred in purchasing furniture and other items required to establish the child in new accommodation. Clearly, these are examples of situations where the child's immediate needs provide the justification for the order. The question arises, however, as to whether a lump sum may be appropriate in a case where it would not be directed at meeting the child's immediate needs.

It may be sensible for the court to order the payment of a lump sum as a form of capitalised maintenance where, in a 'non-benefit case' the father intends to have nothing to do with the child but has the resources to fund a lump sum of sufficient size. However, where it is anticipated that the father will continue to maintain the child, the court is likely to be reluctant to make lump sum orders as pure capital provision. The practice of the divorce court indicates that the breakdown of the parents' relationship is not normally to be regarded as an occasion for bestowing a bounty upon children which they would not normally expect to receive until the death of either or both of their parents (see eg *Chamberlain v Chamberlain* [1973] 1 WLR 1557: inappropriate to settle house for children's benefit after mother's death where there were no special circumstances entitling children to make demands on their parents after conclusion of full-time education; and see also *Kiely v Kiely* [1988] 1 FLR 248; *Lilford v Lord Glyn* [1979] 1 WLR 78; *Draskovic v Draskovic* (1981) Fam Law 87).

On the other hand, cases involving the children of divorcing parents are distinguishable to the extent that the divorce court also has the power to reallocate 'family assets' *as between the parents* and is likely in most cases to exercise that power in a manner which confers on the mother some share of the parties' joint capital assets from which, it may reasonably be supposed, the children will reap some benefit. When the court is dealing with a child of unmarried parents, there is no such power to redistribute capital assets as between the parents and any provision has to take the form of provision for the children. In a few cases, this may make it less difficult to justify capital orders in their favour.

Preservation of the home

Where there has been stable and comparatively long-lasting cohabitation, the court will place as high a priority on preservation of the home as it does when dealing with the home of divorcing parents and their children (as to which, see §3.4.8 above). Thus, in *K v K (Minors: Property Transfer)* [1992] 2 FLR 220, a desire to preserve the home for exclusive occupation by the mother and the children led the judge at first instance to make an order requiring that the father's interest under the joint tenancy of the family's council house be transferred to the mother for the benefit of the children. The Court of Appeal affirmed that the requirement that the transfer be 'for the benefit of the child' does not restrict the court to a consideration of *financial* benefit. However, in the particular circumstances of the case, the judge at first instance had failed to give proper consideration to the effect of his order on the father's position as a sitting tenant who had the right to buy his home at a substantial discount. The case was remitted for rehearing.

In the case of an owner-occupied home, the court may be persuaded to impose a settlement to preserve it for occupation by the children but it is submitted that an outright transfer for this purpose will rarely be justifiable unless the net equity is very small.

4.3.3 Orders for maintenance

The scheme established by the Child Support Act 1991 has been considered above, and reference was made in that account to the provision which prevents the court exercising any of the powers it would otherwise have to make, vary or revive periodical payments orders in respect of any child who is a 'qualifying child' for the purposes of that Act. Reference was also made to transitional arrangements under which, for some time after April 1993, the court may continue to exercise its powers to vary existing orders which require the making of periodical payments. The present account is concerned only with the residual power of the court to make orders for periodical payments, assuming the Child Support Act framework to be fully operational.

The court will obviously retain the power to make a periodical payments order in respect of any child who is not a 'qualifying child' for the purposes of the CSA 1991. The following cases may be identified as still susceptible to the court's powers.

(a) Where the CSA does not apply because the child is not habitually resident in the United Kingdom, but the parent from whom maintenance is sought is resident in England or Wales, the court may make an order for periodical payments (secured or unsecured) against that parent (see CA 1989, Sch 1, para 14). In such a case, the court may wish to be provided with some indication of the effect of applying the CSA formulae, and may use that as a guide to the payments it should order.

(b) Where it is sought to recover maintenance in respect of a child who is not the natural or adopted child of the respondent, but who was a child of the family in relation to any marriage to which he was at any time a party (eg step-children), the exclusive concentration of the CSA on *natural* children means that court proceedings will remain the sole method of recovering maintenance.

(c) In respect of children who are between 17 and 19 and are not in full-time education, the CSA is inapplicable and, if the circumstances are unusual enough to justify a continuing maintenance obligation, that maintenance must be sought from the courts.

(d) Where children are aged 19 or over but remain dependent on parents (by reason, perhaps, of disability or of involvement in education or training), only the court will have power to make an order for continuing support (see CA 1989, Sch 1, para 3).

Apart from cases falling within (a), the cases listed above are all likely to present unusual or special features. It is therefore impossible to offer any general guidance as to the likely manner of exercise of the court's powers.

The court will also be able to exercise its powers in situations contemplated by the CSA as likely to require the continued exercise of those powers *as a supplement to* the operation of the statutory scheme. Three such situations are envisaged:

(1) *'Top-up' payments*: The CSA 1991, s 8(6) provides that the court may exercise its powers where a maintenance assessment is in force with respect to the child but the court is satisfied that the circumstances of the case make it appropriate for the absent parent to make payments additional to the maintenance assessment. As has been noted at §4.2.4 above, under the CSA scheme an absent parent who has sufficient resources will not only be required to

meet the child's maintenance requirement, but will also be required to pay an additional sum up to the prescribed maximum. Thus, the 'top-up' power preserved by s 8(6) will be exercisable only in cases where the absent parent has a very high income. It is unlikely that the court will be easily persuaded to order 'top-up' periodical payments except, perhaps, where unmarried parents had been living together for a lengthy period during which the child had been accustomed to a very high standard of living.

(2) *Educational expenses*: The CSA 1991 provides, by s 8(7), that the court is not prevented from exercising its powers to make maintenance orders where the child is (or would be if an order were made) receiving instruction at an educational establishment or undergoing training for a trade, profession or vocation (whether or not the child is in gainful employment). However, the order must be made by the court solely for the purpose of requiring the making of payments to meet some or all of the expenses incurred in connection with the provision of the instruction or training. Thus, it is open to the court to make an order for the payment of school fees (and in such cases an order for *secured* periodical payments may be particularly appropriate as a guarantee against disruption of the child's education caused by default in making payments). It may be noted that the court may exercise its powers pursuant to this subsection whether or not a maintenance assessment has been made under the CSA.

(3) *Disabled children*: The court is not prevented from making a maintenance order in relation to a child who is disabled, provided that the order is made solely for the purpose of requiring the making of payments to meet some or all of any expenses attributable to the child's disability (see CSA 1991, s 8(8)). For this purpose a child is disabled if he is blind, or deaf or dumb, or is substantially and permanently handicapped by illness, injury, mental disorder or congenital deformity. Regulations may prescribe other disabilities. Again, the court may exercise its powers pursuant to this subsection whether or not a maintenance assessment has been made under the CSA.

5 DEATH

5.1 Introduction

This chapter is primarily concerned with the situation which arises when one cohabitant dies and it is necessary to ascertain the rights and entitlement of the surviving cohabitant. The position of children is considered in outline but, since the position of children of unmarried parents has been substantially assimilated to that of the children of married parents, it is not proposed to consider their rights in detail. However, attention will be drawn to considerations which have a particular application to the children of unmarried parents.

5.2 Succession

5.2.1 Testate succession

The surviving cohabitant

Where it is intended that a cohabitant should benefit on the death of his or her partner, it is vitally important that a will be made to give effect to that intention: a surviving cohabitant has no rights under the rules governing intestacy. There may be a right to apply under the Inheritance (Provision for Family and Dependants) Act (I(PFD)A) 1975 for provision from the deceased's estate, but such proceedings will be costly and the provision that may be made by the court is limited (see §5.3 below).

If property is to be left by will to a surviving cohabitant, it is extremely desirable that the cohabitant be identified in the will by name. Problems are likely to arise where the will includes a provision which is intended to refer to a cohabitant but which does not identify that person by name and, although the task of the court is to ascertain the testator's intention as expressed in the will (when read as a whole and in the light of any extrinsic evidence which satisfies the rules governing admissibility), it will not always be possible for the court to give effect to the testator's wishes in the face of a hopelessly ambiguous, inadequate or inaccurate description of the intended beneficiary.

Faced with a description of a beneficiary not identified by name, the court may be able to conclude that a particular person was intended even where the description used was inaccurate. For example, in construing a will, the court must normally give the words used their 'strict, plain, common meaning' so that, *prima facie*, 'my wife' means the woman to whom the testator was lawfully married. Where there is no one to whom the testator was lawfully married, but he is survived by a woman with whom he had been living, the court may conclude that she is the person to whom the description was intended to refer (see, eg *Re Brown* (1910) 26 TLR 257). In *Re Lynch* [1943] 1 All ER 168, the testator appointed 'my wife AEL' as one of his executors, and left part of his estate 'to my wife during her widowhood'. The testator and AEL were not in fact married, and were unable to marry because they were within the prohibited degrees of relationship, but they had cohabited for five years and had held themselves out as man and wife. It was held that, in the appointment of the executrix, the testator had 'provided his own dictionary'. (It may be noted that the 'wife' in *Re Lynch* would be entitled to the property even if she were already married to another man at the date of the testator's death (see *Re Wagstaff* [1908] 1 Ch 162), and would remain so entitled unless and until she subsequently contracted another valid marriage.)

It may be possible to rebut the presumption in favour of the ordinary meaning of words and to adopt a secondary meaning even where there is a person to whom, in its ordinary meaning, the phrase could apply. In *Re Smalley* [1929] 2 Ch 112, the testator left all his property 'to my wife EAS'. He was survived by his lawful wife, EAM, and by his cohabitant, EAS, with whom he had gone through a bigamous ceremony of marriage, who believed herself to be his wife, and who was reputed in the neighbourhood to be his wife. The court concluded that the testator had used the words 'my wife' in their secondary meaning of his *reputed* wife.

Life interests and gifts over: The Administration of Justice Act 1982, s 22 deals with bequests which appear to give a life interest with a gift over, but which are likely to have been intended not to impose a fetter on the apparent life tenant's powers of disposal as, for example, in the case of a bequest in a home-made will in the form: 'I give all my property to my wife and after her death to my children'. Unless a contrary intention is shown, s 22 operates to give effect to the bequest as the gift of an absolute interest to the spouse. This statutory provision does not apply to unmarried cohabitants. Thus, a bequest in the form given above will create only a life interest.

'Stale' wills: Each new will revokes its predecessor. Moreover, unless made in contemplation of marriage, a will is revoked by the subsequent marriage of the testator. Divorce does not revoke a will but, unless a contrary intention appears in the will, any devise or bequest to the former spouse lapses and any appointment of the former spouse as executor (or as executor and trustee) is treated as omitted (Wills Act 1837, s 18A; and see *Re Sinclair (Deceased); Lloyd's Bank PLC v Imperial Cancer Research Fund* [1985] FLR 965). Problems arise, however, where there is an unrevoked will made many years before the testator's death in which a bequest is made to a spouse from whom he was never divorced. In this situation, a surviving cohabitant must give consideration to applying for provision from the deceased's estate under the Inheritance (Provision for Family and Dependants) Act 1975 (see §5.3 below).

Children

The Family Law Reform Act (FLRA) 1969, s 15 provided that, in wills made after 1969, unless a contrary intention appears, any references to the child or children of any person are to be construed as including any illegitimate child of that person, and any other words of relationship are to be construed as including any person whose relationship depends on an intermediate illegitimate link. However, these rules apply only to references to a person who is to benefit or be capable of benefiting under the disposition or, for the purpose of designating such a person, to somcone else to or through whom that person is related. (Thus, a testator's appointment of 'my eldest son' as executor would fall outside the provisions of the 1969 Act with the result that only the eldest surviving legitimate son would qualify as executor.) The effect of the Family Law Reform Act (FLRA) 1987, s 19 is to remove that limitation with respect to provisions contained in wills made on or after 4 April 1988. It is also provided that the term 'heir', or any expression used to create an entailed interest, is not to be taken as showing an intention to exclude a person whose parents have not been married to each other.

It remains open to a testator to exclude the operation of these rules by making clear a contrary intention, for example by naming each individual child who is to benefit, or by specifying that the bequest is in favour of his *legitimate* children only.

Whether or not a child of the deceased has received a bequest, he has a right to apply to the court under the I(PFD)A 1975 for provision from the deceased's estate (see §5.3 below).

Witnesses' cohabitants

It may be noted that a person who witnesses a will is disqualified from taking any benefit under the will, as is his or her spouse, but a witness's cohabitant is not so disqualified from taking a benefit.

5.2.2   Intestate succession

The Administration of Estates Act (AEA) 1925 provides a statutory scheme which governs the distribution of estates of persons who die wholly or partly intestate. In the case of an intestate who was married, the scheme gives a high priority to the surviving spouse who is absolutely entitled to the entire estate if the deceased leaves no issue or other close relatives. If the deceased leaves issue or other close relatives, the surviving spouse receives (amongst other entitlements) a substantial 'statutory legacy' (at the time of writing, £75,000 where there are issue; £125,000 where there are close relatives but no issue). In many cases, the statutory legacy will exhaust the deceased's estate. Where there is no surviving spouse, any issue take the entire estate absolutely. Where there are no issue, the deceased's relatives become entitled (in order of priority laid down by statute). In default of any relatives, the estate will pass as *bona vacantia* to the Crown.

The surviving cohabitant

As can be seen from the above brief outline, there is no provision under the statutory scheme for a surviving cohabitant. However, a cohabitant may have a right to apply to the court under the I(PFD)A 1975 for provision from the deceased's estate (see §5.3 below). Moreover, where a deceased's estate has reverted to the Crown as *bona vacantia*, provision may be made as a matter of grace for 'dependants' (whether related to the deceased or not), and for other persons for whom the deceased might reasonably have been expected to make provision (AEA 1925, s 46(1)), and this power to make an *ex gratia* payment may be exercised in favour of a surviving cohabitant.

Children

Since amendments effected by the FLRA 1969, the AEA scheme has made no distinction between legitimate and illegitimate issue and, by the FLRA 1987, s 18, a child of unmarried parents now has rights of succession not only in respect of both his parents, but also in relation to remoter members of both his paternal and maternal families. Thus, a child of unmarried parents whose mother has predeceased his maternal grandfather may succeed on the grandfather's intestacy, and this applies irrespective of whether his mother was herself an illegitimate child. It remains impossible for a child of unmarried parents to succeed to a title of honour or property devolving therewith.

The statutory scheme provides not only for succession by children on the intestacy of their parents, but also for succession by parents on the intestacy of their children. However, a child of unmarried parents is rebuttably presumed not to have been survived by his father or by persons related to him through his father (FLRA 1987, s 18(2)).

The FLRA 1987, s 20 removed (in relation to deaths occurring after 4 April 1988) the special protection which was extended to trustees and personal representatives by the FLRA 1969, s 17 (which enabled trustees and personal representatives to distribute property without having ascertained that no person whose parents were not married to each other at the time of his birth or who claims through such a person, is or may be entitled to an interest in the property). Protection for trustees and personal representatives is still to be found in the Trustee Act 1925, ss 27 and 61. Although the trustee may thus be protected from personal liability either by virtue of having advertised for claims (s 27) or because he has 'acted honestly and reasonably, and ought fairly to be excused' (s 61), the beneficiary retains his right to claim against the recipients of property already distributed.

Whether or not a child of the deceased has benefited under his intestacy, the child has a right to apply to the court under the I(PFD)A 1975 for provision from the deceased's estate (see §5.3 below).

5.2.3 *Donationes mortis causa*

The doctrine of *donatio mortis causa* applies where a gift is made in contemplation of impending death, on condition that it is to be absolute and perfected only on the donor's death, being revocable until that event occurs. There must be delivery of the subject-matter of the gift whereby the donor parts with dominion over it. In *Sen v Headley* [1991] 2 FLR 449, the Court of Appeal held that land could be the subject of a *donatio mortis causa* by means of constructive delivery of the title deeds. In that case, in conjunction with clear words of gift, the donor gave the donee two keys, one of which was the only key to the box in which the deeds were kept, while the other was the key to the cupboard in which the box was kept (the donee already had keys to the house itself). It was held that an effective *donatio mortis causa* had been made.

5.3   The Inheritance (Provision for Family and Dependants) Act 1975

5.3.1   Eligibility to make a claim

The surviving cohabitant

A surviving cohabitant who has received no benefit from the deceased's estate or who considers the benefit received to be inadequate, may seek an order from the court under the 1975 Act awarding financial provision from the estate. The eligibility condition which must be satisfied is that contained in s 1(1)(e) of the Act which provides that a claim may be made by:

> 'any person (. . .) who immediately before the death of the deceased was being maintained, either wholly or partly, by the deceased.'

'Being maintained': The phrase 'being maintained' is further explained in s 1(3), as follows:

'For the purposes of [s 1(1)(e)], a person shall be treated as being maintained by the deceased, either wholly or partly, as the case may be, if the deceased, otherwise than for full valuable consideration, was making a substantial contribution in money or money's worth towards the reasonable needs of that person.'

It has been held that this provision constitutes an exhaustive definition of what amounts to 'being maintained' (see *Re Beaumont* [1980] Ch 444; *Jelley v Iliffe* [1981] Fam 128), so that no claim may be made unless the arrangement between the parties satisfies those requirements. To this end, a number of hurdles must be overcome.

'Otherwise than for full valuable consideration': It has been held that this requirement does not merely exclude cases where consideration is furnished under a contract. It applies also to benefits conferred and received under informal arrangements which are not legally enforceable. Thus, in every case where it is asserted that the would-be claimant was being maintained by the deceased, it will be necessary to consider whether the claimant in fact 'gave as good as he got' (*Jelley v Iliffe*, above). A balancing exercise must be undertaken in which the contributions made by the deceased to the claimant's maintenance are weighed against the contributions made by the claimant to the deceased and, moreover, this balancing exercise must take account of *non*-financial contributions. Clearly, the payment to a claimant of a regular housekeeping allowance from which to meet both the claimant's and the deceased's needs would constitute maintenance. Likewise, the provision of rent-free accommodation is regarded as a substantial contribution towards a person's reasonable needs, as would the payment by the deceased of bills for food, heating, etc, without requiring any contribution towards these expenses. However, the recipient of these benefits, although not making any direct financial payment for them may nevertheless be providing something in return on which the court may have to attempt to place a value, such as nursing services, or cooking and housekeeping duties. Even companionship and affection are benefits which have to be brought into the equation (*Re Wilkinson* [1978] Fam 22) and it has to be established that, when all these various forms of contribution are weighed, the deceased's *net* contribution to the claimant's support was substantial.

Cases of traditional 'housewife' dependency will normally present no problem. However, in less straightforward cases the balancing exercise may be less easy to resolve as, for instance, where a couple live in the home owned by one partner while the other pays all outgoings on food, fuel, etc. In these circumstances it may be found that there has been mutual dependency (*Re Beaumont*, above; *Jelley v Iliffe*, above). In such a case, although perhaps neither partner could have maintained the same standard of living without the contribution made by the other, no claim will be possible under the 1975 Act. 'Pooling' of resources will not prevent eligibility if the contributions are unequal (see *Re Kirby* (1982) FLR 249).

In view of the court's preparedness to take account of services it has been observed that, in theory, the more deserving the applicant, the less likely he or she is to be eligible to claim. However, it will often be possible to avoid this consequence by taking a broad view of the case. For example, during a terminal illness, devoted nursing care may be provided by a financially dependent cohabitant to a standard and for a duration which, if commercially valued, would far outweigh the value of the support received during that period, but it has been stressed that the court must take a common-sense approach to these matters (*Jelley v Iliffe*, above; *Bishop v Plumley* [1991] 1 FLR 121).

In practice, the issue of full valuable consideration for the benefits received is likely to arise on a preliminary application to strike out the applicant's claim. At this stage, all that is required is for the court to be satisfied that the applicant *may* be able to establish dependency at a subsequent full hearing. The claim will be struck out only if it is clear that this onus could not be discharged (*Jelley v Iliffe*, above).

Assumption of responsibility: In addition to *de facto* dependency, it must also be shown that the deceased 'assumed responsibility' for the applicant's maintenance (see *Re Beaumont*, above; and see s 3(4)). In practice, proof of the making of payments will raise a presumption that there has been an assumption of responsibility (*Jelley v Iliffe*, above), but there remains the possibility of that presumption being rebutted by evidence, for instance, that the deceased made payments under protest, or with a disclaimer of any intention to assume responsibility. However, it is not necessary to prove that the deceased intended to maintain the applicant after his or her death (*Jelley v Iliffe*, above).

It should be noted also that it is possible to mount a challenge to eligibility on the basis that, although there had indisputably been provision for the claimant in money or money's worth, this provision was not on the facts a contribution towards the applicant's *reasonable* needs. Thus, payments to stave off bankruptcy as the result of profligate behaviour on the applicant's part might be held to fall outside s 1(3) (see further the arguments raised in *Re Dennis* [1981] 2 All ER 140). It is, however, unlikely that the generality of cohabitation cases will involve reliance only on provision of a kind that might invite such a challenge.

'*Immediately before the death of the deceased*': The requirement that the applicant be maintained by the deceased immediately before his death has been held to refer to the settled basis of the arrangement. For example, a surviving cohabitant will not be debarred from making a claim by virtue of the fact that the deceased spent a lengthy period immediately before his death in hospital and was not in fact providing financial support. What is required is that the underlying basis of dependency should continue to the date of death (*Re Beaumont*, above). Thus, a surviving *former* cohabitant will be ineligible to claim no matter how long the period of cohabitation if the relationship had in fact been ruptured prior to the death (see *Kourkgy v Lusher* (1983) FLR 65: applicant had been the deceased's mistress intermittently for ten years but, on the facts, deceased held to have abandoned responsibility for her nine days before his death: applicant therefore ineligible to claim).

Children

Any child of a deceased parent is eligible to claim financial provision from the parent's estate (I(PFD)A 1975, s 1(1)(c); and see *In the estate of McC* (1979) Fam Law 26 which indicates that, in principle, illegitimate children are to be treated on the same basis as legitimate children; and see further *Re Collins* [1990] 2 FLR 72). As noted above (at §5.2), non-marital children have the same rights as, and rank equally with, marital children in respect of succession to their parent's estate on intestacy. Thus, where a cohabiting parent dies without leaving a will, any children of the cohabitation relationship will be deprived of any interest in the deceased parent's property only where that parent was a party to a marriage which had not been dissolved, and where the surviving spouse's statutory legacy exhausts the estate. Where this occurs, it may be appropriate for a non-marital child to claim provision out of the intestate parent's estate.

This may also be the case where the terms of the deceased's will exclude his non-marital children from any interest, as may well

happen through inadvertence in the case of a 'stale' will made prior
to the commencement of the cohabitation and which makes bequests
by name to existing children of the deceased. An application for
provision may also be indicated where provision is made by a will
or by the rules governing intestate succession, but is considered
inadequate. Such a situation might arise, for example, where the
rules governing intestacy result in an estate being equally divided
among the deceased's adult and self-supporting children by an
earlier marriage, and the dependent minor children of the cohabitation relationship.

5.3.2 Basis of claim and exercise of the court's powers

Where eligibility to apply is established, the basis of the claim is
that the distribution of the deceased's estate (whether by will or on
intestacy) is not such as to make reasonable financial provision for
the applicant (s 1(1)).

In the case of all applicants other than a surviving spouse, 'reasonable financial provision' means such provision as it is reasonable
for the applicant to receive *for his maintenance* (see s 1(2)(b)), and
'maintenance' means such financial provision as would be reasonable in all the circumstances of the case to enable the applicant to
maintain himself in a manner suitable to his circumstances by meeting the recurring expenses of living (see *Re Coventry* [1980] Ch 461;
Re Dennis, above).

The applicant must establish that the distribution of the
deceased's estate is not such as to make reasonable financial provision for him. It is not sufficient to prove simply that it would
have been reasonable for the deceased to have made such provision:
it must be proved that the provision in fact made (if any) leads to
an unreasonable result. It will obviously be of great assistance if
the applicant is able to show a desire to make provision (as where,
for instance, the will contained a bequest to the applicant of specific
property which, by the time of the death, was no longer in existence)
or if there is evidence of a declared intention to make provision,
albeit that the required steps were not actually taken. However, it
is not *necessary* to prove that the deceased intended to make provision for the applicant (see *Jelley v Iliffe*, above), since the object
of the Act is to remedy the injustice of a person being put in a
position of dependency and then deprived of financial support after
the deceased's death. Again, however, any statement made by the

deceased as to his reasons for making or not making provision will be relevant to the court's deliberations (and is admissible in evidence; see s 21).

In deciding whether there has been a failure to make reasonable provision and, if so, whether and in what manner to exercise its powers, the court is directed to have regard to the matters listed in s 3. These matters essentially concern the size and nature of the estate (and this may include consideration of the source and origin of the available funds; see *Re Callaghan (Deceased)* [1985] FLR 116), the needs and resources of the applicant, the obligations and responsibilities which the deceased had towards the applicant and towards those entitled under the will or intestacy, and the needs and resources of those beneficiaries since, if provision is to be made for the applicant, it can only be made at the beneficiaries' expense. The court is also directed to have regard to any other matter, including the conduct of the applicant or any other person, which in the circumstances of the case the court may consider relevant (s 3(1)(g)).

Surviving cohabitant

As applicant: Where an application is made by a person eligible to claim under s 1(1)(e), the court is directed to have regard (in addition to the factors listed in s 3(1)) to the basis upon which the deceased assumed responsibility for the applicant's maintenance, the extent of that responsibility and the length of time for which it was discharged by the deceased (s 3(4)). Clearly, each case will be dependent upon its own special facts but it is submitted that the success of a claim by a surviving cohabitant will depend substantially on the needs and resources of the beneficiaries and the nature of the obligations which the deceased owed to them. When these are compared to the needs and resources of the cohabitant, an able-bodied applicant with an earning capacity may be left without further support from the estate if the estate is modest and the court concludes that the beneficiaries are in greater need and have not been guilty of any conduct which would justify reducing or depriving them of their entitlement. Notwithstanding that the applicant was in fact dependent upon the deceased immediately before his death, it may nevertheless be reasonable in all the circumstances of the case for no financial provision to have been made for him or her.

It should not be supposed that it will necessarily be easier to persuade a court to interfere with the distribution of the estate of an intestate than with provision made by will. It will be helpful if there is evidence of an (unfulfilled) intention to make provision for the applicant but, in the absence of such evidence, it cannot be assumed that the deceased died intestate through inadvertence: he may have been well aware of the distribution that would occur on intestacy, and have been content to contemplate that result.

As beneficiary: A surviving cohabitant may be involved in proceedings under the 1975 Act not as applicant, but as beneficiary seeking to resist the claims of some other qualified applicant (such as a surviving spouse or former spouse). In respect of a claim by a surviving spouse, it may be noted that the powers of the court are not limited to making provision merely for the spouse's maintenance (see s 1(2)(a)), and the court is directed to have regard to the provision which the applicant spouse might reasonably have expected to receive if the marriage had been terminated by divorce rather than by death (s 3(2); and see *Moody v Stevenson* [1992] 1 FLR 494). Thus, particularly where the marriage had been in existence for many years before the breakdown, a cohabitant entitled under a deceased husband's will may find that a substantial sum by way of capital is awarded to the man's widow (see also the remarkable case of *Jessop v Jessop* [1992] 1 FLR 591 where, for some 20 years, the deceased (who died intestate) had divided his time between two families, maintaining a wife and children in Middlesbrough and a cohabitant and children in Portsmouth: award of £10,000 made on widow's application for provision, the court having treated as part of the deceased's estate his severable share in the joint 'cohabitational' home; see s 9(1)).

Where there are minor children for whom the deceased has failed to make provision and who are not in the care of any other person who will receive provision from the estate, an order providing for their maintenance is likely to receive a high priority (see *Re Sivyer* [1967] 1 WLR 1482; but note also the warning given in *Moody v Stevenson*, above, at 508, that cases decided under the Inheritance Act 1938 must be approached with caution).

Children

Although the needs of minor children are likely to be given a high priority (see *Re Sivyer*, above; and see also *In the estate of McC*, above), the courts are less sympathetic to claims made by adult children of the deceased. Thus, it has been said that claims for maintenance by adult and able-bodied young men in employment and able to maintain themselves must be relatively rare and should be 'approached with a degree of circumspection' (*Re Coventry*, above). The court will be likely to ask: 'Why should anybody else make provision for you if you are capable of maintaining yourself?' (*Re Dennis*, above). Nevertheless, an award might be made, for example, where an adult child has a disability rendering him vulnerable or in special need (see, eg *Re Debenham* [1986] 1 FLR 404; see also *Re Collins*, above), or where he has been prejudiced in his efforts to pursue a career by having undertaken the duty of caring for the deceased parent (see further *Re Callaghan (Deceased)* [1985] FLR 116).

5.3.3 The court's powers

In addition to orders for periodical payments and lump sum payments the court may make orders providing for the transfer or settlement of property, the variation of ante-nuptial and post-nuptial settlements, and the purchase of property and its transfer to the applicant (s 2(1)). Although applicants other than a surviving spouse are entitled only to awards providing for their maintenance (see, eg *Re Collins*, above), this does not mean that the order must be by way of periodical payments. Indeed, in many cases, the expense that would be involved in administering the estate so as to provide continuing payments would render such an order impracticable. Where the estate is relatively modest, the most sensible order will often be an order for the payment of a lump sum to the applicant, but it may be the case that there is particular property in the estate which can be applied to meet the applicant's reasonable needs, as in *Harrington v Gill* (1983) FLR 265, where the deceased's house (and its contents) were ordered to be settled on the applicant for life. Where an order of this type is made, the court has the power to include consequential provisions in order to ensure that the award in favour of the applicant does not operate unfairly as between one beneficiary and another (s 2(4)).

Where the deceased was beneficially entitled to a joint tenancy in any property immediately before his death, the court may bring the deceased's severable share in that property into his estate by treating the joint tenancy as if it had been severed immediately before his death (s 9(1); and see *Jessop v Jessop*, above).

The court also has the power to review dispositions made with the intention of defeating a claim to financial relief (s 10). There is no presumption of such an intention, and no disposition can be set aside if it occurred more than six years before the death.

The court has the power to make an interim order in favour of an applicant who is in immediate need (s 5).

Provision for variation of certain types of order is contained in ss 6 and 7.

5.3.4   Time-limit

An application under the Act must be made within six months of the date on which representation was first taken out. Application may be made after that date only with leave of the court (s 4).

5.4   Compensation for wrongful death

5.4.1   The Fatal Accidents Act 1976

The Fatal Accidents Act (FAA) 1976 enables an action to be brought for the benefit of dependants of a person whose death occurs in circumstances which would have given rise to an action in tort on the part of the deceased against the wrongdoer if death had not ensued. A person is only entitled to seek damages under the Act if he or she falls within one of the categories of 'dependant' set out in the Act.

The categories include 'any child or other descendant of the deceased' (s 1(3)(e)). It is provided that, in deducing any relationship for the purpose of s 1(3), an illegitimate person shall be treated as the legitimate child of his mother and reputed father (s 1(5)). This rule apparently operates to enable a claim to be made not only by an illegitimate child of the deceased but also by an illegitimate grandchild, including a grandchild whose relationship to the deceased derives from a parent who was also born illegitimate.

The statute also enables a claim to be made for the benefit of:

'any person who
    (i) was living with the deceased in the same household immediately before the date of the death; and
    (ii) had been living with the deceased in the same household for at least two years before that date; and

(iii) was living during the whole of that period as the husband or wife of the deceased' (s 1(3)(b)).

Thus it is necessary to establish that there has been a minimum period of two years' cohabitation *as husband and wife* – a requirement that may occasionally cause difficulties where life in the same household began on a different footing (eg a live-in housekeeper), but gradually evolved into life together as husband and wife. On the other hand, it is clear that the requirement of a shared household *immediately before the date of the death* will not operate to prevent a claim in a case where the deceased partner spent a lengthy period in hospital before ultimately succumbing to the injuries received at the hands of the tortfeasor (see, for an analogy, *Jelley v Iliffe* [1981] Fam 128).

A claimant under the Act must show that he or she belongs to one of the statutorily defined categories of 'dependant' and, since the essence of an action in tort is compensation for loss suffered, must also prove financial loss (ie loss of dependency) resulting from the death, and the extent of that loss will determine the damages awarded in accordance with the normal principles of the law of damages (and subject to deduction for any contributory negligence on the part of the deceased).

A claim on behalf of a surviving cohabitant will therefore be quantified according to normal principles, but with the additional consideration that the dependent cohabitant had no enforceable right of support from the deceased as a result of their living together (see s 3(4)). Clearly, if the deceased had lived, he could have terminated his support of his cohabitant at any time. The court will therefore inevitably have to form a view as to the stability of the relationship between the deceased and the dependant taking into account for example, the length of time that the relationship had been subsisting by the date of the death, in order to determine the likelihood of continued dependence had the deceased not died, for the purpose of selecting the appropriate multiplier.

Damages for bereavement

In addition to any other damages recoverable, the statute provides for the recovery of damages for bereavement for the benefit of the wife or husband of the deceased, but does not provide for the award of such damages to a surviving cohabitant.

Damages for bereavement are also recoverable in respect of the death of a minor. Indeed, in respect of the death of a minor child, damages are recoverable *only* for bereavement, and are set by order at £7,500. In the case of an illegitimate child, such damages may be claimed only for the benefit of the child's mother (s 1A(2)).

5.4.2   Cohabitants excluded from the Fatal Accidents Act 1976

It may be that cases will present themselves in which a cohabitant has died leaving a child or children eligible to claim under the FAA 1976 but also leaving a surviving partner who fails to qualify as a dependant within the meaning of the Act. Such a situation could arise, for instance, if the parties had not cohabited for the required two-year period immediately prior to the death. In such a case, only the child(ren) would be qualified to receive damages as a dependant. However, prior to the extension of the FAA 1876 to cohabitants, the courts had already found an indirect means of compensating the surviving cohabitant for *some* of her lost financial support. In *K v JMP Co Ltd* [1975] 1 All ER 1030, it was recognised, for example, that the loss of financial support which the mother had received from the father while she fulfilled the task of caring for the children would constitute a pecuniary loss to the children to the extent that the care which the mother could give them was diminished by her loss of the father's support. The cost of her support would not be recoverable in its entirety, but elements of the damages payable to the children, for example, in respect of the cost of holidays and outings which the father would have provided for them, had to include sums to enable the mother to accompany them so as to enable the children to continue to enjoy those benefits. The court also considered that the cost of electricity, gas, rent, television and washing machine were 'family expenses' not apportionable between mother and children and, for instance, refused to disallow the extra cost of any electricity which the mother might use for light or heat after the children had gone to bed.

5.4.3   Relationship with Law Reform (Miscellaneous Provisions) Act 1934

Damages are recoverable under this Act for the benefit of the deceased's estate. The heads of damage recoverable under this Act are limited but include damages for pain and suffering endured by the deceased as a result of the tortious injury which caused his death. Where a deceased endured a long period of pain and suffering before ultimately succumbing to his injuries, his estate may be entitled to a substantial sum by way of damages. Clearly the possibility of a substantial award under this head will be particularly significant in a case where a surviving cohabitant does not qualify as a dependant under the FAA 1976 but is entitled to benefit from the estate or is intending to apply for provision from the estate under I(PFD)A 1975.

5.4.4 Other compensation

Criminal injuries

If the deceased died after sustaining injuries criminally inflicted upon him, any dependant (within the meaning of the FAA 1976) may apply for compensation under the Criminal Injuries Compensation Scheme (see Criminal Justice Act 1988, s 111).

Pneumoconiosis and related diseases

Where a deceased's death was the result of pneumoconiosis or a related disease and the conditions of the Pneumoconiosis, etc (Workers Compensation) Act 1979 are satisfied, certain dependants are entitled to claim a lump sum payment. In addition to children of the deceased, 'dependant' for this purpose includes a 'reputed spouse', but a reputed spouse may claim the payment only in the absence of a *de jure* spouse or minor child (s 3). No guidance is given as to the conditions that must be satisfied in order to qualify as a 'reputed spouse'.

Part III
CHILDREN

INTRODUCTION

The Children Act (CA) 1989 (implemented 14 October 1991) has transformed the landscape of child law, repealing in their entirety many of the landmark statutes of the previous complex system and establishing in their place a scheme which aims to integrate and rationalise those areas which were formerly compartmentalised into 'private law' and 'public law'. Virtually no area of child law remains unaffected. Even in areas where the principal governing statute remains largely intact, the general expansion of the court's powers effected by the CA 1989 and the impact of the philosophy underlying that Act are together effecting change. In general, in the chapters that follow, an attempt has been made to explain the relevant law without undue or unnecessary reference to concepts and rules which have been swept away by the Children Act 1989.

Although the legal status of illegitimacy has not been abolished, the Family Law Reform Act (FLRA) 1987 and the CA 1989 do not use the term 'illegitimate child'. In its place, a form of words is used which avoids labelling children, concentrating instead on the marital status of parents. Thus, an illegitimate child is referred to as a child whose parents were not married to each other at the time of his birth. The FLRA 1987, s 1 explains these terms and makes clear that references to a child whose parents were married to each other at the time of his birth, include any child who is treated in law as legitimate (eg an adopted child or a child who has been legitimated by the marriage of his parents subsequent to his birth).

In the spirit of this approach, the term 'illegitimate child' is avoided in the following chapters and, in the absence of an alternative short label provided by statute, the term 'child of unmarried parents' is employed. For convenience, the terms 'unmarried father' and 'unmarried mother' are used to refer to the parents of such a child, but it should be borne in mind that either (or both) of the parents may be married to someone who is not the child's other parent.

It may be noted that the FLRA 1987, s 1 provides that in that Act and in enactments passed and instruments made after 4 April

1988, references (however expressed) to any relationship between two persons shall, unless the contrary intention appears, be construed without regard to whether or not the father and mother of either of them, or the father and mother of any person through whom the relationship is deduced, have or have not been married to each other at any time. By s 2, this general principle of construction is also specifically applied to a number of existing enactments.

6 ESTABLISHING AND RECORDING PATERNITY

6.1 Registration of births

By the Births and Deaths Registration Act (BDRA) 1953, s 10 (as amended), when the birth of a child of unmarried parents is recorded in the Register of Births, the registrar cannot enter the name of any person as father of the child unless:

(a) that mother and father jointly request that his name be entered, in which case both must sign the Register; or

(b) the mother requests his name to be entered and produces declarations by them both that he is the father; or

(c) the father requests his name to be entered and produces declarations by himself and the mother that he is the father; or

(d) either the mother or the father requests his name to be entered and produces a parental responsibility order or agreement or an order requiring him to make financial provision for the child or one of a specified range of orders made under the former law relating to children and for which a finding of paternity was a prerequisite.

A father who requests registration under (c) or (d) when the birth is first registered is to be treated as a 'qualified informant' for the purposes of the Act so that registration at his request discharges the duty of any other qualified informant to register the birth (s 10(2)).

The BDRA 1953 also provides for reregistration if the child becomes a legitimated person (s 14(1)). Where the Registrar-General believes a person to have become legitimated by virtue of the marriage of his parents to each other but the parents fail to furnish the information necessary for reregistration within three months of the marriage, the Registrar-General may require the parents to give such information as he considers necessary with a view to reregistration (s 14(2)).

Section 14A requires the Registrar-General to authorise the reregistration of a person if he is notified (by the court) that a declaration of parentage has been made in respect of that person under the Family Law Act 1986, s 56, and it appears to him that the birth of that person should be reregistered.

The entry of a man's name as the father of a child constitutes *prima facie* evidence of paternity (BDRA 1953, s 34).

6.2   Establishing paternity

6.2.1   Who is a father?

Essentially, subject to the possibility of formal adoption, paternity is simply a matter of biological fact. However, the Human Fertilisation and Embryology Act 1990, s 28(3) provides that where licensed AID (artificial insemination by donor) treatment is provided for an unmarried woman and a man together, that man is to be treated as the child's father.

6.2.2   Establishing paternity in proceedings

As a necessary preliminary to substantive relief

It may be important to establish paternity as a necessary preliminary to seeking substantive relief. For example, in order to establish that he has standing to seek a parental responsibility order, a man will need to establish his paternity of any child of whom he claims to be the father. In such a case the court can adjudicate on paternity. Its findings will bind the parties to those proceedings and, although the rights of non-parties will not be affected (see *Re JS (A Minor) (Declaration of Paternity)* (1981) FLR 146), those findings will provide *prima facie* evidence of parentage which would have to be rebutted in any subsequent proceedings. While the court clearly has jurisdiction to make a finding of paternity when hearing an application for which paternity provides the *locus standi*, it seems that the court could decline to reach a decision on the (jurisdictional) question of paternity if it was plain at the outset that, in the particular circumstances of the case, the substantive application had no prospects of success (as, for example, where there is abundant evidence that the putative father's motives are such as to render a

parental responsibility order inimical to the child's interests). In
A v B and Hereford and Worcester County Council [1986] 1 FLR 289,
in the wardship jurisdiction, it was said that the issue of paternity
should not be tried unless determination of that issue will have a
material bearing on some other issue in the proceedings and it will
be in the child's interests that his paternity should be investigated.

Declarations of paternity

The Family Law Act (FLA) 1986, s 56 (as amended by the FLRA
1987, s 22) provides that any person may apply to the court for a
declaration that a person named in the application is or was his
parent, or that he is the legitimate child of his parents. A declaration
may also be sought in respect of legitimation.

A declaration may only be sought in respect of the applicant's own
parentage or legitimacy. Thus, it is not open to a person claiming to
be the father of a child to bring proceedings for a declaration of
paternity.

When a declaration is sought and the truth of the proposition to
be declared is proved to the court's satisfaction, the court must
make the declaration unless it would be manifestly contrary to
public policy to do so (FLA 1986, s 58(1); apparently embodying
the power exercised in *Puttick v Att-Gen* [1980] Fam 1: declaration
of validity of marriage sought by West German terrorist to prevent
extradition). The declaration is then binding on everyone, unless
obtained by fraud (see *The Ampthill Peerage* [1977] AC 547).

6.2.3 Matters of proof

Presumptions

When a married woman gives birth to a child, the presumption of
legitimacy operates and the child is presumed to be the child of her
husband. However, where a married woman alleges paternity by a
man other than her husband and that man admits to being the
father of her child, this acknowledgement of paternity can suffice
to rebut the presumption of legitimacy (*R v King's Lynn Justices
and Another, ex parte M* [1988] 2 FLR 79). There has been some
uncertainty in the case-law with respect to the standard of proof
required to rebut the presumption (see *S v McC; W v W* [1972]
AC 24; *Serio v Serio* (1983) FLR 756) but the practical significance

of the point has been greatly diminished by the advent of DNA tests, if such tests are ordered (as to which, see below).

Cohabitation does not, as a matter of law, raise a presumption of paternity by the male cohabitant, but entry of the man's name as the child's father in the Register of Births is *prima facie* evidence of paternity (see §6.1 above).

Blood tests and scientific evidence

In any civil proceedings in which the paternity of any person falls to be determined, the court may, on the application of any party to the proceedings, give a direction for the taking of blood samples from that person, the mother of that person, and any person alleged to be the father of that person (Family Law Reform Act (FLRA) 1969, s 20(1); and see Blood Tests (Evidence of Paternity) Regulations 1971 (SI 1971/1861, as amended by SI 1989/776)).

Blood tests cannot be ordered where paternity is not in issue (see *Hodgkiss v Hodgkiss* [1985] Fam Law 87). The purpose of the tests must be to show whether *a party to the proceedings* is excluded from paternity, and there is thus no power to order blood tests in administration proceedings where the issue is whether a person is the child of a deceased person about whose blood information happens to be available. On the other hand, where a declaration of parentage is sought, the court's power to give a direction for blood tests extends to any person named in the application (FLRA 1969, s 20(2A)).

It is open to adult parties to agree on the taking of blood tests for evidential purposes and where there is such an agreement, unless the child is a ward of court, it is unnecessary to obtain the court's consent to the taking of samples from the child for the purpose of testing.

In the absence of consent, the court's power is one of direction and not of compulsion. Thus, testing cannot actually occur without the consent of the parties to the giving of blood samples. It will be necessary to obtain the consent of the person having care and control of the child unless the child is aged 16 or over, in which case the child may himself give a sufficient consent (FLRA 1969, s 8). However, if a party refuses to consent to the taking of a blood sample, it will be open to the court to draw such inferences, if any, from that fact as may appear proper in the circumstances (FLRA 1969, s 23(1); and see *McV v B* [1988] 2 FLR 67; but see also

B v B and E [1969] 3 All ER 1106: husband's refusal held to be reasonable).

Conventional blood tests are *exclusionary* in effect. They cannot establish that a particular man is the father of the child but there is a 97–99 per cent chance of being able to exclude him from paternity where paternity is wrongly asserted. Where tests cannot exclude a particular man, they can indicate the degree of probability that he is the father (by indicating, for example, that the characteristics of the child's blood are such that, if not derived from the alleged father they could be derived from only one man in a thousand of the general male population; see eg *Turner v Blunden* [1986] 2 FLR 69).

It is now possible for scientific testing of blood or other bodily samples to establish conclusively that a particular man is the father of the child, by means of the 'DNA fingerprinting' technique. A direction may be given for such tests using *blood* samples, but at the time of writing it is not possible for a direction to be given in respect of testing of other bodily samples. DNA testing is more costly than the traditional blood tests. It has been held, in the county court, that a local authority has a duty to a child in its care to establish paternity where it is in the child's interests to do so and it was noted that, if the child were later to be placed for adoption, the failure to establish paternity could hold up adoption proceedings. Thus it was reasonable to expect the local authority to pay for a DNA test (*Re B (A Minor) (Child in Care: Blood Test)* [1992] Fam Law 533).

Where a blood test direction is given, it will be the responsibility of the party on whose application the direction was made to pay the costs of the blood tests, but the amount so paid will be treated as costs incurred in the proceedings (FLRA 1969, s 20(6)).

In *S v McC; W v W* [1972] AC 24, the broad proposition was stated that, once a question mark has arisen over the paternity of a child, it is generally in the child's best interests for the truth to be ascertained. However, cases can arise where the court does not consider that the child's best interests will be served by a direction for the taking of tests. For example, if a child has been conceived and brought up as a child of the family within an existing marriage and the mother's association with the man claiming to be the child's father had terminated before the child's birth, then, if that relationship coexisted with sexual relations between the spouses, the court may feel that a direction for blood tests should be refused on the basis that it is not in the child's interests for the presumption of legitimacy to be disturbed (as in *Re F (Minor: Paternity Tests)* [1993] 1 FLR 225, where an application for parental responsibility or contact by the man seeking to establish paternity was unlikely to succeed; see also *Re JS (A Minor) (Declaration of Paternity)* [1981] 2 FLR 146). By contrast, in *Re T (A Minor) (Bood Tests)* [1992] 2 FCR 663, after separating from her husband the mother herself had raised doubts about the paternity of her child. She had initially opposed her husband's request for blood tests, but had withdrawn her objection by the time the appeal was heard. The Court of Appeal considered that it was in the interests of the child's long-term relationship with the parties that the tests be ordered. On the other hand, in *Hodgkiss v Hodgkiss* [1985] Fam Law 87, it was held in divorce proceedings that there was no power to order a test merely to satisfy the husband's curiosity since, the husband having conceded that the children were 'children of the family', paternity was not an issue in the proceedings (but see now the implications of the Child Support Act 1991, as a result of which it is generally *only* in respect of step-children and the like that maintenance may be sought from the courts).

7 THE CHILDREN ACT 1989 – INTRODUCTION

7.1 Parental responsibility

'Parental responsibility' is a key concept which, according to the Lord Chancellor, 'runs through the [CA 1989] like a golden thread, knotting together parental status and the effect of orders about a child's upbringing . . .' (Joseph Jackson Memorial Lecture (1989) 139 NLJ 505).

7.1.1 Meaning and nature of parental responsibility?

'Parental responsibility' means all the rights, duties, powers, responsibilities and authority which by law a parent of a child has in relation to the child and his property (CA 1989, s 3(1)). There exists no further statutory explanation of those rights, duties, etc. In addition to the right to physical possession of the child, the principal 'rights' include the right to determine the child's education and religious upbringing and to use moderate and reasonable corporal punishment to discipline the child; to consent or withhold consent to the issue of a passport to or emigration from the UK by the child; and to consent or withhold consent to the medical treatment of a child under 16 (but see *Gillick v West Norfolk and Wisbech Area Health Authority and Another* [1986] 1 FLR 224). (For a detailed examination of parental powers, see Bromley and Lowe, *Bromley's Family Law* 8th edn (1992) pp 301–312.)

In reality, none of the 'rights' mentioned above are absolute. First, the manner in which a parent chooses to exercise any one or more of them may be challenged in proceedings brought under the CA 1989 (or, in exceptional circumstances, in wardship proceedings) and, if found not to be in the child's best interests, may be controlled by a court order. Secondly, there is an increasing recognition that parental rights are not susceptible to an arbitrary 'cut-off point' by reference simply to a child's age. Lord Denning

MR recognised the practical realities of life with older children over 20 years ago when he observed that the notion of 'custody' 'starts with a right of control and ends with little more than the right to give advice' (*Hewer v Bryant* [1970] 1 QB 357, at 369).

This aspect of parental 'rights' was emphasised in the *Gillick* case, above, where it was stressed that parental 'rights' exist not for the benefit of the parent but for the benefit of the child, and that they exist only for so long as they are needed to enable the parent to perform his parental duties to protect and maintain the child and to secure the child's education up to the age of 16. The decision of the House of Lords in the *Gillick* case and, in particular, the opinions of Lord Fraser of Tullybelton and Lord Scarman are regarded as a significant milestone in the development of adolescents' rights, with implications going far beyond the limited question in dispute in those proceedings. However, the practical reality must surely be that the court is unlikely to accept a child's decision if the child is intent upon a course of action that the court considers harmful. As Lord Donaldson MR observed in *Re W (A Minor: Consent to Medical Treatment)* [1993] 1 FLR 1 at 12, 'good parenting involves giving minors as much rope as they can handle without an unacceptable risk that they will hang themselves'. Nevertheless, by rejecting the simplistic approach to parental rights, the *Gillick* approach leaves a considerable degree of uncertainty and it must be acknowledged that the precise relationship between parents' responsibilities and children's rights remains incapable of exact definition. (In *Gillick* itself it was held that the statutory provision in the FLRA 1969, s 8 (which enables a child over 16 to give a sufficient consent to medical treatment) does not exhaust the power of children to consent to medical treatment: an adolescent of sufficient maturity and understanding may give a sufficient consent even while under the age of 16. However, if such a child *refuses* treatment, it remains open to parents or the court to authorise it; see *Re R (A Minor) (Wardship: Medical Treatment)* [1992] 1 FLR 190; *Re E (A Minor) (Medical Treatment)* [1992] Fam Law 503; *Re W (A Minor: Consent to Medical Treatment)* above.)

The CA 1989 reflects the decision in *Gillick* insofar as

(i) it rejects the former statutory term 'parental rights' in favour of the term 'parental responsibility';

(ii) it recognises practical realities by providing that no order under the Act may be made in respect of a child over the age of 16 save in exceptional circumstances; and

(iii) it specifically contemplates the notion of the so-called 'Gillick-competent' child in a number of provisions, most notably those which enable a child to obtain leave to seek an order on his own behalf, and those which empower a child to refuse to submit to a medical or psychiatric examination directed by a court which has made an emergency protection order or a child assessment order in respect of the child.

7.1.2   Who has parental responsibility?

The Children Act 1989 provides that, in the case of married parents, each of them has parental responsibility for their child, and each may act alone and without the other in meeting that responsibility (save insofar as any statute requires the consent of more than one person in a matter affecting the child) (CA 1989, s 2(1)(7)). In the case of a child of unmarried parents, the mother alone has parental responsibility for the child unless the father acquires it in accordance with the Act. For that purpose, two means are provided, either of which may be used irrespective of whether the parents are cohabiting. These alternative methods are considered further below.

A person who has parental responsibility for a child may not surrender or transfer any part of that responsibility to another. However, a person who has parental responsibility may arrange for some or all of it to be met by one or more persons acting on his behalf (CA 1989, s 2(9)).

7.1.3   Acquisition of parental responsibility by unmarried fathers

Parental responsibility orders (PRO)

The CA 1989 preserves a right first conferred on the unmarried father by the FLRA 1987 to apply to the court for an order conferring on him parental responsibility for his child (CA 1989, s 4). The court cannot deprive the mother of her parental responsibility by an order under s 4, nor can it confer on the father anything less than *all* the parental rights and duties which parental responsibility represents.

In deciding whether to grant the order sought, the court must apply the principle that the child's welfare is the paramount consideration (see §7.3 below). Since the Act provides parents with a simple alternative means of conferring responsibility on the father where both parents are agreed that this should occur, it is likely that most applications for court orders under s 4 will be in cases where the mother resists the father's attempts to acquire parental responsibility, or where the mother is no longer involved in the child's life and the child is in the care of some person other than the father.

In *Re C (Minors) (Parental Rights)* [1992] 1 FLR 1, where the mother was opposed both to contact between her former cohabitant and their young children and to the making of a PRO in his favour, the father appealed against the refusal to make a PRO in his favour (but not, apparently, against the refusal of contact). Waite J set out the following test (at 8):

> 'was the association between the parties sufficiently enduring, and has the father by his conduct during and since the application shown sufficient commitment to the children, to justify giving the father a legal status equivalent to that which he would have enjoyed if the parties had been married, due attention being paid to the fact that a number of his parental rights would, if conferred on him by a PRO, be unenforceable under current conditions?'

In practice, where parents are living apart and the child is being cared for by the mother, the father's main concern is likely to be to secure generous arrangements for contact with the child. If there is some specific matter in dispute relating to the child's upbringing, the father will be able to seek a specific issue order resolving that dispute irrespective of whether he has parental responsibility. Nevertheless, parental responsibility has considerable symbolic significance for many unmarried fathers, and can have important practical consequences also, as noted in *Re H (Minors: Parental Responsibility)* (1992) *The Times*, September 7, where the Court of Appeal found that a judge who had refused to make a contact order in favour of the father had been plainly wrong in also refusing to make a PRO. In that case, the father had a genuine and loving relationship with his child, but contact was denied because of the attitude of the child's step-father, an unstable character who had threatened to leave the mother if contact were resumed. Applying the principles set out in *Re H*, above, the Court found that the father was entirely qualified to be granted a PRO and held that the matter of his parental responsibility ought not to be left 'in the air', there being a possibility that the step-father would apply to adopt the child (in which case the existence of a PRO would mean that the father's agreement to adoption would have to be given or dispensed with).

Where the child is being cared for by someone other than his parents, a PRO may have a more important role to play and will often be sought for tactical reasons. For example, as noted above, possession of parental responsibility has significance in relation to adoption proceedings. It also assumes importance where a local authority is providing a child with accommodation. These and other instances where a PRO affects a father's position are noted where relevant in Chapters 8 and 9 below.

Relationship with residence orders

If a residence order is made in favour of an unmarried father who does not already have parental responsibility, the court which makes the residence order *must* also make an order under the CA 1989, s 4 giving the father parental responsibility for the child (see further §8.2.1 below).

Parental responsibility agreements

The CA 1989, s 4 enables the father and mother of a child to make a 'parental responsibility agreement' providing for the father to have parental responsibility for the child and this agreement, if made in the prescribed form and lodged at the Principal Registry, will operate to confer parental responsibility on the father. The requirement of concurrence by both parents necessarily means that such agreements are most likely to be contemplated while the parents' relationship subsists or, perhaps, following the ending of their relationship in circumstances in which they remain on good terms, and are anxious to work together in the future for the sake of their child(ren). It is submitted that such agreements will be relatively uncommon: they will be made only where:

(i) the parents realise that the unmarried father does not automatically possess parental responsibility (as to which there is considerable public ignorance);

(ii) the father's lack of parental responsibility is perceived to be a problem (notwithstanding his *de facto* exercise of parental responsibility);

(iii) the parents become aware that a remedy exists to deal with the perceived problem, and

(iv) it is perceived to be a problem justifying the expenditure of time, effort and money in order to bring the legal position into conformity with the reality of their daily lives.

(In the first year of operation, some 2,500 agreements were filed. In the same period, well over 100,000 illegitimate children were born.)

Where parents are in harmony, a decision to enter into such an agreement is more likely to be based on a principle of parental equality than on any immediate practical considerations. However, there may arise some cases where the opportunity to make a parental responsibility agreement will be a particularly valuable option. For example, where the mother is diagnosed as being terminally ill, it may be important to cohabiting parents to establish the father's position during the mother's lifetime rather than by a guardianship appointment to take effect after her death.

7.1.4   Termination of parental responsibility orders and agreements

A parental responsibility order or agreement may be brought to an end only by an order of the court. Thus, while it is open to the parties to *confer* parental responsibility on the father by agreement, it is not open to them to *terminate* his responsibility by agreement or by any unilateral act of revocation.

As noted above, where a residence order is made in favour of an unmarried father who does not already have parental responsibility, the court must make a s 4 parental responsibility order in his favour. If the child's residence changes and some other person obtains a residence order in his favour, this does not automatically end the father's parental responsibility.

An application for the termination of a parental responsibility order or agreement may be made by any person who has parental responsibility for the child or, with leave of the court, by the child himself. The court may grant leave for an application by the child himself only if satisfied that the child has sufficient understanding to make the proposed application. In practice, most applications for termination are likely to be made on the breakdown of the parents' relationship, but it may be noted that parental responsibility is acquired by persons other than parents if a residence order is made in favour of the non-parent (see further §8.2.1 below). Thus, it will not necessarily be the child's mother who applies for the termination of the father's parental responsibility.

7.2 Orders – a summary

7.2.1 Section 8 orders

Section 8 orders (residence and contact orders, specific issue and prohibited steps orders) may be made in any 'family proceedings' in which a question arises with respect to the welfare of any child. A section 8 order may be made if application has been made for such an order or the court considers that the order should be made even though no such application has been made (CA 1989, s 10). The meaning and effect of each of these orders is considered in Chapter 8.

'Family proceedings' means (s 8(3)):

(a) proceedings under the inherent jurisdiction of the High Court in relation to children; and
(b) proceedings under a number of enactments (listed in s 8(4)) of which the following are likely to be of most relevance to unmarried parents and their children:
    (i) Parts I, II and IV of the CA 1989 (Part I relates to parental responsibility and guardianship, Part II to family proceedings and Part IV to care proceedings);
    (ii) the Domestic Violence and Matrimonial Proceedings Act 1976;
    (iii) the Adoption Act 1976.

7.2.2 Care and supervision orders

The court has no power of its own motion to commit a child to the care or supervision of a local authority. Care and supervision orders may be made only in response to an application by a local authority (or the NSPCC) under Part IV of the Act. In any family proceedings in which a question arises with respect to the welfare of any child, if it appears to the court that it may be appropriate for a care or supervision order to be made with respect to him, the court may direct the appropriate authority to undertake an investigation of the child's circumstances, and the local authority will then be obliged to consider (*inter alia*) whether it should seek a care or supervision order with respect to the child. If the local authority decides not to apply for a care or supervision order, it must report to the court its reasons for that decision and this information must be given to the court within eight weeks of the direction requiring the investigation (CA 1989, s 37).

The CA 1989, Part V enables local authorities to seek emergency protection orders and child assessment orders. These are orders intended to have effect for short periods to protect children from imminent harm, or to assess their need for protection. Proceedings under Part V of the CA are not within the definition of 'family proceedings'.

7.2.3   Family assistance orders

In any family proceedings where the court has power to make a s 8 order, if it is satisfied that the circumstances of the case are exceptional the court may make a 'family assistance order' requiring a probation officer or the local authority to 'advise, assist and (where appropriate) befriend' any person named in the order. The order may name any parent or guardian of the child, the child himself, and any person with whom the child is living or in whose favour a contact order is in force with respect to the child. A family assistance order may be made only with the consent of any person to be named, save that the consent of the child is not required. A family assistance order will have effect for six months, unless the court specifies a shorter period and may be made whether or not the court also makes a s 8 order (s 16).

7.2.4   Impact on wardship and the High Court's inherent jurisdiction

One of the objectives of the Act is to incorporate into the general law relating to children the flexibility (of both powers and procedure) which was formerly largely confined to the High Court's jurisdiction in wardship. In consequence of this increased flexibility and, in particular, the 'open door' policy with respect to the making of applications by non-parents, it is inevitable that the use of wardship will very substantially diminish in 'private law' cases. While it is still possible to envisage cases where wardship may be indicated, such cases will be most unusual. Accordingly, no further consideration is given in this book to the use of wardship in this context.

With respect to 'public law' cases, local authorities are prevented from using either wardship or the High Court's inherent jurisdiction as a means of obtaining care of a child, and their use of the inherent jurisdiction for other purposes is closely circumscribed (see s 100). Again, therefore, while there will clearly be some situations in which it will be appropriate for a local authority to apply for leave to seek the assistance of the High Court, such cases will be exceptional and, having no special bearing on the children of unmarried parents, are not considered further in this text.

7.3   The welfare principle

The CA 1989, s 1 provides that when a court determines any question with respect to:

(a) the upbringing of a child; or
(b) the administration of a child's property or the application of any income arising from it

the child's welfare shall be the court's paramount consideration.

The welfare principle is not applicable to applications for leave to apply for s 8 orders (*Re A and W (Minors) (Residence Order: Leave to Apply)* [1992] 2 FLR 154, and see §8.1.2 below). Nor is it applicable to applications for adoption orders, as to which the Adoption Act 1976, s 6 makes specific provision. Nor is it directly applicable to applications to oust a parent from the family home since, although the child's future will clearly be affected by the outcome, such proceedings are not proceedings in which the child's upbringing is directly in question (*Richards v Richards* [1984] FLR 11; and see also *Gibson v Austin* [1992] 2 FLR 437).

In essence, the CA 1989, s 1 has the effect of making the child's welfare the only relevant consideration. Weight should not be given to any factor unless it is shown to have some bearing on the child's interests. In certain circumstances, when seeking to determine how the child's welfare may best be served, the court is required to have regard to factors listed in a statutory checklist (s 1(3) and (4)). The checklist is considered further in Chapter 8.

7.4   Avoidance of delay

In any proceedings in which any question with respect to the upbringing of a child arises, the court shall have regard to the general principle that any delay in determining the question is likely to prejudice the welfare of the child (CA 1989, s 1(2)). Moreover, in all cases where any question of making a s 8 order arises it is the duty of the court to draw up a timetable with a view to determining the question without delay and to give whatever directions it considers appropriate with a view to ensuring that, so far as is reasonably practicable, the timetable is adhered to (CA 1989, s 11(1)). The same duty applies to proceedings relating to care and supervision orders (see s 32(1)).

Section 1(2) refers to a 'general principle' not an irrebuttable presumption, and cases may arise where a speedy final determination is not in the children's best interests, as in *S v S (Minors: Custody)* [1992] Fam Law 148 where, after a period of disturbance in the children's lives, the case called for a purely temporary order to allow time for the mother to demonstrate herself to be a stable parent, and to allow the children's wishes and feelings to be watched and tested in the altered surroundings (see also *Re A (A Minor) (Care Proceedings)* [1993] 1 FCR 164, 'planned and purposeful' delay can be beneficial).

7.5   Restrictions on the making of orders

7.5.1   Presumption of no order

An underlying theme of the CA 1989 is that, so far as possible, families should be left free from intrusive intervention in the form of court orders. The CA 1989 therefore adds to the welfare principle a requirement on any court which is considering making an order under the CA 1989 *not* to make any order unless the court considers that making the order will be better for the child than making no order at all (CA 1989, s 1(5)). This has become known as the 'no order presumption' and, again, it should be noted that it is only a presumption. Thus, for example, it would be wrong to say that a residence order should *never* be made in cases where the parents are agreed and are clearly able to co-operate with each other for the sake of their child: an order may be desirable to meet the child's need for stability and security. Moreover, the existence of an order can be of considerable assistance to a parent when dealing with outside agencies, such as local authority housing departments and education authorities (see *B v B (A Minor) (Residence Order)* [1992] 2 FLR 327).

7.5.2 Age of child

Unless the circumstances of the case are exceptional, a court may not make a residence order, a contact order, a specific issue order or a prohibited steps order (the s 8 orders) which would have effect for a period that would end after the child has reached the age of 16 (CA 1989, s 9(6)). Thus, normally, the court will not expect to make any such order in respect of a child who has already attained the age of 16. Where the child concerned is approaching 16 and there are no exceptional circumstances to justify continuance of the order after the child's sixteenth birthday, the practical utility of making the order for such period as remains is likely to be called into question.

7.6 Procedure

It is not within the scope of this book to offer a detailed guide to procedure under the Act, and the reader is referred to specialist publications. However, it may be observed that many of the disadvantages suffered by unmarried fathers under the former procedures have been removed by the Rules which now apply to Children Act proceedings (The Family Proceedings Court (Children Act 1989) Rules 1991, SI 1991/1395, as amended by SI 1992/2068; The Family Proceedings Rules 1991 Part IV, SI 1991/1247, as amended by SI 1991/2113; SI 1992/2067). In particular, the position of the unmarried father is improved in respect of participation in proceedings affecting his child. Space does not permit the relevant provisions to be set out here in full, but it may be noted that, in respect of *all* applications under the Act, the persons who are to be made respondents include every person whom the applicant believes to have parental responsibility for the child, and notice of the application must be given (*inter alia*) to any other person who is caring for the child at the time the proceedings are commenced. Moreover, in respect of applications for s 8 orders, notice is also required to be given (*inter alia*) to every person whom the applicant believes to be named in a court order with respect to the child which has not ceased to have effect (save that notice need not be given where the applicant believes that the court order is not relevant to the application), and to any person with whom the child has lived for at least three years prior to the application. In respect of applications for care orders, notice must also be given to any person whom the applicant believes to be a parent without parental responsibility for the child. The notice requirements are significant since the Rules further provide for applications to be joined as a party (FPC(CA 1989)R 1991, r 7; FPR 1991, r 4.7). It should therefore be possible for an unmarried father who is genuinely interested in his child's welfare and upbringing to participate fully in relevant proceedings.

7.7 Choice of court

'Free-standing' applications for s 8 orders may be made to the magistrates' (family proceedings) court; the county court, or the High Court. Provision is made for the transfer of cases between different levels of court where it is felt that they can be more appropriately dealt with at a level other than that at which they have been initiated, and for 'sideways' transfer (eg from one magistrates' court to another) (see Children (Allocation of Proceedings) Order 1991, SI 1991/1677). In the county court, all contested applications for s 8 orders must be dealt with by a court which is a 'family hearing centre' and where certain judges are 'nominated family judges' for the purpose of hearing such cases. Where an application for a s 8 order is made in existing family proceedings, the application should be made to the court where those proceedings are already in progress.

'Public law' proceedings (ie applications for care orders and related applications, such as for contact with a child in care) must normally be initiated in the family proceedings court. However, if a local authority decides to make an application for a care order as the result of an investigation directed by the court under s 37, the application must be made to the level of court which gave the direction. Where proceedings are commenced in the family proceedings court, complex rules govern the transfer of such proceedings to the county court and High Court (see Children (Allocation of Proceedings) Order 1991). If a case is transferred to the county court, it must be transferred to a county court which is a care centre to be dealt with by a 'nominated care judge'.

Family Courts Business and Services Committees monitor the operation of the Act in relation to each care centre. These committees are chaired by the 'designated family judge' for that centre, who has full jurisdiction in both 'public law' and 'private law' matters.

8 THE UPBRINGING OF CHILDREN

8.1 Introduction

8.1.1 Orders under the CA 1989, s 8

The orders available under the Children Act 1989 in connection with the upbringing of children by private individuals are defined by s 8 as follows:

Residence order: 'an order settling the arrangements to be made as to the person with whom a child is to live'.

Contact order: 'an order requiring the person with whom a child lives, or is to live, to allow the child to visit or stay with the person named in the order, or for that person and the child otherwise to have contact with each other'.

Specific issue order: 'an order giving directions for the purpose of determining a specific question which has arisen, or which may arise, in connection with any aspect of parental responsibility for a child'.

Prohibited steps order: 'an order that no step which could be taken by a parent in meeting his parental responsibility for a child, and which is of a kind specified in the order, shall be taken by any person without the consent of the court'.

8.1.2 Who may apply?

Entitlement to apply

Any parent or guardian of a child is entitled to seek any s 8 order with respect to the child (s 10(4)), and the Act does not draw any distinction for this purpose between married and unmarried parents, or between unmarried fathers who have parental responsibility and unmarried fathers who do not have parental responsibility. Various categories of non-parents are also entitled to apply for residence and contact orders, and these provisions are considered in detail below at §8.2.3 and §8.3.2. Any person (including the child concerned) may apply for any s 8 order if the court grants leave for that purpose.

Applications with leave

As noted at §7.2 above, it was the intention of the CA 1989 to incorporate in the general law relating to children much of the flexibility which was previously confined largely to the High Court's jurisdiction in wardship. Accordingly, provision is made for applications for s 8 orders to be made by *any* person, subject to the requirement that leave of the court be obtained (s 10(1) but see also s 9(3) which restricts the right of local authority foster-parents to apply for leave).

An application for leave must be in writing, setting out the reasons for seeking leave and providing a copy of the application for the making of which the leave is sought. It has been held that applications for leave to apply are not proceedings in which the child's welfare is the paramount consideration (*Re A and W (Minors) (Residence Order: Leave to Apply)* [1992] 2 FLR 154), and it is provided (by s 10(9)) that a court considering whether or not to grant leave must have particular regard to:

(a) the nature of the proposed application;
(b) the applicant's connection with the child;
(c) any risk there might be of that proposed application disrupting the child's life to such an extent that he would be harmed by it; and
(d) where the child is being looked after by a local authority, the local authority's plans for the child, and the wishes and feelings of the child's parents.

It may be noted that the phrasing of para (c) above encompasses not only the disruption of the child's life that might result if the substantive application was successful but also the disruption that might flow (eg in the form of family tensions and strain) from the granting of leave to make that application.

As noted above, it has been held that applications for leave to apply are not proceedings to which the welfare principle applies and, in relation to an application for leave by the foster-mother of a child in care, it was held that the court should approach the application on the basis that the authority's plans for the child's future were designed to safeguard and protect the child's welfare and that a departure from those plans might well disrupt the child's life to such an extent that he would be harmed by it (see *Re A and W (Minors) (Residence Order: Leave to Apply)*, above).

Child as applicant

The Act contemplates applications for s 8 orders by children themselves, but a child will require leave to make such an application and s 10(8) provides that where a child is applying for leave the court may grant leave only if it is satisfied that the child has sufficient understanding to make the proposed application. It has been said that an application by a child to bring proceedings under the Act should be made to the High Court or be transferred to the High Court as quickly as possible (see *Re AD (A Minor)*, noted at [1993] Fam Law 43).

Renewed applications

On disposing of any application for an order under the Act, the court may (whether or not it makes any other order) order that no application for an order under the Act of any specified kind may be made by the person in the order without leave of the court (s 91(14)). This power should be used sparingly, and only after hearing representations and, in *F v Kent CC* (1992) *The Times*, July 21, where justices had made such an order in conjunction with a consent order granting a father limited contact with his children in care, it was held to have been an improper exercise of their discretion, given that it was accepted that the father had not been vexatious, frivolous or unreasonable in making his application.

8.1.3 Availability of orders

It should be borne in mind that orders may be sought not only in proceedings commenced for that purpose under the Children Act, but also in other family proceedings which are already in progress. Thus, for example, an unmarried father whose child has been living with the mother and her husband may, if the mother's marriage ends in divorce, apply in those divorce proceedings for a residence order or contact order in his favour.

It should also be borne in mind that the court has the power to make a s 8 order in family proceedings even though no application for such an order has been made. This power may fail to be exercised in two distinct situations.

First, there may be cases where an application for an order has been made but where, as the full picture has emerged in the course of the hearing, it appears to the court that it would be better for the child to make an order in favour of some person other than (or in addition to) the applicant. Two examples will suffice, both presupposing applications by fathers who have work commitments involving frequent extended absences from home.

EXAMPLE 1: On the father's application for a residence order where the mother is unfit to care for the child, it may emerge that, while the child has been in the father's care for some time, in reality the care of the child is being undertaken almost entirely by the paternal grandmother, with whom the father lives when not working away from home. In such a case the court may consider it more appropriate to make a residence order in favour of the grandmother.

EXAMPLE 2: A father who is serving in the army applies for a contact order. He is shortly to be posted to Germany for two years. Despite some resistance from the child's mother, he has been having regular contact with the child, that contact taking place at the home and in the presence of the child's paternal grandparents. In view of the impending overseas posting, the court may make a contact order in his favour (which may provide for forms of contact other than visits in person (see §8.3.1 below)), but may also consider it appropriate to make a contact order ensuring the preservation of the child's attachment to the grandparents.

Secondly, in family proceedings where the child's upbringing is not directly in issue, it may appear to the court to be desirable to make a s 8 order despite the absence of any formal application. For example, contested ouster proceedings may result in an order requiring a father to leave the family home, but it may be apparent that, notwithstanding violence to the mother, the father poses no risk to the children and that it is not in their interests for the rupture of the father's relationship with the mother to place their own relationship with him in jeopardy. It may be helpful if the court considers and deals with the question of his contact with the children, not least because it may be necessary to attach some exemption to the terms of the ouster injunction to enable him to collect and return the children from the home or premises in its vicinity at the start and conclusion of the contact afforded to him.

8.2   Residence orders

8.2.1   Introduction

Save for a prohibition on the making of a residence order in favour of a local authority (see s 9(2)), there are no restrictions with respect to the person(s) in whose favour a residence order may be made. A residence order may be made in favour of more than one person (eg grandfather and grandmother in whose joint household the child is to live). Moreover, a residence order may be made in favour of two or more persons who do not themselves live together, in which case the order may specify the periods during which the child is to live in the different households concerned (s 11(4)). Thus, it is possible for the court to sanction 'shared care' arrangements under which a child's time is divided between two households, as where a child lives with one parent during school terms and with the other during school holidays, or with one parent during the week and with the other at weekends. It is generally considered important for the child to have the stability of a single settled home, and orders which enshrine 'shared care' arrangements are not viewed with enthusiasm: the court may take the view that the better form of order will be a residence order in favour of one parent with provision for extensive contact with the other parent (for an exceptional case resulting in an order endorsing 'shared care' arrangements, see *J v J (A Minor) (Joint Care and Control)* [1991] 2 FLR 385). Moreover, since 'shared care' arrangements are usually dependent upon an uncommonly high degree of cooperation between the adults involved, it may be expected that in most such cases the 'no order presumption' will militate against the making of an order (see further §7.5.1 above).

Effect of residence orders

The making of a residence order does not affect the existing parental responsibility of either parent but the fact that a person has parental responsibility for a child does not entitle him to act in any way which would be incompatible with the residence order (see s 2(8)).

Where a residence order is made in favour of an unmarried father who does not already possess parental responsibility, the court which makes the residence order must also make an order under s 4 conferring parental responsibility on him. That s 4 order then exists independently of the residence order, cannot be brought to an end while the residence order remains in force, and does not automatically terminate if the residence order ceases to have effect.

Where a residence order is made in favour of a non-parent, that person automatically has parental responsibility for the child for so long as the residence order remains in force, but that parental responsibility ceases if the residence order ceases to have effect (eg on the making of a further order providing for the child to live with some other person). It is specifically provided, however, that where a non-parent has parental responsibility by virtue of a residence order, (s)he shall not have the right to consent or refuse to consent to the making of an adoption order, or to the making of an application for an order freeing the child for adoption, nor will (s)he have the right to appoint a guardian for the child (s 12(3)).

While a residence order is in force with respect to a child, no person may cause the child to be known by a new surname or remove him from the United Kingdom without either the written consent of every person who has parental responsibility for the child or the leave of the court (s 13(1)), save that the person in whose favour the residence order was made may take the child out of the United Kingdom for a period of less than one month (s 13(2)). In cases where leave is required under s 13(1) for the child to be taken out of the United Kingdom (ie where the required consents are not forthcoming to his removal by some person other than the person with whom he lives, or to his removal by that person for a period in excess of one month) that leave may be given either generally (as where the residential parent anticipates annual foreign holidays lasting more than a month) or for specific purposes (as for a particular trip overseas with a non-residential parent to visit his family).

A residence order may be made subject to conditions (s 11(7)). The court may, for example, impose on a Jehovah's Witness a condition that (s)he shall not take the child(ren) out on house-to-house religious work, or a condition designed to ensure that such a parent does not deny the child necessary blood transfusions or other medical intervention.

Short-term orders

A residence order may be made *ex parte* in circumstances of urgency
(as where, at the end of a visit to the parent with whom they have
not been living, children are unilaterally retained by that parent)
(see *Re G (Minors)* (1992) *The Times*, October 9).

In any proceedings where the court has power to make a s 8 order
it may do so at any time during the course of the proceedings even
though it is not in a position finally to dispose of those proceedings.
The Act does not refer to orders made in such circumstances as
'interim' orders, but the interim nature of such an order may be made
clear by the exercise of the court's power (under s 11(7)) to stipulate
that the order shall have effect for a specified period (eg until the final
hearing; and see *S v S (Minors) (Custody)* [1992] Fam Law 148, the
facts of which are outlined at §7.4 above; see also *Re H (A Minor)
(Custody: Interim Care and Control* [1991] 2 FLR 109; a child's temporary needs may not be the same as her long-term needs; following
death of mother of child of divorced parents, child's interests best
served through period of bereavement by living with grandmother
rather than with father; order for child to live with grandmother for
three months; and *Re H (A Minor) (Interim Custody)* [1991] Fam Law
375: children neglected by mother retained by father after access;
father in cramped conditions, had criminal record and faced possibility of further prison sentence; order that children live with maternal
grandmother pending final hearing).

In some cases where the order is intended to be only of temporary
effect, the court may wish to exercise the power (noted above) to
attach conditions to the residence order. For example, in a case
where allegations of misconduct towards the child(ren) have been
made against a mother's new boyfriend but the mother alone has
satisfactory accommodation, the court may make a residence order
in favour of the mother but may direct that during the subsistence
of the order (ie pending the final hearing) the mother is not to
permit her boyfriend to enter her home or otherwise to come into
contact with the child(ren).

Transitional provisions

Transitional provisions exist to achieve consistency of consequences
between orders under the CA 1989 and orders made under the
former law. Thus, where a non-parent has custody/custodianship

or care and control of a child under an order made before 14 October 1991 or made after that date at the conclusion of proceedings which were pending on that date, that order remains in force, and that person has parental responsibility for the child so long as the order continues, but the parental responsibility of the child's parents is not suspended (as was formerly the case when a custodianship order was made) (Sch 14, para 7).

Where an unmarried father already had custody or care and control of his child under a court order made prior to 14 October 1991, or after that date but at the conclusion of proceedings which were pending on that date, an order under s 4 shall be deemed to have been made in his favour, and where such an order is deemed to have been made it cannot be brought to an end while the father retains care and control of the child by virtue of the original order (Sch 14, para 6).

Variation of the custody provisions in an existing order is to be made by the substitution of a residence order.

8.2.2   Residence orders as between unmarried parents

Residence not in dispute

Where unmarried parents have separated (or, indeed, have never lived together) and they are agreed that their child shall live with the mother, there is in principle no necessity for a residence order since the father lacks any parental power to remove the child from the mother's care.

Where the father possesses parental responsibility but agrees that the child shall live with the mother, any application for a residence order in the mother's favour may encounter difficulties arising from the 'no order presumption' (see §7.5.1 above). However, even where the father has signified his agreement to the child residing with the mother, the mother may feel in need of the security which an order can provide and it may be possible to persuade the court, in the circumstances of a particular case, that the mother's need for that sense of security is such that, if an order is not made in her favour, the lack of it may adversely affect her care of the child. The making of a residence order in her favour may also reduce the attractions to her of an application to terminate the father's parental responsibility since, once a residence order is in force in her favour, the father will not be entitled to exercise his parental responsibility in any way which would be incompatible with that order (s 2(8)).

Where unmarried parents are agreed that their child(ren) shall live with the father, it will be desirable for the father to acquire parental responsibility, if he does not already have it. Although s 3(5) provides that a person who does not have parental responsibility for a child but has care of the child may do what is reasonable in all the circumstances of the case for the purpose of safeguarding or promoting the child's welfare, it will be preferable for there to be some formal recognition of the father's position. It may, however, suffice if he acquires parental responsibility by an agreement under s 4, rather than by reference to the making of a residence order in his favour (but it should always be borne in mind that a residence order may be of assistance in a parent's dealings with third parties; see §7.5.1 above).

Residence in dispute

Where there is a dispute between parents with respect to the day-to-day care of their child and the father seeks a residence order, if his application is unsuccessful and the court considers that the child should reside with the mother, the father's application for a residence order will obviously be dismissed but, for the reasons given above, it will be strictly unnecessary to make a residence order in the mother's favour unless the father already possesses parental responsibility. Normally, however, the fact that there have been contested proceedings will provide sufficient justification for the making of an order. Indeed, in some cases, it will be appropriate to make a prohibited steps order to ensure that the father does not seek to remove the child from the mother's care.

The application of the statutory checklist to contested applications for residence orders is considered at §8.2.4 below.

Effect of subsequent cohabitation

Where a residence order has been made as the result of which the child lives with one of two parents who each have parental responsibility for him, the residence order will cease to have effect if the parents live together for a continuous period of more than six months. However, if the residence order was made in favour of the child's father, the automatic lapse of the residence order will not deprive him of his parental responsibility even if the s 4 parental responsibility order was made only in consequence of the making of the residence order.

8.2.3   Residence orders in favour of non-parents

Entitlement to apply

The patchwork quilt of statutory procedures which comprised the former system of child law enabled some orders to be sought by non-parents who satisfied certain qualifying conditions. Broadly, the CA 1989 framework accommodates all those categories of persons by entitling them to apply for all or some of the s 8 orders. Thus, in addition to the right which each parent or guardian has to apply for a residence order, such an order may also be sought by:

(a)   any party to a marriage (whether or not subsisting) in relation to whom the child is a child of the family;

(b)   any person with whom the child has lived for a period of at least three years (for which purpose the three-year period need not be continuous and need not immediately precede the hearing, provided that it did not begin more than five years before and did not end more than three months before the making of the application).

(c)   any person who has the consent of each person in whose favour a residence order is in force;

(d)   any person who has the consent of the local authority in the case of a child who is in the care of a local authority;

(e)   in any other case, any person who has the consent of each person who has parental responsibility for the child (s 10(4)(5)).

Applications with leave

As noted above (at §8.1.2), any person may apply for a residence order if granted leave to make the application, and the child concerned may seek leave to make an application for a residence order in respect of himself.

It is likely that the majority of applications by non-parents (whether made as of right or with leave) will be made by other relatives of the child. For example, it seems that cases where the qualifying condition relied on is that the child has lived with the applicant for at least three years are particularly likely to involve grandparents (for whom the Act makes no special provision). However, the same provision may be relied on, for example, by private foster-parents who have been caring for a child under informal arrangements with the child's parent(s).

8.2.4   The statutory checklist

In determining with whom a child is to live the court must apply the principle that the child's welfare is the paramount consideration. However, in cases which involve more than one child, it may not always be possible to accord paramountcy to the welfare of *each* child. For example, in *Clarke-Hunt v Newcombe* (1982) FLR 482 the court felt unable to separate two brothers and, since the younger boy's interests required that he live with his mother, the older boy was also placed in her care even though this was against his wishes and possibly slightly detrimental to his interests. All too often, 'nobody but a lunatic would think there was an ideal answer' (*Re DW* [1984] Fam Law 17, per Cumming-Bruce LJ at 18).

In ascertaining how best to safeguard and promote the child's welfare when an application for a residence order is contested, the court is required to have regard *in particular* to the matters listed in the s 1(3) statutory checklist (see s 1(4)). The checklist is thus not intended to be an exhaustive list of the relevant factors, but any factor not contemplated by the checklist can be taken into account only if and to the extent that it has a direct bearing on the child's welfare.

The application of the checklist is not to be conducted in a mechanical manner: it remains important to recall Megarry J's comment in *Re F (An Infant)* [1969] 2 Ch 238 that the exercise on which the court must embark cannot be conducted on the basis of some kind of 'points system' and that the weight to be attached to particular factors must ultimately be a matter for the exercise of judicial discretion on the facts of each individual case.

There is nothing in the content of the statutory checklist which is inconsistent with the manner in which disputes over custody were argued and determined under the former law. Accordingly, the matters listed in the checklist are considered individually below with reference to the body of case-law which had evolved prior to the CA 1989:

(a) *The ascertainable wishes and feelings of the child concerned (considered in the light of his age and understanding)*

It is possible to discern in cases decided before the Children Act 1989 strong reservations about attaching great weight to the wishes of children. In *Re S (Infants)* [1967] 1 WLR 396, the wishes of a 13-year-old boy for which he gave 'perfectly sensible reasons' were respected by not compelling him to leave England to live with his mother and attend school in California, but Cross J observed (at 408):

'In many cases it is unfortunately plain that [the child's wishes] are reflections of the wishes of one of the parents which have been assiduously instilled into the [child] and are not anything which could be called an independent exercise of his own will. Sometimes again the [child's] wishes, although genuinely his own, are so plainly contrary to his long-term interest that the court may feel justified in disregarding them.'

(See also *Re C (Minors)* (1978) Fam Law 202: 'slim' evidence of wishes of boy aged 12, wishes not respected: it is 'a situation not infrequently met with . . . when children will express a wish often for the most unreliable or even fickle motives'; *Cossey v Cossey* (1981) Fam Law 56: children aged eight are 'apt to express their views upon no truly reasonable grounds'; *Guery v Guery* (1982) Fam Law 184: dangerous to place decisive weight on wishes of children aged 12 since at that age children were extremely suggestive and reluctant to upset their parents; *Doncheff v Doncheff* (1978) Fam Law 205: girls aged 15 and 14 wished to live with father which would have involved separation from younger brother, their wish to be with their father found to be 'not a very strong wish' and very much influenced by their father, and held not sufficient to outweigh the undesirability of the separation from their brother; and see *Re DW* [1984] Fam Law 17: wishes of 'mature' boy aged ten over-ridden).

However, as Butler-Sloss LJ observed very shortly before the CA 1989 came into force, the courts have over recent years become increasingly aware of the importance of listening to the views of older children:

'not necessarily . . . doing what they want, but paying proper respect to older children who are of an age and the maturity to make their minds up as to what they think is best for them, bearing in mind that older children very often have an appreciation of their own situation which is worthy of consideration . . .' (*Re P (A Minor) (Education)* [1992] 1 FLR 316 at 321: school preference of 14-year-old of decisive weight, observations (at 322) as to detrimental effect on child of possible feelings of resentment if his views were not respected; and see *M v M (Transfer of Custody: Appeal)* [1987] 2 FLR 146).

In *Re P*, Butler-Sloss LJ referred to the court's statutory duty under the CA 1989 'to pay close attention to the wishes and views of children of an age and maturity which may give valuable help to the courts' and, in *M v M* (1992) *The Independent*, August 12, the Court of Appeal set aside the decision of a county court judge who had done no more than pay lip service to the views of two 'intelligent and articulate' children aged 10 and 11 who were of an age when considerable weight should be given to their wishes; the judge had been aware of the need to take account of their views under the CA 1989, s 1, but had not in reality done so and had been plainly wrong in allowing their mother to remove them to Israel when they wished to remain in this country with increased contact with their father (but see also *Re P (Minors) (Wardship)* (1992) *The Times*, May 11: court should have regard to but not be restricted by children's wishes if they diverged from the child's future welfare).

Although it is clearly not without symbolic significance, the fact that the child's wishes are the first-mentioned factor in the checklist does not give them priority over other items: in any given case other factor(s) may have an importance sufficient to outweigh the child's own wishes. In particular, a desire to keep siblings together or to reunite siblings may cause a child's wishes to be overridden. This was the dominant consideration in *Cossey v Cossey*, above; *Doncheff v Doncheff*, above; and *Clarke-Hunt v Newcombe*, above; and see also *Re DW*, above).

(b) *The child's physical, emotional and educational needs*

A dispute with respect to a child's residence cannot be decided merely by reference to the standard of living enjoyed by each claimant: in any given case the inadequacy of the accommodation or resources available to one of the parties may be conclusive but mere disparity in the level of material comforts offered by each home does not by itself determine how the child's interests can best be served and will normally be of little weight unless all other factors leave the case finely balanced (*Stephenson v Stephenson* [1985] FLR 1140).

In general, greater importance is attached to protecting and promoting the child's *overall* well-being, both physical and emotional. A child's emotional needs may well encompass the need to buttress and preserve attachments within the family, and the desirability of keeping young siblings together has been described as a proposition which really does not call for legal authority to establish it (*C v C (Minors: Custody)* [1988] 2 FLR 291, per Purchas LJ at 295; and see *Cossey v Cossey* above; *Doncheff v Doncheff*, above; *Adams v Adams* [1984] FLR 768; *Guery v Guery* (1982) Fam Law 184). On the other hand, in any given case it may be possible to show that the comfort, security, and emotional support which children can derive from being brought up together will not be a significant factor in the life of the particular children concerned. For instance, in *B v B (Minors) (Custody, Care and Control)* [1991] 1 FLR 402, two children aged ten and nine had chosen to live with their father and the dispute concerned only the parties' two-year-old child. The court had the benefit of expert evidence on the likely impact of separation of the siblings and held that, having regard to the age gap between the two older children and the younger child, the importance of bringing up siblings together was not such as to override a preference for the mother's care in circumstances where the father's work commitments would oblige him to leave the youngest child with a child-minder during the day (and see *B v T (Custody)* [1989] 2 FLR 31: case remitted for rehearing where justices had failed to consider possibility of children being divided between the two parents; see also *Re B (Minors) (Custody)* [1991] 1 FLR 137 where four siblings would be split in any event and the issue was whether the second child (a girl strongly attached to both parents) should be reunited in the mother's home with her younger brothers to whom she was 'devoted' or should remain with her father and older brother).

Educational needs may be of particular significance where a change of residence would also entail a change of school, and this aspect of educational needs would therefore form part of the court's consideration of item (c) below. In *May v May* [1986] 1 FLR 325, the greater emphasis placed by the father on academic attainment appears to have been influential in the court's decision that the child should live with him rather than with the mother.

Having identified the child's physical, emotional and educational needs in accordance with this item, the court is required (by (f) below) to consider the capacity of each parent to meet those needs. There may be a difference between a child's short-term and long-term needs and, if necessary, a short-term order may be made to accommodate this consideration (see *Re H (A Minor) (Custody: Interim Care and Control)*, noted at §8.2.1 above).

(c) *The likely effect on the child of any change in his circumstances*

Continuity of care has been described as one of the most important single factors in deciding what is in the best interests of young children (*S(BD) v S(DJ) (Children: Care and Control)* [1977] Fam 109; *Dicocco v Milne* (1983) FLR 247) and this consideration has given rise to the so-called 'status quo' argument. The more satisfactory the status quo, the stronger the argument for not interfering (*S v W* (1981) Fam Law 81; *Re C (Minors)* (1978) Fam Law 202; *Stephenson v Stephenson* above; but see *Greer v Greer* (1974) Fam Law 187). On the other hand, even if the transfer of a child from one parent's care to the other parent's care might entail risks, the court should not hesitate to take risks if the paramount consideration of the child's interests points to that course of action (*W v P (Justices' Reasons)* [1988] 1 FLR 508; and see *Faulkner v Faulkner* (1981) FLR 115).

An argument based on the desirability of maintaining the status quo depends on establishing that a sufficient status quo in fact exists. In *Bowley v Bowley* [1984] FLR 791, for instance, an argument based on a status quo of two months was described as 'almost vanishingly thin' (see also *Re W (A Minor) (Residence Order)* [1992] Fam Law 493: three weeks in life of four-week-old child). In *Re DW*, above, in a contest between a mother and a step-mother, the status quo argument was held not to benefit a step-mother who had cared for the child for eight and a half years, since for most of that period she and the child's father had been together: the breakdown of their marriage created a new situation altogether.

Moreover, the status quo argument will lose much of its force where there has been regular and successful contact with the other parent, as in *Re K (A Minor) (Custody)* [1990] 2 FLR 64 and *Allington v Allington* [1985] FLR 586. In *Allington*, a girl aged 18 months had been left with her father but during the ten weeks following the parents' separation her care was effectively shared by both parents and the bond with her mother was unimpaired. Cumming-Bruce LJ observed (at 593) that there was not really any status quo at all to justify depriving the child of the mother's care 'which, at this age, *prima facie*, she needs'. (The decision in this case was also based in part on the consideration that, if the father continued to have custody for the time being, arguments for maintaining the status quo *would* come into play so as to render a later transfer of custody traumatic, fraught with long-term dangers and possibly even altogether impracticable.)

In general, the court will not be well-disposed towards a parent who seeks to rely upon a state of affairs wrongfully achieved, for example, by failing to return the child after a visit, but there is no principle requiring the child's *automatic* return: the child's welfare must be the paramount consideration (*In Re J (A Minor) (Interim Custody: Appeal)* [1989] 2 FLR 304).

(d) *The child's age, sex, background, and any characteristics of his which the court considers relevant*

It has been described as 'natural' for young children to be with mothers (*Re S (A Minor) (Custody)* [1991] 2 FLR 388 at 390; and see *M v M (Custody of Children)* (1983) FLR 603). This theme runs through many of the decided cases (eg *H v H* [1984] Fam Law 112; *M v M* (1980) FLR 77; *J v J* (1979) Fam Law 91; *Re W (A Minor) (Custody)* (1982) FLR 492; *Re W (A Minor) (Residence Order)* [1992] 2 FLR 332). According to Butler-Sloss LJ in *Re A (A Minor: Custody)* [1991] 2 FLR 394 at 400:

'In cases where the child has remained throughout with the mother and is young, particularly with a baby or a toddler, the unbroken relationship of the mother and child is one which it would be very difficult to displace unless the mother was unsuitable to care for the child. But where the mother and child have separated, and the mother seeks the return of the child, other considerations apply, and there is no starting-point that the mother should be preferred to the father and only displaced by a preponderance of evidence to the contrary' (see also *Re S (A Minor) (Custody)*, above, per Butler-Sloss LJ at 390; but see also *Re W (A Minor) (Residence Order)*, above: parents had agreed before the birth that father would care for the child, mother changed her mind and wanted to breastfeed; held there is a rebuttable presumption of fact that a baby's best interests are served by being with mother).

In practice, contested cases which result in an order in favour of the father of young children are frequently cases where the status quo argument operates strongly in the father's favour (eg *B v B (Custody of Children)* [1985] FLR 166; *B v B (Custody of Child)* [1985] FLR 462).

In *Re S* above (at 390), Butler-Sloss LJ referred also to the relevance of the child's sex:

'It used to be thought many years ago that young children should be with mother, that girls approaching puberty should be with mother and that boys over a certain age should be with father. Such presumptions, if they ever were such, do not, in my view, exist today.'

A child's background can include his religious upbringing and where a change of carer would result in a change in that aspect of the child's life it will be relevant to consider any emotional disturbance which may result. In some cases, the restrictions imposed by strict religious observance may have a decisive part to play where one parent but not the other adheres to the religion or sect concerned (see eg *Hewison v Hewison* (1977) Fam Law 207: Exclusive Brethren; and see *Re B and G (Minors) (Custody)* [1985] FLR 493: scientology) but in many cases any difficulties arising from matters of religion may be adequately dealt with by conditions attached to the residence order (see §8.2.1 above).

(e) *Any harm which the child has suffered or is at risk of suffering*

The word 'harm' in this provision has the same broad meaning accorded to it by s 31(9) (see s 105(1)). Thus, while it includes actual physical harm (see, eg *Hutchinson v Hutchinson* (1981) FLR 167, where the mother's new husband was considered to be a possible danger to the child), it also encompasses, for instance, impairment of the child's emotional or social development (and see, eg *M v M (Transfer of Custody: Appeal)* [1987] 2 FLR 146: relevance of harm likely to result from overriding child's strongly held wishes).

A problem that continues to trouble the court is the extent to which a mother's lesbianism is to be regarded as posing a risk to a child living with her. In *B v B (Minors) (Custody, Care and Control)*

[1991] 1 FLR 402, the court had the benefit of expert evidence from an eminent child psychiatrist concerning the impact of the mother's lesbianism on the child's sexual identity and the possibility of stigmatisation by the child's peers. His view was that there was no evidence to support fears of psycho-sexual development being distorted if a child was reared in a lesbian household, or fears that the child would be subjected unduly to taunts and teasing or be ostracised. In the psychiatrist's view, the dangers to a child of living in a lesbian household tended to be overestimated. In the light of that evidence, and despite concern expressed by the welfare officer with respect to the mother's lesbianism, the judge awarded care and control of the parties' two-year-old son to the mother, stressing the importance of distinguishing between lesbians who, like the mother, were private persons who did not believe in advertising their lesbianism, and militant lesbians who tried to convert others to their way of life. The case demonstrates the potentially decisive contribution that may be made by expert evidence (and compare *C v C (A Minor) (Custody: Appeal)* [1991] 1 FLR 223), and in this connection it may be noted that in *Re R (A Minor) (Experts' Evidence) (Note)* [1991] 1 FLR 291 judicial guidance was given on preparing for a hearing involving expert evidence, and on the approach which experts should adopt.

(f) *How capable each of the child's parents, and any other person in relation to whom the court considers the question to be relevant, is of meeting his needs*

Reference has already been made to the court's duty to identify the child's various needs (para (b)), and to the relevance of the child's age and sex when considering parental capacity to meet those needs (para (d)). Where no question of parental unfitness arises much may depend on the court's assessment of the character and personalities of the individuals involved or likely to be involved in the day-to-day care of the child. The child's relationship with a parent's new partner can be a very significant factor.

Where a parent's work commitments do not enable that parent to care for the child without the assistance of others, the nature and extent of the child-minding arrangements will be of considerable importance, and the court is likely to prefer full-time care by one person to arrangements which depend on the contributions of a number of different persons, however worthy (*Re K (Minors) (Chil-*

dren: Care and Control) [1977] Fam 179; *Dicocco v Milne* (1983) FLR 247; *S(BD) v S(DJ) (Children: Care and Control)* [1977] Fam 109). This is likely to present particular difficulties for working fathers, especially if the child-minding arrangements are dependent on the goodwill of other members of his family, for the court will be concerned as to the reliability and durability of such assistance.

The definition of 'contact order' in the Act gives a clear endorsement of the view already taken by the courts that contact (access) with a non-residential parent is a right of the child and not a right of that parent (see *M v M (Child: Access)* [1973] 2 All ER 81), and contact with a non-residential parent is regarded as of very real importance to the child's emotional health (*M v M* above; *Re B (A Minor) (Access)* [1984] FLR 648; and see further §8.3 below). Accordingly, there may be cases in which one parent's greater willingness to facilitate contact with the other parent will influence the court's decision as to the parent with whom the child is to live (but see *M v M* (1980) FLR 77).

Non-parents: Where a dispute concerning the child's residence is between a parent and a non-parent, the question will arise as to the weight to be attached to the 'blood tie' between parent and child. This matter was considered in *Re K (A Minor) (Custody)* [1990] 2 FLR 64. In that case, the natural father of a boy aged four and a half years sought to recover the child from the aunt and uncle who had cared for him for 12 months following the suicide of the child's mother. Prior to the mother's death, she and the father had cohabited during most of the child's life, albeit that the relationship was a stormy one owing to the mother's mental illness. At first instance, the judge had carried out a careful and detailed assessment of the merits of the two competing households in terms of the standard of care which each could provide, and balancing the consideration of 'normal family life in an exceptionally good home' with the aunt and uncle against the fostering of the natural relationship which exists between a father and son. The Court of Appeal concluded that, in so doing, the judge had embarked upon an exercise 'misconceived in law'. The father was clearly in a position to provide the boy with adequate housing and care. In those circumstances, comparisons with the care offered by the aunt and uncle were not in point; the question should be: 'Are there any compelling factors which require me to override the *prima facie* right of this child to an upbringing by its surviving natural parent?' and, on the facts of that case, 'a risk of physical or emotional damage to the child of a very high order would have been necessary to dislodge the primary claim upon [the boy's] welfare of an upbringing by his father' (per Waite J at 70; and see *Re K (A Minor) (Wardship: Adoption)* [1991] 1 FLR 57; see also *Re DW (A Minor) (Custody)* [1984] Fam Law 17).

It is arguable whether the Court's strictures with respect to the judge's conduct of the balancing exercise could be legitimately repeated if a similar case were to arise under the CA 1989, given the obligation of the court to give specific consideration to the matters in the checklist. In any event, *Re H (A Minor) (Custody: Interim Care and Control)* [1991] 2 FLR 109 indicates that *Re K* (1990) should not be taken too far or applied too rigidly. However, the question still arises as to the extent to which the court's consideration of each party's capacity to meet the child's needs is to be weighted in favour of the natural parent simply by virtue of his relationship to the child. In the seminal case of *J v C* [1970] AC 668, Lord MacDermott observed that parental care 'can be capable of ministering to the total welfare of the child in a special way, and must therefore preponderate in many cases' and, as Lord Donaldson MR explained in *Re H*, above (at 113):

'. . . all that *Re K* is saying, as I understand it, is that of course there is a strong supposition that, other things being equal, it is in the interests of the child that it shall remain with its natural parents. But that has to give way to particular needs in particular situations.'

(g) *The range of powers available to the court under the CA 1989 in the proceedings in question*

This consideration is most likely to be significant when the court is hearing an application for a care order (see further Chapter 9). However, it is possible to envisage cases exclusively involving private individuals in which the court may consider it appropriate to go beyond the application(s) formally before the court (see the examples given at §8.1.3 above).

Removal from the jurisdiction

Where parents in dispute as to their child's residence themselves reside (or intend to reside) in different countries, the comparative advantages to the child of living in each of the countries concerned will form part of the court's consideration of the statutory checklist (see, eg *Guery v Guery* (1982) Fam Law 184). However, where there is no dispute that the child is to live with a particular parent and that parent wishes to remove the child from the jurisdiction indefinitely or for an extended period, leave of the court will be required. The child's welfare is the paramount consideration but, in the ordinary run of cases, the court will be slow to refuse leave and will do so only where the interests of the child and those of the parent caring for him are clearly incompatible (see *Poel v Poel* [1970] 1 WLR 1469). This was found to be the case in *Re K (A Minor) (Removal from Jurisdiction)* [1992] 2 FLR 98, where an American mother wished to return with the child to live in the United States. Leave was refused, first and foremost because the continuation and development of the relationship between father and child (a girl, then aged four) was of very great importance, and a proposal reducing that contact to something like annual visits would be an extremely retrograde step. Secondly, the mother's proposals for her own future were essentially unrealistic, with no sensible plan for achieving any ultimate goal by reasonable stages (but note also the observation that, generally, 'it is a very strong thing for this court to make an order which will prevent the following of a chosen career by the person who has custody': *Nash v Nash* [1973] 2 All ER 704, per Davies LJ at 706; and see *Re F (A Ward) (Leave to Remove Ward out of the Jurisdiction)* [1988] 2 FLR 116; *Lonslow v Hennig (formerly Lonslow)* [1986] 2 FLR 378).

In *Re K*, the court was conscious that the refusal of leave would do nothing to alleviate the mother's depression, disenchantment and sense of isolation in this country, but considered that she had an underlying resilience that would enable her to cope with the decision of the court so that the decision would not have an adverse effect on her care of the child (see also *Tyler v Tyler* [1989] 2 FLR 158; *M v M (Minors) (Removal from Jurisdiction)* [1992] Fam Law 291).

Irrelevant considerations

It will be noted from the above account that the checklist itself does not easily accommodate allegations of misconduct by adult parties *in relation to each other*, it having been established many years ago that decisions concerning the care of children cannot be used as a means of punishing a parent for misconduct or rewarding a parent who is 'unimpeachable' if the child's interests require some other order (see generally *J v C*, above; *S(BD) v S(DJ)* [1977] Fam 109). Accordingly, it must be stressed that such allegations of misconduct will be relevant to the decision which the court has to make only if and to the extent that a parent's alleged misconduct suggests the likelihood of deficiencies in the care which the parent will bestow on the child. To take a simple example, a mother who has a succession of brief affairs with lovers who are never brought into contact with the child and whom the parent sees only while the child is at school or similarly absent from the home will be in a different category to a mother who entertains successive lovers in the home while the child is present or whose lovers constitute such an irresistible attraction to her that the child is frequently left in the home alone or with young, inexperienced or otherwise inappropriate babysitters.

Unless the allegations can be shown to have some direct bearing on parental capacity and fitness, attempts to use residence proceedings as a means of ventilating a long history of adult grievances are likely to receive short shrift from the court.

8.3   Contact orders

8.3.1   Introduction

The definition of a contact order is set out at the start of this chapter. That definition is so phrased as to reinforce the view already expressed in cases decided under the former law that contact between the child and a non-residential parent (or other relevant person) is a right of the child, and not a right of the parent or other person concerned (see, eg *M v M (Child: Access)* [1973] 2 All ER 81). The child's welfare is, of course, the paramount consideration, and in contested cases the court will be required to give specific consideration to the statutory checklist.

The definition also makes it clear that, although the most common form of contact will be contact in person, the court may where appropriate make an order providing for other forms of contact, of which the most obvious possibilities will be the exchange of letters, cards and gifts and which could, for instance, envisage 'video letters' and contact by telephone calls.

There are no restrictions with respect to the persons in whose favour a contact order may be made. However, no contact order may be made under s 8 in respect of a child who is in the care of a local authority (s 9(9)). The making of a contact order does not operate to confer parental responsibility on the person in whose favour the order is made. However, any person who lacks parental responsibility for a child but in whose care the child is at any given time (eg as the result of a contact order) may do what is reasonable in all the circumstances of the case for the purpose of safeguarding or promoting the child's welfare. Thus, for example, if the child suffers accidental injuries during a contact visit, consent may be given for the administration of an anti-tetanus injection if such an injection is advised.

Before making a contact order the court will need to be satisfied that making the order will be better for the child than making no order at all. Where contact has been taking place without apparent difficulty, the court is likely to resist the request that an order be made. In any event, the court will prefer, wherever possible, to make an order simply for 'reasonable contact', so as to permit flexibility by leaving the details to be agreed between the parties. Where necessary, however, the court can spell out with considerable precision the contact arrangements that are to apply. In particular, where the court's decision will result in a resumption of contact after a lengthy interval the court may lay down a detailed timetable under which contact begins at a very modest level and gradually builds up over a period of time, to allow for the re-establishment of familiarity, trust and confidence.

The court may also consider it necessary in some cases to exercise its power (under s 11(7)) to impose conditions which must be complied with in connection with the contact order. For example, it may impose a condition that a parent in whose favour the contact order is made shall not bring the child into contact with his or her new partner. It may also be appropriate in some cases for a contact order to contain restrictions (or, indeed, impose obligations) with respect to the activities in which the child is to be involved during contact visits or the premises to which the child may be taken, and this power could, for instance, be exercised to regulate religious observance.

If it is not necessary for a child's residence to be regulated by a court order, a contact order may be the only order made with respect to the child.

Where a contact order requires the parent with whom a child lives to allow contact between the child and his other parent, that order will cease to have effect if the parents live together for a continuous period of more than six months (s 11(6)).

8.3.2   Who may apply?

In addition to each parent of the child, entitlement to apply for contact orders is also extended to all those who have the right to seek residence orders, and the categories of persons so eligible are set out at §8.2.3 above. Persons not falling within any of those categories require leave to make an application for a contact order, as will a child seeking an order in respect of him/herself. The matter of obtaining leave is considered at §8.1.2 above. Provision is also made for applications for contact orders by any persons who have access to children under orders which were made prior to 14 October 1991 or at the conclusion of proceedings which were pending on that date (see Sch 14, para 9).

Although the Act contemplates applications by non-parents, it may be anticipated that the court will be reluctant to make orders where this would involve any substantial interference with the freedom of a residential parent to lead his or her own life with the child. In particular, for instance, where a child is living with the mother and contact arrangements already exist in favour of the father the court may expect arrangements to be made between the father and his relatives so that the child's links with them are maintained in the course of the father's own opportunities for contact rather than by imposing further constraints on the mother. On the other hand, where a father is showing no continuing interest in his child it may be possible to obtain a contact order in favour of (for example) the paternal grandparents, if the court is satisfied that they have a valuable contribution to make to the child's life.

Much more problematical is the situation that sometimes arises where parents are united in their view that certain other relatives should be excluded from contact with the child. It is submitted that in these circumstances the court is unlikely to make a contact order (or grant leave to apply for such an order) unless there is compelling evidence as to the benefits that will accrue to the child if the parental wishes are overridden.

8.3.3   The statutory checklist

The matters listed in the checklist have already been considered individually (at §8.2.4 above) in relation to disputes concerning a child's residence. Where there is dispute over contact, the considerations particularly likely to be influential are the child's wishes (para (a)), any harm he has suffered or is at risk of suffering (para (e)), the child's needs (para (b)), and each parent's (and any other relevant person's) capacity to meet those needs (para (f)). Those matters are considered here with specific reference to disputes over contact as between the child's parents.

Child's needs and parental capacity to meet them

As already noted, contact with a non-residential parent is regarded as a right of the child, and not as a right of the parent (*M v M (Child: Access)* [1973] 2 All ER 81). Such contact is normally regarded as being of very real importance to the child's emotional health and long-term best interests (see *Re B (A Minor) (Access)* [1984] FLR 648). This principle is equally applicable to children of unmarried parents (*S v O (Illegitimate Child: Access)* [1982] FLR 15), and where the parents have lived together for some time after the birth so that a bond exists between father and child contact should be refused only if and because it has been shown that the enforcement of contact would have adverse effects on the child. The court should be slow to reach the conclusion that this will be the case, bearing in mind Latey J's observation (in *M v M*, above, at 88) that:

'where the parents have separated and one has care of the child, access by the other often results in some upset in the child. These upsets are usually minor and superficial. They are heavily outweighed by the long term advantages to the child of keeping in touch with the parent concerned.'

This passage was cited with approval in *Re H (Minors: Access)* [1992] 1 FLR 148, where the court's order provided for a resumption of contact after a three-year interval, pending a welfare officer's report (but see also *M v J (Illegitimate Child, Access)* (1982) FLR 19: father had a drink problem and had attempted suicide; contact refused; and see also *Re F (A Minor) (Access)* [1992] Fam Law 484: future would hold only distress and disruption if contact were granted).

Contact with a child of unmarried parents may be granted where there has been little or no cohabitation subsequent to the child's birth (as in *S v O*, above: no cohabitation but father had shown an interest in and paid maintenance for the child; child had no father-figure and father's desire to get to know his son and do all he could for him was of benefit to the child).

On the other hand, where there is no existing attachment, a father seeking to establish a relationship with the child may find that, in the court's view, the needs of the child are already adequately met and that the introduction of a new adult in his life would not be in his interests, as in *Re W (A Minor) (Access)* [1989] 1 FLR 163, where the existence of the blood tie with the applicant father and his fitness to have contact with his child were outweighed by the child's need for stability in the new family unit comprising himself, his mother and her new husband. It was held that the child's interests required that the relationships developing within that new unit be given protection against intrusion (see also *Re SM (A Minor) (Natural Father: Access)* [1992] Fam Law 308; *Re A (Minors) (Access)* [1992] Fam Law 67; *Starling v Starling* (1983) FLR 135; and see *Re H (Minors: Parental Responsibility)* (1992) *The Times*, September 7: father had genuine and loving relationship with son but assumption in favour of contact displaced in view of attitude of step-father, an unstable character who had threatened to leave mother if contact were resumed).

Harm to the child

The court will not be justified in refusing contact simply because the residential parent (usually the mother) opposes it (see *Evans v Jackson* (1986) 150 JPN 702: contact granted to former cohabitant father despite opposition from mother and her new husband; but see also *Re H (Minors: Parental Responsibility)*, above). However, the court will take into consideration the impact that an order for contact will have and may refuse contact if it is satisfied that a mother's fear and stress arising from contact would affect the quality of her care for the child. Thus, if a mother will be disturbed by every instance of contact, even if this is overreaction, if the court finds that her disturbance will genuinely exist and will result in emotional disturbance in the child, contact with the father may be refused (see *B v A (Illegitimate Children: Access)* (1982) FLR 27;

A v C [1985] FLR 445; *Re BC (A Minor) (Access)* [1985] FLR 639; *Wright v Wright* (1981) FLR 276; and see *Re C (Minors) (Parental Rights)* [1992] 1 FLR 1; *Re F (A Minor) (Access)* [1992] Fam Law 484).

A finding or suspicion that a father may have engaged in sexually inappropriate behaviour towards the child will not necessarily result in the denial of contact (*C v C (Child Abuse: Access)* [1988] 1 FLR 462; but see also *Re R (A Minor) (Child Abuse: Access)* [1988] 1 FLR 206; *S v S (Child Abuse: Access)* [1988] 1 FLR 213; and *Re CB (A Minor) (Access)* (1992) 5 Practitioners' Child Law Bulletin 63: grandfather with conviction for indecently assaulting child's mother believed to pose a continuing risk to child).

Where a father poses no risk to the children, but is prone to eccentric or bizarre behaviour, that behaviour, even though capable of baffling or distressing a child, is not of itself sufficient to displace the assumption that a child should be allowed to enjoy the advantage of continuing contact with that natural parent (*Re B (Minors: Access)* [1992] 1 FLR 140).

Child's wishes

The court is unlikely to persist with orders for contact if the child is implacably opposed to contact with the non-residential parent even though that parent is in no way unfit to have contact (*B v B* [1971] 3 All ER 682). The fact that contact under a court order has been thwarted by a residential parent and that her actions have caused distress to the child does not of itself render contact inimical to the child's interests (*Re E (A Minor: Access)* [1987] 1 FLR 368) but, if all attempts to establish or maintain contact fail, the time may come when the court has to say 'enough is enough' (see *Churchard v Churchard* [1984] FLR 635: boys aged ten and eight implacably opposed to seeing father having taken mother's side in marital conflict; *Williams v Williams* [1985] FLR 509: children aged five and four, uncooperative mother indoctrinating them and stimulating their fears of father; see also *Sheppard v Miller* (1982) FLR 124: failure to establish contact after a long struggle, mother uncooperative, court forced to accept that contact not in interests of a five-year-old child upset by friction between parents, child knew of mother's attitude and not wanting to offend mother, child opposed to contact).

8.3.4   Transitional provisions

Where, on 14 October 1991, an order was in force which provided for access to a child, that order remains in force following implementation of the CA 1989 and is susceptible to variation. A party wishing to obtain a variation of the access arrangements may do so by applying for a contact order (see §8.3.2 above).

8.4   Specific issue orders and prohibited steps orders

8.4.1   Introduction

The flexibility conferred by specific issue orders and prohibited steps orders was intended to replicate the wide-ranging powers enjoyed by the High Court in wardship. When a child becomes a ward of court, 'custody' is vested in the court and no important step in the child's life can be taken without leave of the court.

By contrast, under the CA 1989 any person having parental responsibility for a child may act alone in discharging that responsibility. However, he is not entitled to act in any way which would be incompatible with any order made with respect to the child under the Act (s 2(7)(8)). Thus, where there is concern as to a specific aspect of a child's upbringing, the court's aid may be invoked by means of an application for a specific issue or prohibited steps order.

Neither a specific issue order nor a prohibited steps order may be made to achieve a result which could be achieved by a residence or contact order or which could not be achieved by the High Court in the exercise of its inherent jurisdiction (see eg *Nottinghamshire County Council v P* [1993] 1 FCR 180).

Where a residence order exists, or is being made in the same proceedings, it may be possible to deal adequately with any dispute relating to some specific aspect of the child's upbringing by attaching conditions to the residence order, but a specific issue order or a prohibited steps order may be sought and made where there is no residence order in existence. Such orders can be made *ex parte* where necessary. The issues that may be dealt with by such orders are many and various and all that can usefully be achieved here is to offer a few examples.

Specific issue orders

Where there is dispute as to which school a child shall attend, a specific issue order may be made to determine the child's education. It may also be desirable to seek a specific issue order where (for example) the child is in need of medical treatment but there is dispute as to which of two alternative treatments should be given, or where there is dispute over whether a terminally ill child should be cared for in the child's own home or the home of relatives, or should be admitted to a hospice. Where necessary, detailed directions may be given. Parents in dispute over whether or not their child should receive the standard range of vaccinations and immunisations would be able to seek resolution of that issue. It would also be appropriate to seek a specific issue order requiring a child to be returned to this country where the child has wrongfully been kept abroad (see *Re D (A Minor) (Child: Removal from Jurisdiction)* [1992] Fam Law 243).

Prohibited steps orders

It should be noted that a prohibited steps order can only be made to prohibit the taking of any step which could be taken by a person in discharging his parental responsibility for a child. Thus, the power to make a prohibited steps order does not give the court the right to regulate a person's life generally, but only to restrain actions in relation to the child concerned. However, such restraint may be addressed to any person, whether or not that person has parental responsibility. Thus, for example, an unmarried father or a grandparent may be forbidden to attempt to make contact with the child (and see, eg *S v C* [1992] Legal Action, March 18: prohibited steps order against paternal grandmother to prevent interference with mother's care of child; and note that the court also granted an injunction to prevent the grandmother molesting the mother; see also *M v M (Ouster: Children Act)* [1992] Fam Law 504). More importantly in practice, a prohibited steps order may be sought (*ex parte*, if necessary) to ensure that an unmarried father does not remove his child from the mother's care (and see also *Re D (A Minor) (Child: Removal from Jurisdiction)*, above).

It may be anticipated that prohibited steps orders will commonly be sought by a parent with whom the child lives, and be directed at the other parent or some other person, but a prohibited steps order may be made to prevent the parent with whom the child is living from taking some specified step. For example, a parent could be forbidden to involve the child in particular activities, such as participation in protest demonstrations or rallies.

8.4.2 Who may apply?

Any parent or guardian of the child may apply, as may any person in whose favour a residence order is in force. Any other person (including the child concerned) requires leaves to make an application. It is submitted that exceptional circumstances will be required to justify the granting of leave to apply. However well-intentioned the applicant may be, the court will be slow to accept that it would be justified in interfering with the discharge of parental responsibility by those who have the day-to-day care of the child, especially where the order would, if granted, impose burdensome restraints on the freedom of action of the carer. It is likely that, before granting leave, the court will require it to be demonstrated that, *prima facie*, the child's health or well-being will be put at risk in some significant respect unless the applicant is permitted to seek the substantive order to which the application for leave relates.

8.5 Enforcement of s 8 orders

8.5.1 Residence orders

The CA 1989, s 14 provides that where a residence order is in force in favour of any person and any other person is in breach of the arrangements settled by that order and has been served with a copy of the order, the order may be enforced under the Magistrates' Courts Act 1980, s 63(3), as if it were an order requiring the other person to produce the child to the person who has the benefit of the residence order. The magistrates' court has the power to impose a fine or imprisonment.

This provision is expressed to be without prejudice to any other remedy open to the person in whose favour the residence order is in force (see s 14(3)). With respect to orders made in the county court, the Family Proceedings (Amendment No 2) Rules 1992 (SI 1992/2067) provide for the application to s 8 orders of CCR Ord 29, r 1(3), which deals with the endorsement of a penal notice on an order enforceable by committal. However, CCR Ord 29, r 1(3) requires that the order be 'in the nature of an injunction', which will not generally be the case in respect of residence orders, and it will therefore not be within the court's jurisdiction to attach a penal notice (see *Re P (Minors) (Custody Order: Penal Notice)* [1990] 2 FLR 223, which held that the same objection applied in respect of directions in a custody order that the children should not be removed from the jurisdiction without leave and that their surnames should not be changed; but prohibited steps orders to the same effect and addressed to a particular person would clearly be enforceable by committal; see below).

Where a person is required by a s 8 order to give up a child to another person and the court that made the order is satisfied that the child has not been given up, it may make an order authorising an officer of the court or a constable to take charge of the child and deliver the child to the person to whom the order required him to be given up (Family Law Act 1986, s 34, as amended by CA 1989, Sch 13, para 62).

Contact orders

As noted above, the application to s 8 orders of CCR Ord 29, r 1(3), enables s 8 orders to be endorsed with a penal notice, but a penal notice is only to be endorsed at the discretion of the court. There is no doubt that a contact order will be enforceable by committal within the meaning of CCR Ord 29, r 1(3) provided that the order spells out what the person with care of the child is to do or abstain from doing, but an order simply providing that the parent with care shall allow 'reasonable contact' will not be capable of such enforcement and it will be necessary to apply to the court for the contact arrangements to be defined with the required precision (see *D v D (Access: Contempt: Committal)* [1991] 2 FLR 34).

Committal orders in family proceedings are remedies of very last resort and should be considered only where there has been a continuing course of conduct designed to detach the child from a relationship with the non-residential parent, and where all other efforts to resolve the situation have been unsuccessful (see *Re M (Minors) (Access: Contempt: Committal)* [1991] 1 FLR 355). Moreover, as *Re N (A Minor) (Access: Penal Notice)* [1992] 1 FLR 134 indicates, committal is entirely inappropriate where *the child* objects to contact, albeit that the residential parent may have exerted a strong influence on the child. (For a rare example of committal, see *C v C (Access Order: Enforcement)* [1990] 1 FLR 462; and see also the order made at first instance in *D v D*, above). A contempt of court (inviting condign punishment) would also be committed by a party's legal adviser who incited or encouraged that party to breach a court order (*Re K (Minors) (Incitement to Breach Contact Order)* [1992] 2 FLR 108).

Specific issue orders and prohibited steps orders

Provided that a penal notice has been attached to the order, breaches of specific issue orders and prohibited steps orders are punishable by committal, and much of what has been said above in relation to contact orders applies equally to specific issue and prohibited steps orders.

A person who considers that, owing to the passage of time or a change of circumstances, a particular restriction should no longer apply should seek a variation or discharge of the order concerned and should not rely on being able to persuade the court in any committal proceedings that the contempt should simply be condoned.

8.6 Guardianship

8.6.1 Introduction

The CA 1989, s 5 substantially revised the law relating to the appointment of guardians. The relevant provisions are considered below with particular reference to the situations that may arise in the case of unmarried parents. The position differs according to whether or not a residence order and/or parental responsibility order or agreement was in force at the time of the parent's death.

It should be borne in mind that the absence of a residence order (and/or a parental responsibility order or agreement) may be attributable to a wide variety of causes. For example, the parents may have been living together in a settled and secure relationship up to the date of one parent's death and have been unaware of the father's legal position or of the availability of s 4 agreements. On the other hand, the lack of any orders may equally be attributable to the fact that a father has never lived with the mother and their child and has never sought to play any significant role in the life of his child. Between these two extremes, there exists a wide range of possibilities.

Where there are proceedings with respect to a child during the parents' joint lives, there may be cases where it is particularly desirable that a parent with whom the child is to live should be able to make a guardianship appointment which would take effect immediately on the parent's death and, where necessary, the importance of residence orders in this context may assist in rebutting the 'no order presumption'.

Any parent with parental responsibility may appoint an individual to be his child's guardian (and it should be borne in mind that an unmarried father who has the benefit of a residence order will also necessarily have been granted parental responsibility). The appointment may be made either by will or simply in writing, dated and signed by the person making the appointment (or it may be signed at his direction in his presence and in the presence of two witnesses who attest the signature). Where parental responsibility is possessed by a non-parent by virtue of a residence order in his/her favour, that does not give the non-parent the power to appoint a guardian. An unmarried father who has not acquired parental responsibility has no power to appoint a guardian. A guardian has parental responsibility for the child, and has the right to appoint a guardian to act in succession to himself.

8.6.2   On the mother's death

No residence order in force

Where a father has acquired parental responsibility for his child (see §7.1 above), any appointment by the mother of a guardian for the child will not take effect until the father has also died or otherwise ceases to have parental responsibility for the child (eg by an order made on the application of a person in whose favour a residence order is in force). Likewise, if the mother has died without appointing a guardian, the court will have no power to appoint a guardian for the child where the father has parental responsibility.

Where the father has not acquired parental responsibility for the child, any guardianship appointment made by the mother will take effect on her death, and that guardian will have parental responsibility for the child (s 5(6)). Any dispute between the guardian and the father with respect to the upbringing of the child may be resolved by order(s) made under s 8, for which each of them is eligible to apply. The fact that a guardianship appointment has taken effect does not prevent a father from applying for a parental responsibility order with respect to his child but, if he is granted parental responsibility, it seems that this will not retrospectively affect the guardian's appointment (presumably, however, it would prevent the taking effect of any appointment by the guardian of a successor to himself).

Where the father has not acquired parental responsibility for the child and the mother has made no appointment of a guardian, any person may apply to the court for appointment as the child's guardian. However, it would also be open to the father at this stage to apply for a parental responsibility order and it must be supposed that the fate of the application for appointment as the child's guardian would await the outcome of the father's application for parental responsibility.

Where a residence order was in force

Where a residence order was in force in favour of the mother at the date of her death any appointment by her of a guardian for the child will take effect immediately irrespective of whether the father has parental responsibility. Where a residence order was in force in favour of the mother at the time of her death but she makes no appointment of any person to act as the child's guardian, any person may apply to be appointed guardian of the child, irrespective of whether the father has parental responsibility. If a mother's appointment takes effect or a guardian is appointed by the court, any dispute between father and guardian may be resolved by appropriate order(s) under s 8, for which each of them is entitled to apply. Moreover, if the father has parental responsibility for the child, the guardian is entitled to apply to have the father's parental responsibility terminated. Equally, however, the taking effect of an appointment by the mother will not prevent the father from making an application for a parental responsibility order in his favour. Likewise, where the mother made no appointment and some person applies to the court for appointment, it would be open to the father at this stage to apply for a parental responsibility order and, as noted above, it must be supposed that the fate of the application for appointment as the child's guardian would await the outcome of the father's application for parental responsibility.

8.6.3   On the father's death

As noted above, an unmarried father has no power to appoint a guardian for his child unless he has parental responsibility for the child. Even then, unless a residence order was in force in his favour at the time of his death, no appointment made by him will take effect on his death unless the mother has predeceased him.

8.7   Adoption

8.7.1   Introduction

The broad legal framework of adoption is outlined below only to the extent necessary to consider the particular effect of adoption law on unmarried parents and their children.

Residence requirements

An adoption order cannot be made unless the child has had his home with the applicants for the relevant qualifying period (see Adoption Act (AA) 1976, s 13).

The test

By the AA 1976, s 6 the court's duty, in reaching any decision relating to the adoption of a child is to have first regard to all the circumstances, first consideration being given to the need to safeguard and promote the welfare of the child throughout his childhood. So far as practicable, the court must ascertain the wishes and feelings of the child regarding the decision and give due consideration to them having regard to the child's age and understanding.

Nature and effect

An adoption order vests parental responsibility for the child in the adopters and is irrevocable. As regards the period after the making of the order it extinguishes the parental responsibility of any other person in respect of the adopted child, any duty he has to maintain the child, and any existing order made under the CA 1989 (AA 1976, s 12; and see *Re R (A Minor) (Adoption: Access)* [1991] 2 FLR 78). Moreover, adoption also severs all legal ties with the natural parent's extended family (including the right to inherit on intestacy), and in some circumstances this can appear to entail substantial disadvantages to the child (see *Re LA* (1978) 122 SJ 417). However, it has been said that, whatever the legal effect of an adoption as a matter of theory, there is no reason why the making of an order should prevent the child from seeing his former relatives if that is desirable (see, eg *Re D (Minors) (Adoption by Step-parent)* (1981) FLR 102; *Re GR (Adoption: Access)* [1985] FLR 643). At one time it was said that, if such continued contact was appropriate, that in itself was likely to be a good indication that it would not be in the child's best interests for an adoption order to be made (see *Re V (A Minor) (Adoption: Dispensing with Agreement)* [1987] 2 FLR 89). The view now appears to be that there is not necessarily an inconsistency in finding that the child requires the security provided by adoption while at the same time wishing to preserve for the child the benefits of contact with relatives who are important to him.

Consequently, there has been a notable relaxation in the court's attitude towards the insertion in adoption orders of terms providing for access/contact by a natural parent or other relative (under the power contained in AA 1976, s 12(6) or, now, by making a contact order under CA 1989, s 8). Though such provision remains rare, a term providing for future contact with former relatives may be inserted where there is agreement that contact should occur, even if the prospective adopters resist the making of formal provision for it, and it has been held that a term so inserted would be enforceable in the normal way by committal proceedings in the event of breach (see *Re C (A Minor) (Adoption Order: Conditions)* [1988] 2 FLR 159: term to preserve contact with sibling; but see also *Re C (A Minor) (Adoption Order: Condition)* [1986] 1 FLR 315: inappropriate to include term requiring adoptive parents to send annual reports on child's progress to father). This tendency towards making adoption more 'open' in turn considerably reduces the comparative attractiveness to the court of its power to make a s 8 residence order in place of the adoption order sought (see below).

Under the former law, it was held that a court which makes an adoption order had no power under the AA 1976, s 12(6) to grant an injunction restraining natural mother and grandfather from having further contact with the child (see *Re D (A Minor) (Adoption Order: Validity)* [1991] 2 FLR 66), but it would seem that the availability of s 8 orders (see below) would now enable the court to make a prohibited steps order to achieve that result.

Availability of orders under the CA 1989, s 8

Proceedings under the AA 1976 are 'family proceedings' and the court therefore has the power in those proceedings to make any order under the CA 1989, s 8. In practice, this power is most likely to be exercised where an adoption order would be inappropriate (or where parental agreement is not given and cannot be dispensed with) but the court considers that the child should remain in the care of the applicants, in whose favour it may then make a residence order (with provision for contact between the child and other persons, if appropriate). Alternatively, there may be cases where the court considers that the child's interests will be best served not by remaining with the applicants, but by living with some other person whose involvement with and commitment to the child has impressed the court as the evidence has unfolded. Again, the court may refuse to make an adoption order and may make a residence order in favour of that other person.

Particular situations where the power to make s 8 orders may have a significant impact are considered further below.

Interim adoption orders

In addition to its powers to make orders under the CA 1989, s 8, if the requirements of parental consent are met the court also has the power to postpone the determination of the adoption application and to make an interim order giving parental responsibility for the child to the applicants for a probationary period not exceeding two years (AA 1976, s 25). 'Probationary' period imports a process of investigation or experiment in relation to all the circumstances relevant to the case, and not merely to the suitability of the applicants. In *S v Huddersfield BC* [1975] Fam 113, an interim order was made for the express purpose of providing a period in which the father of an illegitimate child would have visiting and staying contact with the child in order to ascertain whether the child's interests would be best served by a transfer to the father's care.

Parental agreement

An adoption order cannot be made unless each parent or guardian of the child agrees to the making of the adoption order, or his agreement is dispensed with on one of the grounds set out in the

AA 1976, s 16(2). An unmarried father is not a 'parent' for this purpose unless he has parental responsibility for his child. The grounds on which parental agreement may be dispensed with are as follows:

(a) the parent cannot be found or is incapable of giving agreement (see *Re F(R) (An Infant)* [1970] 1 QB 385; *Re R (Adoption)* [1966] 3 All ER 613);

(b) the parent is withholding his agreement unreasonably. Briefly, the requirements for reliance on this ground can be summarised thus:

  (i)   It will be necessary to establish that it would be in the child's best interests to be adopted.

  (ii) It must be shown that the parent's refusal to consent is, in all the circumstances of the case, a decision which no reasonable parent could reach.

  (iii) The ground does not require any culpability independent of the unreasonableness of the refusal to consent, and the circumstances which render a refusal unreasonable may be outside the parent's control and may have arisen through no fault of his/her own.

  (iv) Although the s 6 test is not directly applicable to the question whether a parent is withholding her agreement unreasonably, a reasonable parent will give a high priority to the child's best interests. Thus:

  (v)   where the parent has no (or very little) involvement in the child's life and has little realistic prospect of resuming the child's care or otherwise establishing a relationship beneficial to the child, it will not be open to that parent to withhold agreement for purely sentimental reasons and there is a very real prospect that the refusal to agree to the adoption will be held to fall outside the band of decision-making within which reasonable disagreement is possible (see *Re W (An Infant)* [1971] AC 682; *Re H; Re W (Adoption: Parental Agreement)* (1983) FLR 614; *Re El-G (Minors) (Wardship and Adoption)* (1983) FLR 589; *Re V (Adoption: Parental Agreement)* [1985] FLR 45);

(c) the parent has persistently failed without reasonable cause to discharge his parental responsibility for the child (see *Re P (Infants)* [1962] 3 All ER 789; *Re D (Minors) (Adoption by*

Parent) [1973] Fam 209: failure must be culpable to a high degree: no such failure by father who failed to provide for child or see her for a year where there had been a temporary drifting apart following breakdown of the parents' marriage);

(d) the parent has abandoned or neglected the child (requiring conduct rendering the parent liable to criminal prosecution (see *Watson v Nikolaisen* [1955] 2 QB 286);

(e) the parent has persistently ill-treated the child (connoting a series of acts; see *Re A (A Minor) (Adoption: Dispensing with Agreement)* (1981) FLR 173);

(f) the parent has seriously ill-treated the child (in which case, it must also be shown that rehabilitation of the child in the parent's household is unlikely, whether by reason of the ill-treatment or otherwise; see s 16(5)).

Freeing for adoption (AA 1976, s 18)

The procedure whereby a child may be 'freed for adoption' was created to enable binding parental agreement to be given (or dispensed with) at a stage earlier than the final adoption hearing, and possibly before the child is placed with particular prospective adopters. A freeing order may be sought only by an adoption agency and application cannot be made unless at least one parent with parental responsibility consents to the making of the freeing application, or the child is in local authority care under a care order. No freeing order can be made unless the requisite parental agreement is given or can be dispensed with on the grounds set out in s 16(2) (listed above). Moreover, before making a freeing order, the court must be satisfied that an unmarried father who does not have parental responsibility has no intention of applying for a parental responsibility order under the Children Act 1989, s 4, or for a residence order under that Act, or that if he were to make such an application it would be likely to be refused (s 18(7)).

On the making of a freeing order, parental responsibility vests in the agency. However, where a child who has been freed for adoption remains unadopted one year after the making of the freeing order, and is not then placed for adoption, the child's former parent or guardian may apply for revocation of the freeing order (see AA 1976, ss 19, 20; 'Parent' for this purpose excludes an unmarried father who does not have parental responsibility for the child). These residual rights in relation to a child who has been freed for adoption are a relevant factor in considering whether a parental responsibility order should be made in a father's favour and, where a father has shown a genuine commitment to his child, it may be right to make a parental responsibility order in his favour even though the rights conferred by it are incapable of immediate exercise by him, and even though it is clear that sufficient grounds exist for dispensing with his consent to the making of a freeing order (see *Re H (Illegitimate Children: Father: Parental Rights) (No 2)* [1991] 1 FLR 214. In addition to the extent of the father's involvement with the child, his character and history will also be relevant; see *D v Hereford and Worcester CC* [1991] 1 FLR 205).

Thus, where a father has shown a real concern for and interest in his child, it may be difficult for the court to conclude that an application for a parental responsibility order would be likely to fail. Where such an application is made, the freeing application cannot be disposed of until that outcome of the father's application is known and, of course, if the application succeeds, the father's agreement to the making of a freeing order must then be given or dispensed with.

Unmarried fathers – joinder as party to adoption proceedings

In cases where his agreement to the adoption is not required, an unmarried father must nevertheless be joined as a party to the proceedings if he is liable to contribute to the child's maintenance by virtue of any order or agreement (Adoption Rules (AR) 1984, r 15(2)(h)). The court also has the power to direct that any other person not specifically mentioned in the Rules shall be made a respondent and such a direction could be given in a case where a father has been having contact with his child but, for whatever reason, is not liable to maintain the child within the meaning of the Rules. The Sch 2 report which must be prepared for the court in every adoption case must indicate whether any other person, such as an unmarried father, should be made a respondent to the proceedings. The standard form for Sch 2 reports also makes provision for the inclusion of information with respect to an unmarried father, but there is no requirement that an unmarried father be named, nor does the court have power to order that he be interviewed (see *Re L (A Minor) (Adoption: Procedure)* [1991] 1 FLR 171). However, where the identity of the child's father is known, any involvement which he has in the child's life will be disclosed by the Sch 2 report since that report must deal with the extent of the child's contact with his natural family, including his father, and must indicate the nature of the relationship enjoyed by them.

Adoption proceedings are 'family proceedings'. It is therefore open to an unmarried father to apply within those proceedings for a residence or contact order in his favour (unless the child is in care, in which case any application for contact must be commenced in the family proceedings court but may subsequently be transferred to the court to which the adoption application is made; see further Children (Allocation of Proceedings) Order 1991, art 7). Where such an application is made, the court should hear both applications at the same time (*Re G (A Minor) (Adoption and Access Applications)* (1980) FLR 109), but this does not inhibit the court's power to determine whether there should be interim contact pending the final hearing (see *Re G (A Minor) (Adoption and Access Applications)* [1992] 1 FLR 642).

Renewed applications

When an adoption order has been refused, the court is not permitted to hear a renewed application by the same applicants in respect of the same child unless either the court which refused the original application gave a direction that the prohibition on hearing renewed applications should not apply or it appears to the court that, because of a change of circumstances or for any other reason, it is proper to proceed with the application (AA 1976, s 24).

8.7.2 Adoption by parents

By both parents as joint applicants

It is not possible for an unmarried couple jointly to adopt their own child (or any other child) since an adoption order in favour of joint applicants is possible only where the applicants are married to each other.

By father as sole applicant

After the death of his child's mother, an unmarried father may wish to adopt his child and an adoption order may be made in his favour if the child is at least 19 weeks old and has had his home with the father at all times during the 13 weeks preceding the making of the order (this being the qualifying period applicable to a 'relative' of the child, defined by the AA 1976, s 72, to include the father of an illegitimate child). The death of the mother will take the case outside the statutory provisions which aim to discourage adoption by one parent (see below), leaving the court's decision on whether to make the adoption order to be made simply by reference to the s 6 test (see §8.7.1 above).

Since an alternative procedure now exists whereby a father may obtain parental responsibility for his child, the only additional benefit to be derived from an adoption order will be that adoption necessarily confers on the child the status of legitimacy. To be weighed against that is the effect that an adoption order would have of severing all the child's legal ties with his deceased mother's family. It is submitted that, though still a theoretical possibility, the right of fathers to seek adoption orders in these circumstances is of little practical significance.

While the mother still lives, the court cannot make an adoption order in favour of the father unless it is satisfied that the mother cannot be found or that there is some other reason justifying her exclusion from parenthood and, if an adoption order is made, the court must record that reason (AA 1976, s 15: the burden of proof is a heavy one; see *Re C (A Minor) (Adoption by Parent)* [1986] Fam Law 360).

Moreover, adoption by the father during the mother's lifetime will be possible only if the mother agrees to the adoption or her agreement can be dispensed with under the AA 1976, s 16(2). Where the mother agrees to the adoption and wishes to have nothing more to do with her child, it would presumably be open to the court to find that her attitude towards the adoption itself constitutes a sufficient reason justifying her exclusion from parenthood.

If the mother does not consent to the making of an adoption order but there are clear grounds for dispensing with her agreement *other than* the unreasonable withholding of agreement, it would be open to the court to find that the facts which establish the mother's mistreatment of the child (or other culpability required by the ground relied upon) themselves constitute a sufficient reason for excluding her. Although it is possible for a father who is caring for his child to obtain parental responsibility by means other than the making of an adoption order, it is also possible to envisage cases where the mother's past conduct or her present and likely future state of mental health make it appropriate for her to be permanently excluded from the child's life, and no means exist other than adoption whereby the mother of a child may be deprived of her parental responsibility (and thus her right to apply for CA 1989, s 8 orders). Again, however, in applying the s 6 test, the existence of other members of the mother's family and the child's links with them will be a relevant consideration.

By mother as sole applicant

As noted above, in the case of an adoption application by a parent as sole applicant, there is a statutory prohibition on the making of an adoption order during the other parent's lifetime unless the other parent be found or there is some reason justifying his exclusion from parenthood (AA 1976, s 15). However, where the mother is the applicant the position is significantly different in that, unless the father has parental responsibility, his agreement to the adoption will not be required. Moreover, unless he is maintaining the child he will be a party to the proceedings only if the court exercises its discretion to join him (see §8.7.1 above). Nevertheless, the degree of his past and present involvement with the child will be revealed by the report which must be supplied to the court by the local authority (see §8.7.1 above). There is unlikely to be any sufficient reason for permitting adoption by the mother alone where the father has any continuing involvement in the life of the child and, again, the severing of ties with other members of the father's family may be a relevant consideration.

By a parent as a joint applicant with his/her spouse

Such applications are made where a father or mother who has been caring for the child is married to someone other than the child's other parent. Although known as 'step-parent adoptions', it should be appreciated that, as a matter of law, such adoptions render not only the step-parent but also the natural parent the child's parent by adoption. Section 15 (discussed above) has no application to a case where the father or mother applies to adopt his/her child not as sole applicant but jointly with his/her spouse.

Although the minimum age for adoption applicants is normally 21, where the applicants are the child's parent and step-parent, an application may be made where the parent has attained the age of

18 provided that the step-parent has attained the age of 21. Where the applicants are the child's father and step-mother, the consent of the child's mother will be required (or must be dispensed with) in all cases. Where the applicants are the child's mother and step-father, the consent of the child's father will be required only where he has parental responsibility for the child.

(a) *Where the consent of the other parent is required*

Where the child's other parent consents to the adoption (and provided, of course, that there is no reason to doubt the applicants' fitness to adopt the child) it is unlikely that an adoption order will be refused. As noted at §8.7.1 above, adoption proceedings are 'family proceedings', and the court could refuse to make an adoption order, making instead a residence order in favour of the parent and step-parent jointly. However, the recent practice of the courts demonstrates a reluctance to go against the wishes of adult parties who are united in their desire that an adoption order be made (see, eg *Re D (Minors) (Adoption by Step-parent)* (1981) FLR 102; *Re S (A Minor) (Adoption or Custodianship)* [1987] 2 FLR 331: note, moreover, that the specific statutory provisions central to these two cases were repealed by the CA 1989). This reluctance will be all the more pronounced if the child is old enough to express a view and also favours adoption.

Where the child's other parent does not consent to the adoption, it will be necessary to determine whether his/her consent can be dispensed with. All grounds other than s 16(2)(b) (unreasonable withholding) involve proof of a high degree of parental culpability and, on proof of such a ground, an adoption order is likely to be refused only in unusual circumstances where there are independent reasons for concluding that adoption will not be in the child's best interests.

Where the application to dispense with the other parent's agreement alleges only that agreement is being unreasonably withheld, it will be necessary to demonstrate, first, that it is in the child's interests to be adopted. In the present context, this may be demonstrated, *inter alia*, by evidence that the child needs the sense of security which an adoption order can give (not least by protecting the family against future litigation initiated by the other parent with respect to the child's upbringing). And, for example, where the child has half-siblings born to the parent and step-parent the desirability of integrating the child as a 'full' member of the new family unit may be particularly influential, also serving to demonstrate why a joint residence order in favour of the parent and step-parent would be an inadequate substitute for adoption (see, eg *Re D (Minors) (Adoption by Step-parent)* (1981) FLR 102; but see also *Re P (Minors) (Adoption)* [1989] 1 FLR 1: step-parent adoption refused where application related to only two of three children living with parent and step-parent). If it is shown that it would be in the child's interests to be adopted, the court must then consider the reasonableness of the refusal to consent (see §8.7.1 above).

Where the court concludes that adoption would not be in the child's best interests or that there is insufficient justification for dispensing with the parent's agreement, it may safeguard the child's position by making a residence order in favour of the parent and step-parent. The court may also consider it appropriate to make a direction that AA 1976, s 24 shall not apply. As noted at §8.7.1 above, s 24 normally prevents a renewed application to adopt a child when a previous application by the same applicants has been unsuccessful. Where its application has been waived the court has usually concluded that an adoption order could not be made in the face of evidence that the child has been benefiting from contact with a natural parent whose consent has been withheld, but the court has assessed that relationship as fragile and has contemplated the appropriateness of a renewed application in the event of a change of circumstances (see, eg *Re M (Minors) (Adoption: Parental Agreement)* [1985] FLR 921).

(b) *Where the father's consent is not required*

As noted at §8.7.1 above, even where a father's consent is not required, his views will normally be conveyed to the court and he may be joined as a party to the proceedings. He will, at the very least, normally be permitted to make representations to the court. Where he opposes the making of an adoption order, the court does not need to consider whether sufficient grounds exist for dispensing with his consent but, dependent upon the nature and extent of his relationship with the child, the court's application of the s 6 test may lead it to conclude that an adoption order would not be in the best interests of the child. Again, the court may deal with the application by making a residence order in favour of the applicants and may waive the prohibition on the making of a renewed application in the future.

8.7.3   Adoption by non-parents

As a result of repeals effected by the CA 1989, the adoption legislation no longer draws a distinction between adoption applications by relatives and adoption applications by non-relatives, save to the extent that an adoption order may be made in favour of a relative after a shorter period of caring for the child than applies to non-relatives with whom the child lives other than as a result of an adoption agency placement for adoption (see AA 1976, s 13). Nevertheless, for present purposes it is still convenient to deal separately with the two classes of case.

In relation to all such cases, reference may be made to the dictum of Lord Templeman in *Re KD (A Minor) (Access: Principles)* [1988] 2 FLR 139 (at 141) that:

> 'the best person to bring up a child is the natural parent. It matters not whether the parent is wise or foolish, rich or poor, educated or illiterate, provided the child's moral and physical health are not endangered.' (and see *Re K (A Minor) (Wardship: Adoption)* [1991] 1 FLR 57)

By relatives

The position with respect to required consent(s) is as set out at §8.7.1 above. Where any required consent is not forthcoming, or where opposition is indicated by a father whose consent is not required, the court will investigate closely the nature and extent of any continuing involvement in the child's life on the part of the parent who opposes the adoption. Moreover, other considerations independent of that aspect of the matter may play a part in the court's application of the s 6 test. The courts have on occasions shown reluctance to grant 'intra-family' adoptions because of the resulting distortion of family relationships and the risk of confusing the child's sense of identity. However, where the child has become completely integrated into the family as the child of the prospective adopters, the court may take the view that, far from confusing the child's sense of identity, adoption will reinforce it and is therefore preferable to the residence order alternative (see *Re S (A Minor)* *(Adoption or Custodianship)* [1987] 2 FLR 331; and see *Re W (A Minor) (Adoption: Custodianship)* [1992] Fam Law 64). In particular, where all the adults involved are united in their view that adoption offers the best course, the court will be slow to impose a result which may be perceived as an unwarranted intrusion of authority. Where adoption is opposed by a father who does not have parental responsibility but where there are factors making adoption desirable, the court may make an adoption order, but with a contact order in the father's favour.

By non-relatives

In cases where an adoption order is sought by a parent (with or without his/her spouse), a refusal by the court to make the adoption order will usually not result in any change in the arrangements for the child's day-to-day care. The same result is also comparatively likely where an adoption application by relatives is unsuccessful: the question which the court usually faces is whether the existing care arrangements should be recognised and reinforced by a change in the child's status. As a broad generalisation, in the case of applications by non-relatives the refusal of an adoption order is much more likely to result in a change to the arrangements for care of the child. In consequence, if the adoption application is to be successfully resisted, it will usually be necessary to show that a realistic alternative exists (and see *Re K (A Minor) (Wardship: Adoption)* [1991] 1 FLR 57, endorsing the dictum of Lord Templeman in *Re KD*, quoted above). Thus, for example, the court will pay little heed to the objections of a father who cannot himself make proposals for the care of the child if the child's mother has no wish/capacity to care for the child herself and she has placed the child with an adoption agency. On the other hand, if the father is offering to care for the child himself, the primary position accorded to natural parents means that he is entitled to first consideration as the long-term carer. The question is whether he is a fit and suitable person to care for his child and it is not a matter of a straight balancing exercise between the father and an unknown potential adoptive family (see *Re O (A Minor) (Custody: Adoption)* [1992] 1 FLR 77: it is not for the court to indulge in social engineering; per Butler-Sloss LJ at 79).

Involvement of other family members

The power of the court in adoption proceedings to make orders under the CA 1989, s 8 has been noted above. That power is exercisable at any stage in the proceedings. It may be the case that although the child's parents are unable or unwilling to undertake the child's care, other members of a parent's family wish to assume responsibility for the child's upbringing. In these circumstances, an application for a residence order (with leave, if necessary) offers the extended family members an opportunity to press their case for consideration as alternative carers for the child. In *Re L (A Minor) (Care Proceedings: Wardship) (No 2)* [1991] 1 FLR 29, the judge observed that:

> 'adoption should only be considered in the last resort when no one in the extended family was available and suitable to look after a child. Parentage was not always perfect but parentage in the family is preferable to the unknown risks of adoption . . . We consider that every child has a right, whenever it is possible, to be brought up in its own genetic family. That right should not be taken away except in the last resort when there were strong and cogent reasons for so doing.'

9 CHILDREN AND LOCAL AUTHORITIES

It is beyond the scope of this book to provide a comprehensive account of the powers and duties of local authorities. This chapter concentrates on the principal features of the framework established by the Children Act 1989 as it affects unmarried parents and their children. Save where otherwise indicated, all statutory references in this chapter are references to provisions of the Children Act 1989.

9.1 Provision of accommodation for children

9.1.1 Local authorities' duty to provide accommodation

The 'voluntary care' framework providing for the reception of children into care with parental consent has been replaced by provisions of the CA 1989 under which a child may be *provided with accommodation* by a local authority. A local authority *must* provide accommodation for any 'child in need' (defined by s 17(10)) within its area if it appears to the local authority that the child requires accommodation as a result of:

(a) there being no person who has parental responsibility for him;
(b) his being lost or having been abandoned; or
(c) the person who has been caring for him being prevented (whether or not permanently, and for whatever reason) from providing him with suitable accommodation or care (s 20(1)).

A local authority *may* provide accommodation for any child within its area (even though a person who has parental responsibility for him is able to provide him with accommodation) if it considers that to do so would safeguard and promote the child's welfare.

As they affect children of unmarried parents, these provisions mean, for example, that a local authority will have a duty to provide accommodation for a child of unmarried parents even where the child's father has parental responsibility for him if the child is a 'child in need' and requires accommodation because his mother (or other person with whom he has been living) is unable to continue caring for him, and has a power to provide accommodation for the child if the mother is unwilling (rather than unable) to care for him herself.

However, unless the local authority provides accommodation for a child with the consent of a person in whose favour a residence order is in force (or who has care of the child by virtue of an order made under the High Court's inherent jurisdiction), a local authority may not provide accommodation for a child in the face of objection by a person who has parental responsibility for him and who is willing and able to provide him with accommodation or to arrange for accommodation to be provided for him (s 20(7)). Moreover, where a local authority is proposing to look after a child by providing him with accommodation, before it makes any decision with respect to the child (including, presumably, the decision whether it has the right to provide accommodation), the local authority must, so far as practicable, ascertain the wishes and feelings of (*inter alia*) the child, and his parents (s 22(4)).

Where a child is already being provided with accommodation by a local authority then, unless the local authority is providing accommodation for the child with the consent of a person in whose favour a residence order is in force (or who has care of the child by virtue of an order made under the High Court's inherent jurisdiction) any person who has parental responsibility for the child may at any time remove him from the accommodation provided for him by the local authority (s 20(8)).

The combined effect of these provisions is that where, for example, an unmarried father has parental responsibility in respect of a child living with the mother and the mother experiences difficulties which lead her to request the provision of accommodation for the child, the father may prevent the child being accommodated by the local authority if he is able and willing to provide the child with a home and, if the child is already being accommodated by the local authority, the father may remove him at any time, except that if a residence order exists in the mother's favour her agreement to the provision of accommodation by the local authority will suspend the father's right to prevent or terminate the local authority's provision of accommodation for the child (but see also s 20(11); child aged 16 or over may give a sufficient consent to being accommodated).

Where a father does not have parental responsibility for a child of his who is being accommodated by the local authority, he is entitled to take steps to acquire that responsibility (either by court order or by agreement with the mother) so as to acquire the right to remove the child. However, it may be preferable for him to seek a residence order so that he acquires the right to remove and retain the child not merely as against the local authority, but also as against the child's mother. If a residence order is in force in favour of any person who consents to the provision of accommodation by the local authority, the father will need to obtain a residence order in his favour in any event, whether or not he already possesses parental responsibility.

9.1.2 Local authorities' duties in relation to children for whom they are providing accommodation

Before making any decision with respect to a child for whom it is providing accommodation, it is the duty of a local authority, so far as is reasonably practicable, to ascertain the wishes and feelings of (*inter alia*) the child and his parents and to give due consideration to them.

The local authority has a duty to make arrangements to enable the child to live with (*inter alia*) a parent of his, or a relative (as defined in s 105(1)), friend or other person connected with him, unless that would not be reasonably practicable or consistent with his welfare (s 23(6)). Those 'arrangements' might entail the provision of support services to a parent or (for example) grandparents who would not otherwise be able to provide suitable care.

Where the child cannot be enabled to live with a parent or relative, etc, in accordance with s 23(6), the local authority has a duty, so far as is reasonably practicable and consistent with the child's welfare, to secure that the child is accommodated together with any sibling(s) and in accommodation near his home (s 23(7)).

The Department of Health's *Guidance and Regulations* requires a local authority to draw up a plan in writing for any child it is proposing to accommodate. That plan is to be drawn up in consultation with the child, his parents, and other individuals and agencies who are important in the child's life. The aim should be to reach a clear agreement with parents concerning future arrangements for the child (see generally *Guidance and Regulations, Vol 3 Family*

Placements, 2.17–2.74; and *Vol 4 Residential Care*, paras 2.17–2.74).

9.1.3   Complaints procedure

The Act requires every local authority to maintain a procedure for considering any representations or complaints about the discharge by the authority of its functions under Part III of the Act (which deals, *inter alia*, with the provision of accommodation for children) (see s 26(3)). The procedure must ensure the involvement of some person independent of the local authority in the consideration of the complaint, and in any discussions held by the authority about the action to be taken in respect of it (s 26(4)).

Representations may be made (*inter alia*) by the child himself, a parent (including an unmarried father), and such other person as the authority considers has a sufficient interest in the child's welfare to warrant his representations being considered (s 26(3)).

9.1.4   Adding compulsion to the accommodation of children

If a local authority considers that a child would be at risk if removed from accommodation which the authority is providing for him, a care order offers the only means of adding compulsion to the arrangements. The local authority will thus be required to satisfy the court that the 'threshold conditions' are satisfied; ie that unless a care order is made the child is likely to suffer significant harm arising from shortcomings in the parental care he is likely to receive (see further §9.2 below; and note that the reference to harm specifically attributable to shortcomings of parental care seems to mean that harm resulting purely and simply from the child being (re)moved from the place where he is being accommodated may not satisfy the threshold conditions, no matter how long the child has been in local authority accommodation, and no matter how unprepared the child may be for the change).

It is hoped that in most cases parents will adhere to the agreement reached with the local authority. The agreement will normally include provisions dealing with the removal of the child (eg that the parent will give a specified period of notice). Cases can arise, however, where a parent indicates an intention to remove the child and the circumstances are such that the local authority considers that the child is likely to suffer harm is removed. In such a case, it may be appropriate for the local authority to seek an emergency protection order (EPO) prior to seeking a care order, and an EPO may be granted where there is reasonable cause to believe that the child is likely to suffer significant harm if he does not remain in the place where he is then being accommodated (see §9.3.1 below).

9.2   Care orders

9.2.1   Introduction

As the preceding paragraphs indicate, the possession of parental responsibility by an unmarried father can be of great significance where a question arises as to the right of a local authority to provide accommodation for the child. However, where there are care proceedings, an unmarried father's rights stem solely from the fact of parenthood and the broad framework outlined below makes no differentiation between different categories of parent (married or unmarried, with or without parental responsibility, etc). For reasons of space, this account concentrates on care orders but it should be remembered that a court to which application is made for a care order and which finds the threshold conditions proved may make a supervision order instead of a care order, and may do so in addition to or instead of making any of the other orders (eg s 8 orders) available to it.

9.2.2   Availability of care orders

Application may be made by a local authority or by the NSPCC (as 'authorised person').

A court may make a care order if (and only if) it is satisfied:

(a) that the child concerned is suffering, or is likely to suffer, significant harm; and
(b) that the harm or likelihood of harm is attributable to –
   (i) the care given to the child, or likely to be given to him if the order were not made, not being what it would be reasonable to expect a parent to give to him; or
   (ii) the child's being beyond parental control (s 31(2)).

'Harm' means 'ill-treatment or the impairment of health or development', which are in turn very broadly defined (s 31(9)).

Where the threshold conditions are satisfied, it is by no means automatic that a care order will be made. It must be in the child's best interests to make the order (and be better for the child than making no order at all), having regard in particular to the matters listed in the statutory checklist which requires the court to consider (*inter alia*) the harm which the child has suffered or is likely to suffer (para (e)), the capacity of his parents and any other relevant person to meet his needs (para (f)), and the range of powers available to the court in the proceedings (para (g)). Thus, a local authority which seeks a care order will be expected to lay before the court its proposals with respect to the child's care against which to assess the child's prospects if the care order is refused, with or without the making of some other order. These proposals must include the proposals which the authority makes with respect to contact between the child and his parents while the child is in care (see s 34(11); and see §9.2.4 below).

9.2.3   Power to make other orders

Although no residence order can be made in favour of a local authority, a court seised of care proceedings is nevertheless empowered to make a residence order in favour of some other person. This power may be exercised at any stage in the proceedings. Thus, for example, if a local authority applies for a care order because there is cause for concern in relation to a child's welfare while in the care of his unmarried mother, the court can refuse to make a care order but has the power to make a residence order transferring the care of the child to his father if this appears to be in the child's best interests. This power is exercisable whether or not the father has already acquired parental responsibility under s 4. Where the court makes a s 8 order as an *interim* measure, the court must also make an interim supervision order unless it is satisfied that the child's welfare will be satisfactorily safeguarded without one (see s 38(3)).

9.2.4   Effect of care order

The effect of a care order is to vest parental responsibility in the local authority (s 33(3) and see *Cheshire County Council v M* [1993] 1 FLR 463, but see also *In re B (Minors)* (1992) *The Times*, December

31). The making of a care order discharges any existing residence or contact order (s 91(2)). It does not have the effect of terminating an existing parental responsibility order or agreement by virtue of which a father has parental responsibility but that parental responsibility does not entitle the father to act in any way which would be incompatible with the care order, by virtue of which the local authority has a discretion (which cannot be fettered by the court which made the care order) with respect to the arrangements to be made for the child's care. The local authority is however obliged, so far as reasonably practicable, to ascertain and give due consideration to the wishes and feelings of the child's parents before making any decision with respect to him (s 22(4)(5)) and, so far as is reasonably practicable and consistent with his welfare, to accommodate the child together with his sibling(s) in accommodation near his home (s 23(7)). However, where the local authority forms the view that a child in care should be permitted to live with either of his parents, the authority may only allow him to live with the parent after the authority has complied with the requirements laid down by the Placement of Children with Parent, etc Regulations 1991.

9.2.5   Contact with children in care

The Act contains a statutory presumption in favour of reasonable parental contact with children in care (s 34(1)) and the local authority may only deny contact on the authority of a court order save that it may deny contact for not more than seven days in circumstances of urgency where it is satisfied that the refusal of contact is necessary to safeguard or promote the child's welfare (s 34(6)).

Section 34(11) expressly provides that before making a care order the court must consider the contact arrangements which are proposed by the local authority and must invite the other parties to comment on those arrangements. Moreover, the court is empowered to make a 'care contact order' (or to refuse to make such an order) at the same time as it makes a care order. The power to make a care contact order is exercisable even where no application for such an order has been made.

Section 34(3) provides for application to the court for a contact order in respect of a child in care by the child's parents, any guardian of the child, and any person in whose favour a residence order was in force immediately before the making of the care order. The relevant guidance to local authorities makes it clear that, in addition to those categories of persons, the local authority's consideration of the question of contact between a child in care and his family should include any relevant members of the child's extended family (see *Guidance and Regulations, Vol 3*, para 6.5). When an application is made to the court in respect of contact, it may be necessary for the court to review the local authority's long-term plans for the child (see *In re B (Minors)*, above). Where an application for contact with a child in care has been refused, no further application may be made by the same person within six months of the refusal save with leave of the court (s 91(17)).

9.2.6 Leaving care

The Act provides that the making of a residence order operates to discharge any existing care order (s 91(1)), and it is clear that a residence order may be made in respect of a child in care (see s 9(1)). Thus, a successful application for a residence order may serve as the means of obtaining a child's discharge from care.

Before making a residence order the court must, of course, be satisfied that the making of the residence order is in the child's best interests.

Provision is also made for applications for the discharge of care orders (see s 39), and such an application may be made by:

(a) any person who has parental responsibility for the child;
(b) the child himself; or
(c) the local authority in whose care the child is.

Such an application for discharge would be appropriate in the case of a child of united parents seeking the child's return to their joint care. However, where an unmarried father seeks to assume the care of his child, it is in most cases likely to be more appropriate for the father to apply for a residence order (even if he already has parental responsibility), since the making of the residence order in his favour would thus settle the arrangements for the child not only as between the father and the local authority but also as between the father and the mother (or any other relevant person).

It should be noted that the child is entitled to apply for his own discharge from care, and does not require the leave of the court to make such an application. It has already been noted that a child is also able to seek a residence order with respect to himself, and this would be an alternative to an application for the discharge of the care order. However, leave of the court is required for the making by the child of an application for a residence order.

9.3 Other protective measures

9.3.1 Emergency protection orders (CA 1989, s 44)

An emergency protection order (EPO) can be made on the application of any person if the court is satisfied that there is reasonable cause to believe that the child is likely to suffer significant harm if he is not removed to accommodation provided by the applicant, or if he does not remain in the place in which he is being accommodated. It may also be made on the application of a local authority or the NSPCC where enquiries with respect to the child are being frustrated by the unreasonable refusal of access to the child. An EPO obliges a person who is able to do so to produce the child to the local authority (or other successful applicant). An EPO carries with it parental responsibility for the child, but only to the extent of taking what action is necessary to safeguard or promote the welfare of the child. When an EPO has been made, the applicant must allow the child reasonable contact with (*inter alia*) his parents and any person with whom the child was living at the time when the order was made (s 44(13), subject to any directions given by the court under s 44(6), which empowers the court to give directions as to the contact which is, or is not, to be allowed between the child and any named persons).

In the first instance, the duration of an EPO shall not exceed eight days. An EPO is renewable once only (for up to seven days), and only if the court has reasonable cause to believe that the child is likely to suffer significant harm if the order is not extended (see s 45(5)(6)). After the expiration of 72 hours from the making of the EPO, an application may be made for the discharge of the EPO save that no such application may be made by any person who was given notice of and was present at the hearing at which the EPO was made. Otherwise, application for discharge may be made by (*inter alia*) the child's parents.

If, during the existence of an EPO it appears to the local authority (or other applicant) that it is safe to return the child home or to allow the child to be removed from the place where he is being accommodated, the local authority has a duty to return the child (s 44(10)). The child must be returned either to the care of the person from whom he was removed or, if that is not reasonably practicable, to the care of a parent or someone who has parental responsibility (s 44(11)).

9.3.2   Child assessment orders (CA 1989, s 43)

A local authority (or other authorised person) may apply to the court for a child assessment order requiring any person who is in a position to do so to produce the child for assessment in order to ascertain whether the child is suffering or is likely to suffer significant harm. A court may treat an application for a child assessment order as an application for an emergency protection order (s 43(3); and see s 43(4)). A child may only be kept away from home under a child assessment order in accordance with directions given by the order (s 43(9)) and, where a child is to be kept away from home, the order shall contain such directions as the court thinks fit with regard to the contact that the child is to be allowed to have with other persons while away from home (s 43(10)).

Any person applying for a child assessment order must take such steps as are reasonably practicable to ensure that notice of the application is given (*inter alia*) to the child's parents (s 43(11)). The order may last for a maximum duration of seven days.

9.4   Challenging local authorities' decisions

A decision reached by a local authority in the course of discharging its duties and exercising its powers under the Act may be susceptible to challenge by way of an application for judicial review. Such an application will succeed only where one or more of three grounds of attack is established. There must be either '*illegality*' – where the authority made an error of law in reaching the decision in question, or '*procedural impropriety*' –where there has been failure to observe procedural requirements (and which can involve breach of the rules of natural justice), or '*irrationality*' – where the authority has reached a decision which is 'so outrageous in its defiance of logic or of accepted moral standards that no sensible person who had applied his mind to the question to be decided could have arrived at it' (*Council of Civil Service Unions v Minister for Civil Defence* [1985]

AC 374, per Lord Diplock at 410; interpreting the '*Wednesbury principles*'; see *Associated Provincial Picture Houses Ltd v Wednesbury Corporation* [1948] 1 KB 223).

An application for judicial review may be made only with leave of the court. In most cases, a successful application for judicial review will result in an order quashing the original decision.

INDEX

References are to paragraph numbers.